# Sociology and Social Work

## PERSPECTIVES AND PROBLEMS

BY

## BRIAN J. HERAUD, B.Sc.(Soc.)

SENIOR LECTURER IN SOCIOLOGY,
POLYTECHNIC OF NORTH LONDON

*Foreword by* NOEL TIMMS, MA, DPSA,
PROFESSOR OF APPLIED SOCIAL STUDIES,
UNIVERSITY OF BRADFORD

## PERGAMON PRESS

OXFORD · NEW YORK · TORONTO
PARIS · SYDNEY · FRANKFURT

| U. K. | Pergamon Press Ltd., Headington Hill Hall, Oxford OX3 0BW, England |
| U. S. A. | Pergamon Press Inc., Maxwell House, Fairview Park, Elmsford, New York 10523, U.S.A. |
| CANADA | Pergamon of Canada Ltd., 75 The East Mall, Toronto, Ontario, M8Z 2L9 |
| AUSTRALIA | Pergamon Press (Aust.) Pty. Ltd., 19a Boundary Street, Rushcutters Bay, N.S.W. 2011, Australia |
| FRANCE | Pergamon Press SARL, 24 rue des Ecoles, 75240 Paris, Cedex 05, France |
| WEST GERMANY | Pergamon Press GmbH, 6242 Kronberg-Taunus, Pferdstrasse 1, Frankfurt-am-Main, West Germany |

First edition 1970

Reprinted 1972 (twice), 1973, 1974, 1977

Library of Congress Catalog Card No. 79-119894

*Printed in Great Britain by A. Wheaton & Co., Exeter*

0 08 015854 4 flexicover

0 08 015855 2 hard cover

# Contents

## PART IV

# Foreword

"To my mind there is a very close and direct relationship between sociology and social work. It is only between sociologist and social workers that there is no relation, unless it be a negative one." This comment has a contemporary astringency and relevance, but it was originally made in 1925 at a time when, at least in America, there seemed to be a real chance that social workers and sociologists might together work out the shape and function of their inter-relationship. The debate that ensued was comparatively long—it lasted until about 1932—and completely unproductive. Perhaps some of the reasons for this outcome can be found in the comments of a social worker on a paper by E. Mowrer published in 1929 on "The Sociological Analysis of the Contents of 2,000 Case Records with Special Reference to the Treatment of Family Discord". Mowrer reported that amongst the techniques in general use in ten casework agencies in Chicago were to be found ordering-forbidding, auto-suggestion, and persuasion. The social work comment on this was that "The very phrasing of the list of direct techniques suggests the days of witchcraft, and their serious acceptance would justify the U.S. Census Bureau in continuing to classify social workers as part of the semi-professional group made up chiefly of mediums, fortune tellers, chiropractioners. . . . Perhaps again our records are to blame, but one is tempted to suspect an emotion-driven bias in the selection of these terms on the part of the author." Both "sides" carry responsibility for turning what should have been a patient dialogue into a battle, but the social worker's characteristic belief that the best means of defence is interpretation did not help the sociologists to grasp ways in which their own professional ideologies might prevent them describing, if not explaining, the social workers' reality.

Since those days the relationship between sociology and social work has not been systematically pursued, but, as Brian Heraud points out, sociology is at present attracting the attention of increasing numbers of social workers and at least some sociologists appear to be interested in developing a sociological understanding of the problems social workers face. In this situation, which Heraud rightly characterizes as inter-actional, we must try to ensure that both social workers and sociologists have the maximum freedom for intellectual movement, so that the various forms of collaboration can be adequately explored. There is room for—and we need—a number of texts devoted to this exploration. Peter Leonard has already provided one, and now Brian Heraud offers what I am sure will be found to be a very useful basic text for social-work students and students of social work. Some of the ground covered in this volume has, of course, been traversed by other authors, but the reconsideration by the present author of such central themes as the organizational context of social work will help the reader to grasp that there is no monolithic set of beliefs that can be taken as an exhaustive description of *the* sociological approach. Some of the questions raised in this volume will undoubtedly in their turn have to be considered again. For example, I am not convinced that "the psychiatric deluge" is a sufficiently good historical description of the psychoanalytic influence on social work in the immediate past or that the explanation of this series of events in the status seeking of social workers sounds altogether plausible. But the fact that the reader may soon find himself arguing with the author is a measure of the accomplishment of this book.

Above all, Brian Heraud shows sociology as an activity. For instance, the analysis of Dahrendorf is not simply presented, as it were to be either accepted or rejected, but we are given some guidelines for the critical examination of the analysis.

This book will, I am sure, come to be used on a wide scale. It will do much to prevent any recurrence of the situation described by the writer whose words begin this foreword: "The social worker who reads the sociological literature and who sees great promise and hope for a more scientific type of social work in the sociological point of view, finds himself in the condition of the thirsty wanderer in the desert who sees a mirage and expects to drink his fill only to be bitterly disappointed at the frustration of his hopes."

Brian Heraud has provided a text which gives a good idea of the sociological perspective, which shows how the sociologist works in areas like those of the family, social stratification and community, and which seeks to demonstrate the returns for social work that can be expected from the application of this perspective.

NOEL TIMMS

School of Applied Social Studies,
The University of Bradford.

# Acknowledgements

I SHOULD like to thank a number of people who have read the whole manuscript or separate chapters, or who commented on a draft of a paper on "The teaching of sociology to social workers" which I gave to a meeting of the Teachers Section of the British Sociological Association in 1967 from which the idea of the book originated. My thanks also go to a number of people, too numerous to mention, who have given up their time to talk to me about the problems involved in writing a book of this kind.

Jean Nursten, of the Department of Applied Social Studies at the University of Bradford and Editor of the series in which this book appears, read the whole manuscript and gave invaluable advice and assistance on the planning of the book as a whole. Pamela Smith, tutor in the Department of Child Care and Social Studies, North Western Polytechnic, read several of the chapters in first draft and made important suggestions at an early stage. Jean Hardy, Senior Research Associate in the Department of Social Administration, University of Birmingham, read the earlier paper and thus made important contributions to the book as a whole. Margot Jefferys, Professor of Medical Sociology in the Department of Sociology, Bedford College, London, has made a number of valuable comments on several chapters of the book. The book has benefited considerably from the innumerable conversations I have had about sociology and social work over a number of years with John Mayer, Associate Professor of Sociology at the Albert Einstein College of Medicine, New York. I should also like to thank my colleagues, both sociologists and social workers, at the North Western Polytechnic who have made helpful and critical comments on my attempts to relate sociology and social work. My thanks also to the many students I have taught (and who have taught me) for their contributions to the thinking that has gone into the book. The library staff of the North Western Polytechnic should also be praised for their toleration of my rather erratic borrowing habits.

The book is of course entirely my own responsibility.

London 1970                                    BRIAN HERAUD

# PART I

# CHAPTER 1

# Sociology and
# Social Work—An Introduction

SOCIOLOGY is today attracting the attention of increasing numbers of social workers. This is seen by the number of articles and books appearing in Britain and America which discuss the relationship between the two fields. Sociology is increasingly seen as helping to provide a basis of knowledge on which the social worker can draw in order to work with clients in the context of the complex organizational settings of a modern society. Sociology is not the only social science which makes up this "knowledge base", nor is the relationship between the two of a very recent origin. The whole range of the social sciences are at the disposal of the social worker, or for that matter anybody who wishes to understand human society in a more systematic and scientific manner. In addition to sociology, psychology and social anthropology might be mentioned as disciplines of the most immediate relevance.[1] It is perhaps not sufficiently recognized that it is from these basic disciplines that social workers derive the knowledge that is used. Thus Timms,[2] referring to one of the most important areas of social work, social casework, points out that "the knowledge used derives mainly from the disciplines of psychology and sociology, and there is no body of casework knowledge as such". In this sense the relationship between the social sciences and social work parallels that between the biological sciences and the practice of medicine. Whilst the point made by Timms is clearly valid, it is also possible to suggest that the point at which the social sciences and the practice of social work intersect is, at least potentially, one at which knowledge might also be created.

3

The interchange between the social worker and the social scientist might be described as a "transactional" one in which both sides have considerable contributions to make, a situation which is stimulating in its immediate context and exciting in more distant prospect.

Again, sociology had an important influence on social work in its formative years and played a part in the first courses of training for social workers. The early sociological influence on social work was based mainly on the evolutionary theories of Spencer which, as Leonard[3] has shown, served to reinforce beliefs in the concept of personal inadequacy as the cause of social problems. Spencer's view of society as being in a state of balance in which there should be no interference by the State or other agencies to protect inadequate individuals, influenced social work in Britain and produced, in particular in the Charity Organization Society, a belief in extreme "individualism" and in the need to foster independence and self-reliance in the face of economic insecurity. The work of Booth,[4] which showed that problems such as poverty were due not to personal inadequacy but to such environmental factors as low earnings, was rejected by many social workers at this time.

Again, the first academic institution devoted to the training of social workers was named the School of Sociology and, at its inauguration in 1903, placed sociological studies (based mainly on the theories of Hobhouse) at the forefront of its curriculum.[5] By this time the more evolutionary theories were being modified to include some belief in the need for co-operative action to ensure the welfare of all. In America, sociology was beginning to provide a framework for the understanding of social problems which was useful for social workers. In 1917 Mary Richmond published an influential book entitled *Social Diagnosis* in which she defined social work and the social worker's task in mainly sociological terms, which emphasized the importance of social factors in the understanding of the individual. The social worker was, according to Richmond, concerned to make "as exact a definition as possible of the situation and personality of a human being in some social need . . . in relation to the social institutions of his community". Treatment was to be based on the collection and interpretation of social evidence, which consisted of "all facts as to personal or family history which indicated the nature of a given client's difficulties and the means to their solution".

## THE "PSYCHIATRIC DELUGE"

However, the influence of sociology on the early social workers was considerably diminished by developments in a new area of psychology, namely psycho-analysis and psychiatry. The "psychiatric deluge", as it has been termed,[6] first began to make its impact in America and, although never so influential, has also been of considerable importance in British social work. The concepts and explanations of individual behaviour derived from the clinical experiences of the psychiatrists appeared particularly appropriate for the social worker, who also worked in a face-to-face relationship with an individual client. The psychiatric approach concentrated on the intra-psychic condition of the individual and advanced explanations concerned, amongst other things, with the states of feeling the individual had about his problems. In addition, the dynamic relationship between the psychiatrist or social worker and client was itself seen as part of the process of understanding and aiding the individual. Such an approach seemed to provide a distinctive area of knowledge which the social worker could "operationalize" in her immediate contacts with clients, and removed her from the role of the rather helpless "manipulator" of the social environment in which she had been cast by the social diagnosis approach. One American writer[7] went so far as to claim that 50 per cent of the cases described by Mary Richmond in her *Social Diagnosis* presented "clearly psychiatric problems" while another 15 per cent suggested the possibility of a "psychopathic condition". However, the skills which derived from this new knowledge also helped the social worker in her quest for professional status, and provided a basis on which professional skills might develop. A concern with wider social conditions and the quest for social reform which the sociological approach implied was hardly a sure base for a claim to professional status, for it smacked too much of the politician or labour leader. A more technical exercise on behalf of individuals appeared a far surer basis for such a claim. However, the distinction between "reform" and "therapy" which these two approaches imply, has been a major ideological issue within social work to this day, and will form a basis for much of the subsequent discussion of social work in what follows.

The effect of the move from "cause" to "function" (or from reform to therapy), as it has been called,[8] was to substitute a mainly psychiatric theoretical basis for the previous emphasis on a more sociological framework. This, according to Leonard,[9] led to a "sociological blindness" in which social work became characterized by a "kind of reductionism which explains all social phenomena in terms of individual personality ignoring the structural elements". One must, in fairness, also add that sociologists, particularly in America, were also, as part of their professional development, turning away from a concern with social problems, and thus practical endeavours such as social work, in favour of an interest in more theoretical approaches to society. In Britain, where sociology has never lost its concern with social problems and practical issues, the trend has been less noticeable and sociologists have not lost touch with practical concerns, including social work. As a result British social work has always been able to maintain some balance between its psychological and sociological components.

## A NEW CONVERGENCE

However, it is to sociology that social workers and other practitioners are again turning. In the United States this new and important convergence appears to date from the mid-1950s, when an increase in the number of sociologists working in schools of social work and in social work agencies has been noted.[10]

There is a fresh realization that a sociological approach is a necessary part of the diagnosis of individual behaviour and the treatment of individual problems, and that sociology is of relevance to the understanding of the individual act. As a result of the influence of psychiatry and psycho-analysis, social workers have relied on the handling of "the relationship" between worker and client as an important means of achieving their ends. However, it seems clear that a focus on the "relationship" between worker and client leaves out of account a whole dimension of important social and cultural factors. One of these is the differing social position which worker and client may occupy. For example, social worker and client come from a different kind of family, have had a different kind of educational experience as well as experience of working life, and may have widely differing attitudes to individual or social problems. The social worker, like anyone else, will have a model of society and how it functions, or "ought" to function, gained from his own individual experience. But these two views of the world, those of the client and the social worker, may differ at a number of important points. For example, Leichter and Mitchell[11] have compared the "kinship values" of caseworkers in a New York agency with those of their clients. To the statement "It is usually nice for a young married couple to live near their parents" a significantly higher proportion of clients than caseworkers (42 per cent compared with 14 per cent) replied in the affirmative. An even greater discrepancy was found when the two groups were faced with the statement "it's selfish for someone to cut himself off from his relatives": 65 per cent of clients against only 16 per cent of caseworkers agreed with the statement. This difference in the orientation of caseworker and client to family life may lead to a number of difficulties unless such factors are taken into consideration. Thus the caseworker may attempt to obtain from the client an adherence to forms of behaviour which are not really accepted in the client's social milieu.

A further problem found by social workers in their relationship with clients relates to the intake process, or the first interview. Some clients do not continue beyond this initial contact with the agency, and this has been explained in terms of the different ways in which the two conceive of the initial interview and its purpose. Part of the social worker's "professionalism" lies in the assumption that the first interview should be one of diagnosis and study. However, the client may see the purpose of the interview as the provision of more immediate assistance with problems. This difference implies a difference in the way in which each conceives of the roles appropriate to this situation. Such problems are not so much the result of the different personalities of each individual but of differences in the roles prescribed by each individual's social situation.

These illustrations suggest that an approach which goes beyond a discussion of the "personalities" of individuals is vital to the social worker; in these examples it would appear that some analysis of the differences in cultural values held by social groups, and of the whole theoretical area known as "role theory", is vital to the whole process of casework.

Gordon Hamilton[12] has summed up the problem as follows:

> The social worker of tomorrow can no longer restrict herself to consideration of how the client feels about his situation. He must be equally attuned to the effects on the client of ethnic, class and other significant group determinants of behaviour; the "hard core" family cannot be fully explained as one merely showing character disorders.

This kind of statement underlines the plea made by a number of contemporary writers on social work that the "social" be put back into social work. Although, as Wootton[13] suggests, this may mean a number of things, at the least it implies a reduced emphasis on psycho-analytic theory and a fresh realization that individuals and their families live in streets with neighbours, spend a good deal of time in factories and other workplaces, and are affected by what happens outside their homes as well as by domestic relationships. Taking into account the existence of various forms of counselling it is difficult in fact to see a distinctive role for the social worker except as someone who deploys a range of knowledge about the social as well as the psychological context of social problems.

This raises again the distinction between a therapeutic and a reformist orientation. The adoption of a mainly therapeutic approach, in which measures directed towards individuals are considered important irrespective of any statutory or structural reform, is a distinguishing feature of social work ideology.[14] However, social workers are showing an increasing concern with reform and therefore with more structural issues. The interest of some social workers in such pressure groups as the Child Poverty Action Group and in the wider context of such problems as homelessness, indicates the beginning of a change in orientation.

Other changes in the practice of social work itself may also imply a greater consideration of the importance of the sociological approach. Concepts such as community care and the increased use of preventive measures, although in their infancy, result in a greater need for knowledge about society and its institutional framework. In addition, the organizational basis of statutory social work is undergoing change, whilst a substantial drive is being mounted to increase the numbers of professionally trained workers. With social work in such a furore, this is perhaps an appropriate time for the reconsideration of some of the fundamental assumptions and theories upon which practice is based. Change is in the air, and this gives an opportunity for a fresh look at the basis of knowledge which the social sciences provide for social work. The Seebohm Report,[15] with its recommendations that groups and communities as well as individuals should be made the focus of the social work approach, clearly implies that social workers should widen and sharpen their sociological perspectives. The recent Gulbenkian Report[16] on community work carries a similar message.

The fact that sociology can help the social worker in dealings with clients and with improvements and changes in practice is not, of course, the only reason why sociology should be welcomed by the social work profession. The possession of specialized knowledge which is not generally available is one recognized attribute of a profession and social workers, as well as other occupational groups, have for some time been aspiring to professional status. Thus in the same way as the findings of psycho-analysis were welcomed by the social workers of the 1930's as a means of increasing professional status, so in the 1960's sociology can be seen as performing a similar function. One danger here is that findings derived from sociology might be "taken over" by the social worker with a good deal more confidence than would be attached to them by the sociologist or the research worker. Thus one unfortunate result of professionalization may be the wider dissemination of material of variable quality in the absence of any methodological context. One way out of this dilemma is to increase the social worker's awareness of the whole apparatus of social scientific research which accompanies sociological inquiries. Although a detailed analysis of scientific method will not be a part of this book, certain problems of a methodological nature which face the sociologist and which should also be understood by the social worker will be briefly outlined.

## EXISTING SOCIOLOGICAL
## PERSPECTIVES IN SOCIAL WORK

Social workers and other practitioners will, of course, have a certain kind of social or sociological perspective. Sociologists have even been accused of trying to "teach their grandmothers to suck eggs" in their attempts to impart sociological wisdom to the social worker.[17] Clearly, an experienced social worker who becomes familiar with an area and its inhabitants over a long period has at his disposal a good deal of "social" knowledge, in particular about family and community life. However, the accumulation of such facts does not, in itself, imply a sociological understanding.

Beliefs that one "knows about" or "understands", for example, family and community life, through intimate contact with it are confounded not only by the complexity of these subjects and the subtlety of their relationship with the wider society, but also by the (often unacknowledged) emotional and value-laden content of such "knowledge". Although it seems impossible to stand entirely clear of such values, the social scientist attempts to be at least aware of his value orientations and to take these into account in his work. Although the social worker has, in the last analysis, to act on the basis of values (his own and those of the agency, the profession and society) it also seems important that he attempts to "stand clear" in order to try to understand more objectively the nature of the social interactions in which he is involved.

Thus before a sociological perspective can develop, there must be a progressive "unlearning" of the models of society which are held; here, sociology has the important function in the education of social workers and others of "debunking" certain popular views of society.

Again, the kind of sociological perspective adopted by social work theorists has emphasized a particular approach to society which has for long dominated sociological thought, particularly in the United States. Thus Timms[18] comments that social-work theorists are much concerned with stressing a "consensus" model of society which sees groups as being in fundamental agreement about norms and values and thus about social problems and social deviance. This leads to a conception of social failure and deviance in terms of "maladjustment" and treatment as a process of "adjustment" to some agreed norm. There is, however, less emphasis on a model of society which stresses conflict, rather than consensus, and sees various mechanisms (including social work) as playing a coercive role. This theory, which will be expanded in later chapters, suggests a different framework for the analysis of individual or social problems and presents the social worker with a very different framework in which to view such problems. In the same vein, C. Wright Mills[19] comments that the approach of Mary Richmond, although influenced by a certain kind of sociological thinking, still defines problems in mainly individual terms, which are at the most seen in terms of the immediate "situation" of the individual. However, such situations are rarely linked into structures characterized, for example, by differing and conflicting class interests:

> Thus pathologists tend to slip past structures to focus on isolated situations . . . present institutions train several types of persons—such as judge and social worker—to think in terms of "situations". Their activities and mental outlook are set within the existent norms of society; in their professional work they tend to have an occupational incapacity to rise above a series of "cases".

## SOCIAL WORK
## AS A FOCUS OF SOCIOLOGICAL INTEREST

There is also reason to believe that the subject of social work is beginning to interest larger numbers of sociologists and other social scientists. The development of social-work training has increased the number of social scientists in direct contact with social workers. Small beginnings are being made with research in which both are involved. One reason why social work should interest sociologists is that, like medicine and education, it is a focus for the organization and expression of certain social values in society. Social work as an occupation has also become a focus for professionalization and bureaucratization and provides means by which these can be studied. A number of fields of practice have, in the past, been the subject of sociological interest. Thus in America considerable attention has been given by sociologists to the institution of modern medical practice.[20] Studies have been made of medical education, of hospitals, and of the social significance of illness and its treatment. Here the interest has not been just to achieve a more efficient medical service by analysis designed to help doctors achieve their ends, but the understanding that can be gained through such analysis of significant features of the social system. Thus medicine can be seen as a major focus of the contemporary value system. It enshrines beliefs about life, death, and the quality of man's social as well as physical existence. Examination of this kind of institution provides a short cut to the understanding of the value systems of different groups, of systems of authority, and of complex organizations. In Britain the field of education has served a similar purpose, and there has been relatively little interest displayed in fields like social work except by those working in areas of study such as social administration. There is no reason why a sociology of social work should not develop in Britain, and this might take as one possible model the analysis made of medical practice in America and of education in Britain.

## THE DEVELOPMENT OF SOCIOLOGY

A further reason for the convergence between sociology and social work is the recent enormous expansion and therefore increasingly pervasive influence of sociology as an academic discipline on all fields of practice. By now departments and chairs of sociology exist in most British universities. Between 1962 and 1964 the number of chairs established in the subject increased from three to twenty.[21] Sociologists, as well as other social scientists, are also working in research capacities in fields such as crime and delinquency, housing and town planning, and medicine. The development of the subject is itself an interesting social phenomenon which it would be inappropriate to consider here in any detail. Sociology has developed in an age in which a "scientific" approach to phenomena of all kinds has gained ascendancy. The value of an ordered systematic way of looking at the physical universe has long been accepted, and man has for some time taken almost for granted the fact that the natural and physical universe can to some extent be controlled and used for his benefit. However, human society itself, the social universe, has until recently been reserved for the speculations or dogmatisms of philosophers or religious sages. Only in the eighteenth and nineteenth centuries, that is many hundreds of years after the investigation of certain problems of the physical universe began, did man begin to investigate human society in any kind of systematic way and to suggest that it could be studied in the same way as the physical universe. But today the social sciences offer to the minds of some a way of ordering this social universe. The need for a more systematic and scientific way of looking at human activities is now more recognized, and this has inevitably come to have importance for those who work in the practising and counselling professions. Increasingly expert and professional knowledge is demanded rather than the speculations of amateurs; thus teachers and social workers are increasingly looked to as experts in human relationships, and they in turn must look to the social scientist for a basis of knowledge in order to function in this way. Just as medical practice developed rapidly when it began to use the findings of biologists, physiologists, and other scientists, social practitioners can only develop their skill by using the findings of social science.

## THE NATURE OF APPLIED SOCIOLOGY

The relation between the academic discipline of sociology and practical fields where this knowledge might be applied is a complex one. Certain difficult questions arise. For what purposes or ends is the knowledge made available to be used; that is, how ought sociology to be applied? In what way is this knowledge to be incorporated into professional practice; that is, how can sociology be applied?

In the first place, how is the sociologist distinguished from the practitioner—such as the social worker or the teacher?

Sociology and social work are often confused in the popular imagination, as anybody who interviews candidates for entry to undergraduate courses in sociology will know. As Berger[22] suggests, there exists "an image of the sociologist as a sort of theoretician for social work". This image has developed partly historically as a result of the association between sociology and social problems which developed in the wake of large-scale industrialization. However, sociology is a discipline concerned with understanding such problems and, more importantly developing more general theories of society. Social work is a practical exercise in helping individuals or groups with problems. There is nothing inherent in the sociological enterprise which leads to the practice of social work or anything else. But a sociological understanding is vital to all those who, like social workers, seek to work with people with certain goals or values in mind. Thus it is quite normal for students who desire a career in social work to take a degree in sociology before embarking on professional training.

In a book published in 1931, one of the few wholly devoted to the subject of sociology and social work, McIver[23] distinguishes between the "science" of sociology and the "art" of social work. The former is concerned solely with understanding what is, that is society as it exists. The latter is concerned with the manipulating, controlling, and changing of individuals and society, thus involving the specific use of values to guide such ends. Sociology cannot, however, prescribe these as it would then lose its claim to a scientific status. The function of sociology in relation to social work is, according to McIver, to suggest how social problems arise and how, if change or amelioration of these problems is desired, this might best be secured by a deeper understanding of their characteristics and causation. Sociology cannot directly solve practical everyday problems, and science, as he puts it, is not a "ready reckoner". However, sociology could provide the basic material by which the social worker could develop a social philosophy, or a rational way of harnessing the deep desire to help others. This would involve the knowledge of the social phenomena involved in every case but which transcend the individual case. This would help to set realistic limits to the social worker's aspirations on behalf of her clients.

The distinctions made by Berger and McIver between the sociologist, who is concerned to understand society, and the practitioner, who is concerned to use values in the pursuit of certain ends such as physical or social health, can be summed up in the claim that sociology makes to being "value free". This does not mean that the sociologist has no values or beliefs of his own— a clearly impossible situation. What is implied is that in his work as a sociologist, the individual (so far as it is possible) leaves behind his own personal convictions and feelings and attaches importance to only one value—that of scientific integrity. This, of course, is very difficult; there may be issues on which the sociologist has no particular feelings or beliefs, but this is unlikely. What is necessary, then, is that he tries to understand and control his values and to see them as possible biases in the analysis of any particular social situation. What is important is to attempt to lay bare the facts of any situation and let others, such as social workers or politicians, take action about such facts.

Some social scientists reject the idea of a value-free, disinterested social science both on the grounds that it is in any case impossible to keep values from entering the work and to recognize fully the implications of these values, and because they feel that sociology should, in fact, take up a particular value position. Thus it is felt by some that the social sciences, and sociology in particular, should be the spearhead of social reform and should criticize the *status quo*. Sociology should be the means of building a new and reformed society. It is, of course, equally possible for the sociologist to support the *status quo* and to apply his skills to the support of thoroughly reactionary policies.

The value-free sociologist asserts his right to be interested in knowledge for its own sake and to seek this knowledge. However, he cannot get away from the dilemma that knowledge is not just the property of the scientist and can be used for a variety of ends, some of which he may not accept. This dilemma becomes even greater when the sociologist is working directly in conjunction with a practitioner who is going to apply this knowledge directly to achieve some end.

Gouldner[24] has suggested two alternative ways of looking at the relationship between the sociologist and the practitioner. Accepting that the relationship is one between consultant and client, he distinguishes between two possible approaches for the sociologist. In one, the "engineering" approach, the client's formulation of the problem is accepted by the sociologist whose only concern is to find the most efficient way of attaining the client's ends. In the other, the "clinical" approach, the sociologist is not restricted to the client's own definition of the problem, but is concerned to introduce his own values and may, indeed, even see the client's definition of the situation (for example the social worker's view of social or individual problems) as part of the problem. This approach not only implies the clarification of the client's values or ends, but the examination of possible incompatibilities in these values of ends. In addition the attitudes and values of those who consult practitioners (e.g. the clients of social workers) are also part of the whole problem in which the sociologist becomes involved. Nor, it should be added, should the sociologist be indifferent to the results of his interventions or policy suggestions. The dangers of ignoring such issues can be seen in the application of sociology to industry where, it has been argued, knowledge has been used to make workers more productive and to reduce potential or actual conflict with management. This so-called "cow sociology" (in which workers are made into happy cows) highlights the problem of applied sociology; that is the possible lack of control over the use of knowledge derived from sociology and the uncritical acceptance of the practitioner's definition of the situation or problem. For example, in much of the work carried out for industry the problem has been viewed entirely from the standpoint of management; thus one group has been assisted at the expense of another. The sociologist then becomes a tool of the practitioner.

The clinical approach outlined above corresponds broadly to the position of sociologists like C. Wright Mills and Lynd[25] who have pointed to the dangers of ignoring the uses to which knowledge might be put. Lynd, who posed the question "Knowledge for what?", answered by suggesting that the sociologist had a vital interest and a moral commitment in the use to which his knowledge was to be put.

In the case of social work, which is at base an interference in the moral lives of individuals and society, such dangers are particularly strong. In a society characterized by social inequality, social work may be seen as a means of legitimizing and supporting the *status quo*, in particular of manipulating individuals into accepting under-privileged positions. Thus the sociologist must be particularly on his guard against the consequences of such an engineering approach. One form of protection against such difficulties lies, as Halmos[14] suggests, in taking the ideological foundations of social work as a major focus for sociological analysis. Providing the normative basis of the social work process can be laid bare in a critical manner, the sociologist can to an extent avoid the charge of engineering the goals of one group at the expense of another. What becomes important is an analysis of the value positions of all groups concerned in the social work process.

There appear to be two main ways in which sociology might be applied to practical fields. Firstly, sociology can be seen as providing a broad liberal education together with a systematic framework within which people (whether practitioners or not) can think about human society. Here the function of sociology is to challenge common-sense views and biases and to replace them with a framework of knowledge about the social forces impinging on practical efforts to assist or educate people. However, there is no necessarily deep interpenetration of sociological findings with practice or a focusing on certain specific areas of interest. Instead, as Tropp[26] has put it, "one should not be afraid of introducing students to a wide range of ideas. Both teacher training and social worker training have to teach students to think and I know of no better way than of acquainting them with the ideas of the great philosophers and sociologists." Here sociological material is presented and the practitioner is left to determine how or whether he can use it in his practising relationships with other people.

The second view rests on the belief that the practitioner can best utilize sociological findings by a closer application of them to his actual work and practice. This implies some prior consideration of the basic tasks confronting the social worker. McIver[23] suggests that the concept of individual maladjustment lies at the root of social work and particularly casework, which is the major area of social-work practice. This is the principle by which the task confronting the caseworker is most frequently expressed. He distinguishes between the many individual maladjustments of everyday life and the more specific departures from certain standards which imply more important maladjustments between an individual and a social situation. It is with these latter problems that the social worker is concerned. Here it is important to distinguish between certain absolute maladjustments which most would accept as requiring help from a social worker and relative maladjustments, that is problems of individual nature about which there might be controversy. This is the point at which, according to McIver, sociology is of importance to the social worker because in this situation the social worker is liable to be at the mercy of many conflicting possible courses of action. The social worker has to decide whether or not a problem exists and what course of action to take in relation to it. What is required is an analysis of the social background of each case and a classification of the type of maladjustment which is dominant in each situation. The first implies, among other things, some understanding of the subjective meaning that each social situation has for an individual; the second implies the setting out of the elements which are present in each case and thus the systematic classification of social maladjustment. Both processes are similar to those which a doctor goes through in the diagnosis and treatment of each case. In this instance, the social scientist joins the social worker in the task of diagnosis and treatment.

Greenwood[27] has stressed that the application of sociology to social work does not just imply the understanding of an academic discipline but the translation of its findings into terms which the social worker can use. Thus social science theory must be turned into practice principles which are meaningful to the social worker. This requirement derives from the complex and abstract nature of much of social science and the difficulties the non-specialist has in learning what is virtually a new language. These factors have in the past prevented a greater interaction between the two fields. Two primary needs in this direction are research centred on the systematic classification and analysis of the kinds of diagnosis and treatments common to social work practice, which can be seen as specimens which await classification within a social scientific framework; secondly, social work can be seen as a goal-oriented activity, and thus the clarification of goals becomes important. Social work has become the focus of the interests of a number of different parties (workers, clients, administrators, local councillors, etc.), thus making difficult the clarification of goals. Thus only if the various goals are investigated from the point of view of the various actors in this situation can such a clarification be realized.

The concepts of adjustment and maladjustment can only be utilized within a cultural framework which includes a consideration of the norms and values of all involved. For example, the goals of social-work agencies are related to the goals of the social-work profession which, in turn, are linked to more general norms held by certain dominant groups in society. This involves an analysis of the total value structure, and this in turn leads on to the need to determine the social functions played by social work in a particular culture.

Again, an emphasis on the individual case and the service rendered to an individual by a social worker constitutes, for Halmos,[14] one organizing principle by which a sociological contribution to social work can be made. Thus "the case is the fulcrum of social work and, as a rule, the individual and his family, and this ought to determine the direction of sociological orientation. The sociology of the case is primarily a family sociology and secondarily the sociology of the social structure and culture."

This order is dictated by the logic of the learning process and the practice of social work, in particular casework; a clear link between sociology and casework is provided by a focus on the family.

However, this should not be the limits of the contribution that sociology can make to social work. The emphasis on "the case", as Halmos points out, often means the loss of a wider social or political perspective; this may affect the way in which both diagnoses and methods of treatment are conceptualized. For example, social workers often use, but take for granted, community resources in the process of helping people with problems. There is therefore a need for the meaning of terms like "the community" to be extended and sharpened by sociological analysis.

It is clear, also, that the social worker needs to be able to analyse and classify individual social problems and to relate individual symptoms to broader categories of diagnosis and treatment. Thus the theoretical approach of sociology which stresses broad categories rather than individual cases should be linked in an explicit way with practical training in the social work agency; such practical experience is not only an essential part of social work training, but can also be a complement to the theoretical teaching of the social scientist. Here a sociological empathy could be built up, which is distinguished from the sociological intellectualization of the pure academic, in which the student could be encouraged to get the feel of the situation through applying sociological insights to practical situations.

Finally, social work itself and the ideology which underlies it should itself be the subject of sociological analysis. This enables the student to see something of the political and social framework in which social work has developed and at present functions, and thus encourages the student to locate himself in his profession and his society. Thus, analysis is required of the therapeutic as opposed to the reformist bias in social work, of the value system of the profession and the relationship between this and values held in the wider society, of the functions which social work carries out for the wider society. Again, what is also required is an analysis of the process by which aspirants for professional membership come to adopt certain professional values and develop a professional identity and ideology. In the study of social work training, the function of the sociologists is "to hold up a mirror to the whole situation in which student and teacher find themselves."[14] Unless this is done the student may, because of reliance on ideological principles internalized too rigidly during training, be unable to rethink his approach to social problems in a period of rapid social change. Thus, in a period of change and development (e.g. of an organizational kind) the kind of analysis of the social work profession and its social context which sociology could offer appears of vital importance.

There is, as yet, no definitive statement of the content of a programme in sociology and social work, although several promising preliminary suggestions have been set out.[28]

Meyer et al.[10] distinguish four levels at which sociology and social work can be related which are both extensions of existing trends in practice and also reflect current developments in sociology. The term level means the broad distinctions that can be made in the objectives of social work and the methods used to achieve these ends.

First, there is the level of interpersonal interaction, already stressed by the writers mentioned above, which includes social casework and groupwork and in particular the interpersonal aspects of these approaches, with the idea of the family as client as one illustration of the approach. Secondly, the community level includes efforts by social workers and others to intervene in community processes in order to solve problems and has as its counterpart an increased interest amongst sociologists in community problems and structure.

Thirdly, the agency level includes a concern in the administrative problems of the social work agency, but also the organization in which social workers come into contact with clients; the counterpart in sociology is a growing interest in the sociology of the organization. Finally, the societal level includes the concern of the social worker in a broad attack on social problems through involvement in the controversies about social policy, a development which has a parallel in the growth of political sociology and the study of social movements.

The plan of the book draws on some of the approaches outlined above and makes a distinction between the contribution that sociology can make to the understanding of the social situation of the client (Part II) and of the social worker (Part III). Part II involves discussion of some of the central features of modern society, including the family and kinship, the community, the system of social stratification and social deviance, and the interrelationship between these areas and the social work process. In Part III the functions that social work carries out are discussed, including the maintenance of stability and the facilitation of change. The process of professionalization in social work is also discussed, including the process of professional socialization; finally, there is an analysis of the organizational context of social work, including the nature of professional and bureaucratic authority. Finally, in Part IV some of the problems surrounding the relationship between sociology and social work are discussed.

The presentation of material has inevitably involved selection and this has been carried out with a number of considerations in mind. Material has been selected so as to give a representative account of the work of contemporary sociologists in some of the fields which are of most importance for the social worker. The selection has therefore not been confined to British material but includes a number of studies made in the United States and elsewhere which appear of great significance to social workers wherever they work. Again, it is also important that practitioners gain some understanding of the nature of sociology as a whole if they are to utilize it fully and with the greatest understanding. Thus one chapter has been devoted to the sociological perspective in which certain concepts and theories are introduced, the relationship between sociology and some other social sciences is sketched out, and further problems involved in sociological analysis are suggested. The broad plan of each chapter or set of chapters (apart from those on sociology and the conclusion) is of a short introductory section followed by an exposition of the sociological approach to each particular subject and a conclusion in which some of the implications for social work of the sociological material presented are drawn together.

It is hoped that this book can make a contribution to sociology teaching on the many different types of courses of training and education for social work. The book may, in particular, be useful to students who have little previous knowledge of sociology. It is also hoped that the book will be of value to some of the newer degree courses, both at universities and at other colleges under the auspices of the Council for National Academic Awards, which attempt to give a grounding in social science and a professional qualification in social work at the same time and thus are able to extend and deepen the relationship between the social sciences and practices such as social work.

## NOTES AND REFERENCES

1. These disciplines were selected by UNESCO experts as of greatest relevance to social work; see *The Contribution of Social Sciences in Social work Training*, UNESCO, Paris, 1960.
2. N. Timms, *Social Casework—Principles and Practice*, Routledge & Kegan Paul, London, 1964
3. P. Leonard, *Sociology in Social Work*, Routledge & Kegan Paul, London, 1966.
4. C. Booth, *Life and Labour of the People of London, 1889–1903*, MacMillan, London, 1903.
5. M. Smith, *Professional Education for Social Work in Britain*, Allen & Unwin, London, 1965.
6. K. Woodroofe, *From Charity to Social Work*, Routledge & Kegan Paul, London, 1962.
7. M. Jarrett, The psychiatric thread running through all social casework, Proceedings of the National Conference on Social Work, 1919; cited in R. Lubove, *The Professional Altruist*, Harvard Univ. Press, 1965.
8. Porter R. Lee, cited in Lubove, *op. cit.*
9. P. Leonard, The application of sociological analysis to social work training, *Br. J. Sociol.* **19** (4), Dec. 1968.
10. H. Meyer *et al.*, Social work and social welfare, in P. Lazarsfeld (ed.), *The Uses of Sociology*, Weidenfield, London, 1968.
11. H. Leichter and W. Mitchell, *Kinship and Casework*, Russell Sage Foundation, New York, 1967.

12. In a foreword to H. Stein and R. Cloward, *Social Perspectives on Behaviour*, Free Press, Glencoe, 1961.
13. B. Wootton, *Social Science and Social Pathology*, Allen & Unwin, London, 1959.
14. P. Halmos, Problems arising in the teaching of sociology to social workers, *Int. Soc. Serv. Rev.* (8), March 1961.
15. Report of the Committee on local authority and allied personal social services Cmnd 3703, H.M.S.O., 1968 (the Seebohm Report).
16. *Community Work and Social Change*, Longmans, London, 1968.
17. See Letters, *Case Conference*, vol. 4, no. 9, 1958.
18. N. Timms, The role of the social worker, *New Society*, 3 Sept. 1964.
19. C. Wright Mills, The professional ideology of social pathologists, *Am. J. Sociol.* **49**, 1943.
20. See R. Merton *et al.*, *The Student Physician*, Harvard Univ. Press, 1957; A. Stanton & Schwarz, *The Mental Hospital*, Basic Books, New York, 1954; and T. Parsons, *The Social System*, ch. X, Routledge & Kegan Paul, London, 1952.
21. I. Neustadt, Teaching Sociology, inaugural lecture at University of Leicester, 1964.
22. P. Berger, *Invitation to Sociology*, Penguin, 1963.
23. R. McIver, *The Contribution of Sociology to Social Work*, Columbia University Press, New York, 1931.
24. A. Gouldner, Explorations in applied social science, in Gouldner and Miller (eds.), *Applied Sociology; Opportunities and Problems*, Free Press, Glencoe, 1965.
25. C. Wright Mills, *The Sociological Imagination*, O.U.P., New York, 1959; R. Lynd, *Knowledge for What?*, Princeton University Press, 1939.
26. A. Tropp, A comment on the relevance of sociology to the training of teachers and social workers, in Halmos (ed.), Sociological Review Monograph no. 4, 1961, Keele.
27. E. Greenwood, Social science and social work; a theory of their relationship, *Social Service Rev.* **29** (1) (1955).
28. See P. Leonard, 1968, *op. cit.*; Meyer *et al.*, *op. cit.*; and E. Thomas (ed). *Behavioural Science for Social Workers*, ch. 1, Free Press, New York, 1967.

# CHAPTER 2

# The Sociological Perspective

## INTRODUCTION

What is the nature of a sociological perspective? In the space of one brief chapter it is impossible fully to answer this question; however, it is important for the practitioner to have some general grasp of the approach taken by the areas of knowledge which are used, as this will make the flexible use of this knowledge more possible. One difficulty about attempting to answer the question "what is sociology?" lies in the fact that there is disagreement amongst sociologists on the kind of approach to take: one approach stresses the necessity to use the methods and procedures of the natural and physical sciences; on the other hand, there are those who argue that the meaning of human actions are, in the last analysis, not accessible in this way and who stress a more humanistic perspective.[1] These differences are partly a reflection of the desire of some sociologists for the status which is attached to scientific endeavour in general, and the resistance of others to the reduction of the complexities and uniqueness of human behaviour to what is conceived as the bloodless categories of science.

Another problem relates to the general use of a "social" approach toevents and problems; this implies the exposition or collection of facts or opinions about a range of events from the trivial to the important, but it is not necessarily coexistent with what most sociologists would regard as a sociological perspective. Nor is it sufficient to say that sociologists are interested in studying society or human behaviour, for historians, anthropologists, and psychologists could make the same claim. It is necessary to understand something of the way sociologists look at man in society, or of aspects of society, which distinguishes their approach from that of novelists or social commentators, or from other social scientists. What, for example is the specifically sociological approach to the study of marriage and the family—the professions or religion?

In what follows, some introduction will be given to certain concepts which are common to the thinking of most sociologists, irrespective of the theoretical approach taken, and which will form the framework of the approach in each chapter. One problem here is that sociology employs terms and concepts which are in everyday popular usage (such as culture, value, function, or institution) but invests these with a special meaning of their own which it is necessary to understand.

Some of these concepts will be introduced within a particular framework of thinking about man in society, and in which changes in the way sociologists have approached these tasks can also be briefly outlined.[2]

## THE INDIVIDUAL IN SOCIETY

One strand of thought which has run through sociology, and in particular characterized the approach of the early thinkers in the subject, is the view that the individual is born into a social world that he has not himself made. Thus an individual has to locate himself in society; firstly, in the family group and then within widening circles outside the family. Parents will control a child's behaviour and controls of various kinds will continue during the life of the individual. The concept of *social control* is generally used in sociology to denote the means by which society ensures that its members behave in certain ways; control rests in the last analysis on physical force or violence, but in many societies takes the form of persuasion rather than coercion.

Society is thus able to pass on to its members certain ways of acting. For example, when an individual marries he does so within limits which have been determined beforehand. In Britain the pattern is for marriage to be based on free choice and romantic love after a courtship in which the two individuals involved have got to know one another. But in other societies, such as India, the couple have often not met before the marriage which is arranged by the two families involved. Here very different kinds of behaviour are being shaped by what others expect; there are, therefore, shared *norms*, *values*, and *beliefs* which are referred to as the *culture* of a society. Values are generalized states of affairs which are held up to individuals as worth pursuing (examples are loyalty or independence), but are not specific forms of conduct. Norms are more direct requirements or demands about the behaviour of individuals in social situations. One distinction is between prescriptive norms, which spell out positively what an individual should do, and proscriptive norms, which directs individuals to abstain from certain activities. Norms are backed by positive or negative sanctions, such as rewards or punishments.

Bott[3] considers the various meanings of the terms norm and normal. Normal is used in three ways: to refer to what is "clinically" ideal from the point of view of psycho-analysts and psychologists; to refer to statistically average behaviour; and to refer to behaviour which people feel is expected and customary. The term norm is also used by social scientists to refer to a typical pattern of conduct which is observed in people's behaviour. Social norms are defined as "people's ideas about what behaviour is customary and what behaviour is right and proper in their social circle".

The extent to which actions are influenced by norms and values varies; in some societies, particularly simple ones, a wide range of choice is not available, and therefore norms are important as guides to actions although even here norms may not be precise or consistent. In more complex societies it is easier to ignore certain norms; studies of norms actually held by people have suggested considerable variability. Bott, in her study of the norms of family life, concluded that "informants found it difficult to make familial norms explicit at all". Considerable variation in norms is found even in small-scale societies.

In the examples cited above, the individuals are involved in situations which are subject to differing, but equally powerful, social pressures which have little or nothing to do with the personalities of the individuals involved but stem instead from cultural beliefs concerning, in the case of marriage, the control of sexual behaviour. The game, as it were, is "fixed" before the participants have arrived, often by members of the society who are long since dead.

Where shared norms govern behaviour which is particularly important for the maintenance or survival of the society, the term social institution is employed. Thus the norms which govern the forms of behaviour which lead individuals into marriage can be termed the institution of marriage. Other important social institutions are the law and education. Behaviour becomes institutionalized when it is organized around a formal set of norms which are accepted as important guides to behaviour.

One way of expressing this approach is to see society as set over and above the individual, and acting on him as a social fact; this is the view held by one of the early sociologists, Durkheim[4] (1858–1917), who defined social facts as "ways of thinking, acting and feeling external to the individual endowed with a power of coercion by means of which they control him". Thus institutions such as marriage or the law are facts which confront individuals and determine their behaviour.

## SOCIETY IN THE INDIVIDUAL

Durkheim was reacting, in a sense, to the extreme psychologism which characterized much thinking at this time, in which behaviour was seen largely in terms of the action of individuals; however, the picture conveyed in the last few paragraphs, which sees society almost as a prison in which the individual is doomed to spend his days, is one which does some violence to reality. It is clear, for example, that individuals are not (in the main) literally forced to conform to the will of society; in most cases the rules that exist are obeyed only too willingly. This is not because society's power is any weaker than suggested, but because people are induced to want what society also wants; thus society is in a sense even more powerful because it can determine what people *are* as well as what conduct should be followed. Society, therefore, gets into man.

As already suggested, powerful pressures exist in any situation which serve to define the behaviour that is appropriate. Thus in each situation individuals are confronted with a definite set of expectations and demands, and they have as the American sociologist Thomas (1863–1947) suggested, to define the situation or agree on what behaviour is appropriate.[5] In many cases people's definitions of the situation will coincide. But society has also provided a guide for the individual in these situations; this can be termed the *role* which individuals assume in social situations.[6] In a sense, society provides individuals with scripts which enable them, like actors in a theatre, to play their roles. Roles vary in the exactness with which they make demands on the individual; for example, some occupational roles are very loosely defined, such as those of many unskilled workers, but the doctor or the lawyer is expected to play his part according to a quite distinctive formula.

Roles also relate to *social positions (or statuses)* which individuals hold, such as husband and wife, teacher or student. There are various ways of approaching the concept of role. Emphasis can be given to the incumbent of the role or position, on the focal person, and on the set of individuals with whom this person interacts and who will have expectations relating to the focal role. Roles also have a dual, or pair, quality, in which behaviour in one position is usually specifically oriented to behaviour in one other position; thus a husband is generally expected to be economically active and to support his family, while a wife stays home, looks after the house, and minds the children. The content of roles also changes; more wives are going out to work and more husbands are engaging part of the time in domestic activity. But there are still certain expectations governing the roles of husband and wife.

One way of looking at roles and social positions is in the context of a *social structure:* thus each society can be seen as a formal hierarchy of social positions, and social roles which are attached to such positions, which persist over time irrespective of the individuals occupying them. The idea of social structure is applicable to any set of organized positions; examples include business organizations, factories, or schools.

Individuals gain access to roles through a process of *socialization* in which the child, and later the adult, learn the rules which allow them to become a member of groups and of society. The process of socialization relates not only to the process by which the child is moulded by the family, but to the entry of an individual into any social group; for example, a profession or occupation. One way of looking at roles is to see them as not only external to the individual, who accepts them like a role in a play, but as part of the identity of the individual. Thus at the same time as a child learns what role he has to play, he also begins to form some conception of his "self". G. H. Mead (1863–1931),[7] one of the first thinkers in this field, suggests that the child learns to play roles by "taking the roles of others", in which the child, through play, learns the roles of others around him; initially there are significant others, those persons with whom he is most closely associated; later the child learns that the roles he plays are subject to expectations from society and becomes oriented to generalized others. Through this general conception of society, the child learns to have a clear conception of himself.

Thus identity is bestowed socially; this can be seen by the relative ease with which it is possible to change the identity when the individual is subjected to a totally different set of influences from a new environment, such as a prison or an asylum. A similar process occurs when any group is made to accept a new set of roles, for example recruits to the army or to an occupation or profession; essentially what is created for the individual is a new identity or a definition of himself. In these situations the social world becomes internalized within the child or the adult; thus not only is society external to the individual in Durkheim's sense, but through internalization becomes also part of every individual: as Berger remarks: "society does not stop at the surface of our skins. Society penetrates us as much as it envelopes us. Our bondage to society is not so much established by conquest as by collusion . . . we are betrayed into captivity with our own co-operation."[5]

Another way of understanding the same point is through the

concept of *reference groups*; this is a collectivity which provides individuals with a model with which to compare themselves, and which is therefore decisive in the shaping of opinion and actions. In some cases one is a direct member of a reference group, in others the group influences the directions of behaviour. The world is, therefore, seen through the idea of a variety of groups with which a person associates himself. The need for membership in, and acceptance by, a group can influence the judgement, opinion, and actions of individuals.

In this section the idea of the individual as dominated by society has been supplemented by the view that man is controlled as much by inner as by outer forces.

Here, instead of the prison which society throws around us, social reality resembles more a puppet theatre in which the puppets act out willingly the parts assigned to them.

## CO-OPERATION AND CONFLICT

However, a third view of the relationship of man to society can be suggested. This introduces a new level of sociological analysis in which one of the key terms is that of *social relation*. One difficulty in dealing with the entity "society" (which, in Durkheim's view, had moral authority over the individual) is the vagueness of this concept. The concept of social relation, or the idea of a "network of social relationships", is implicit in use of the term society.[8] The term relates to the behaviour of more than one party and implies that the participants understand something of the significance of each other's behaviour. There will also, most importantly, be expectations about the behaviour of individuals in situations of social interaction which is related, in most cases, to the rules or norms which govern the situation.

In a situation of complete co-operation, the expectations of the participants are identical. But there may be other situations in which the expectations of the participants (or actors) are not in accord, that is a situation of social conflict. At the one extreme there is the possibility of perfect co-operation; at the other of total conflict;

normally situations of social interaction lie somewhere between these two poles. The issue of conflict and co-operation will be taken up again in a concluding section of this chapter.

Thus, although situations may be defined by the actors involved in identical ways, it is still possible for each actor to bring his own definition to each situation and for this to conflict with other definitions. Here the work of Weber (1864–1920),[9] another famous thinker of the early years of sociology, is of considerable importance. Whereas Durkheim stressed the objective reality of society, Weber emphasized the importance of understanding the subjective meaning that every "actor" brings to a social situation. Thus each social situation is established and sustained by the meaning brought into it by participants. In some cases this will be established firmly by tradition and the holding of common norms; but in many situations the actor can apply a deviant interpretation and attempt to get this established in place of the existing interpretation, or he can withdraw (or become alienated from) the situation in a variety of ways. An example of this is the charisma (denoting social authority not based on tradition) of the religious or political leader. Clearly, societies have changed and are changing as a result of the actions of man: one particularly important task for the sociologist is, in fact, to map out the causes and conditions of change. This view helps to add another strand to the Durkheimian view of society, by focusing on a further aspect of social reality; thus, paradoxically, although society defines us, it is in turn defined *by* us. The extent to which individuals rebel or deviate from accepted meaning and from the controls of society will, of course, vary with their social position: thus some have more power to change events than others. But the fact that society is, in this sense, in the hands of its members, cannot be denied.

Thus the notion of *social deviance*, the departure from socially accepted behaviour, constitutes a major area of interest for the sociologist; deviance can range from the refusal of the thief to accept the normal "definition of the situation" in respect to property, to the more subtle disregard of social conventions, characteristic of those defined by society as mentally ill. Again, deviance of an individual, or even small group, nature can be distinguished from *social disorganization*, or the refusal of a mass of individuals to accept common definitions, a situation which can result in revolution and the establishment of a new form of social order. Both types show the possibility of defiance of the established social order. A central part of this process is the withdrawal from such social forms of legitimacy, of a belief in their justification or rightness, on the part of individuals involved in the system.

A further way in which the individual can escape from the bonds of society is by the direct manipulation of events. Rather than rebellion or withdrawal, the individual attempts to structure events according to his own purposes. Thus, although the individual in the prison or asylum suffers a considerable onslaught on his identity, he also attempts to "work the system" by structuring events to suit his ends—in prison a complex underworld exists in which the inmates seek to frustrate or turn to their own advantage the system under which they live. Again, an individual may play his role from a distance, that is deliberately play a role with little or no inner conviction or identification with it: this happens particularly in situations where an individual is subject to coercion (as in many prisons or other closed institutions). Thus roles are not in all cases played automatically and unreflectingly as an almost automatic response to the expectations of the situation.[10]

This third picture of society does not deny that individual "actors" are constrained by external controls and also by the inner demands of the role: but there exist options about how roles should be played and how a situation should be defined. In some cases there is a refusal to play the role. This view leads away from the somewhat rigid determinism which derives from a certain level of the sociological perspective. Using again the analogy with drama to illustrate this view, Berger suggests that

> Social reality now seems to be precariously perched on the co-operation of many individual actors . . . the institutions of society, while they do in fact constrain and coerce us, appear at the same time dramatic conventions . . . they have been invented by past impresarios and future ones may cast them back into the nothingness whence they emerged.[5]

Sociologists are interested not only in the study of specific social relations but also in the connection between sets of relationships, and in the nature of the activities which sustain relationships. As already suggested, individuals are motivated to engage in social relations and to accept norms governing interaction through processes of socialization and also of education; these are carried out in group situations such as the family and the school. The complex of activities which sustain social relationships can be referred to as *the social system*, or, rather more usefully, as separate social systems or sub-systems which can be labelled the family system, the educational system, the economic or political system. One important part is the interrelationship of these systems; for example, as will be shown in more detail later, the family interacts with the economy, the community, and the value systems. Thus the way in which a child is socialized will depend on values held not only in the family but in the community and the wider society. One of the essential tasks of sociology is, in fact, to bring to light the complex interrelationships between these systems.

## SOCIOLOGY AND OTHER SOCIAL SCIENCES

In order to clarify further the nature of the sociological perspective it is useful at this stage to contrast this with other areas of the social sciences;[11] of greatest importance in the present context are psychology and administration.

These distinctions should not be misunderstood to imply that there are rigid distinctions between boundaries of inquiry in the social sciences; indeed, most sociological thinking implies certain psychological assumptions and much of the work of the psychologists is based on sociological assumptions. In addition, a variety of approaches are to be found within both fields.

Both psychology and sociology[12] focus on the understanding of human behaviour, but the former focuses on the different actions of the same individual, while the latter is concerned with interaction between individuals or the relationship of one individual to another, and the complex social structure and culture in which individuals are involved and which derives from social interaction. What the psychologist seeks to discover about the individual, who is for the sake of analysis taken away or abstracted from the environment, the sociologist seeks to discover about the environment, whilst, for the sake of analysis, putting aside the particular individuals which compose it. Thus a division of labour is made in which each social scientist tries to penetrate further into what appears to be a legitimate area of analysis without having to take all other relevant factors into account. Thus in no sense is psychology or sociology better than the other; the distinction simply rests on different levels of analysis. A parallel to the interest which the sociologist has in the social system is the interest of the psychologist in the personality. Again, certain problems appear to be better explained by one or the other kind of approach. For example, in the study of racial prejudice and discrimination, the psychologist could hope to show that people were prejudiced because of their disturbed personalities. But this approach appears inadequate when prejudice and discrimination appear to be part of the behaviour of the majority of the population and are manifested, in particular social situations, amongst those who have not previously behaved in this way.[13] Thus an explanation in terms of the social system, of the structure of social relationships, appears in certain cases a more useful approach. If the social and cultural factors involved in the situation are initially explored, then it may be shown that prejudice and discrimination derive in some situations not from individual personalities but from the social system in which individuals are involved; indeed, the social system may require behaviour of this kind.

An important area of overlap between psychology and sociology is in the developing field of social psychology. From the psychological point of view social factors are taken into account when it is important to study the influence of a person's social characteristics or setting on his behaviour. For the sociologist, social psychology involves the understanding of the way personality influences the outcome of social processes.

The distinction between the two approaches often breaks down in research or teaching, and at times the interests of the sociologist and social psychologist appear very close.

Teaching and research in social work, particularly in the area known as human growth and behaviour, appear to offer a particularly good opportunity for a closer liaison between sociology and psychology as well as an exposition of the important ways in which they differ.

Social administration has developed as a subject in the more recent past but, as yet, scarcely ranks as a discipline in its own right like psychology and sociology. Essentially the product of the development of the Welfare State in Britain, the object of social administration is the analysis of "the development of collective action for social welfare on the part of government, employers, philanthropic bodies and consumers to meet human needs; in brief the social services".[14] Social administration as a field of study arose in part because no other social science sufficiently concerned itself with such questions and with the social problems that derived from industrialization—it is therefore a part of the considerable development and increased specialization in the social sciences. Social administration can be seen, however, as utilizing, in a direct way, other social sciences (in particular sociology and economics). Although some sociologists are interested in the development of social problems and their amelioration, this is often incidental to an understanding of society as such; sociology appeared as too broad in perspective to undertake the necessary detailed analyses of social welfare institutions and the social services that were required: as one of the early thinkers in the field of social administration remarked, "sociology seemed to stand for nothing in particular and everything in general that had any connection with society".[15]

One subject of central concern in social administration is the distribution of income and of wealth and the effects of State action on this distribution. However, this is not studied, as in the case of the sociological approach, as a means of understanding and developing theories about the social system, but because of a more direct concern with the problems arising out of inequality and the merits or demerits of various schemes to redress this condition. There is thus a direct concern with values, in particular with the inequalities and "unfairness" of a modern stratified social system rather than with the analysis of the patterns of social interaction and social relationships generated by this structure.

## THE SCIENTIFIC STATUS OF SOCIOLOGY

It has already been suggested that there is some disagreement about the scientific status of sociology. The argument that sociology is a scientific endeavour rests on the view that both a generally scientific approach to human behaviour and a specifically scientific methodology are possible.

Science in general differs from other kinds of activity in that it claims to be based on the observation and recording of phenomena. It is thus empirical in that it is concerned with verifiable propositions about observable phenomena. It differs therefore from other activities which deal with non-observable phenomena and in which propositions are in no way capable of being verified. However, it is possible to observe the behaviour of physical matter under differing conditions and, it is claimed, of individual and group behaviour.

Thus a considerable amount of attention is given to the collection of data by methods common to much scientific endeavour. It is inappropriate in this context to look at these in any detail,[16] but, for example, in the social sciences various forms of survey methods are in common use in which data is collected (by sampling methods or otherwise) by the use of a questionnaire. Again, more intensive methods of participant observation may be used in which the observer becomes part of a group or community which he is studying and begins to understand it from the inside. This latter method, derived from anthropological field work, has been used in a number of community studies in Britain.

One attempt to solve some of the methodological problems involved is Weber's notion of "ideal type".[17] This refers to the deliberate accentuation of some of the features of the social phenomena under investigation, a process by which such phenomena can be seen in a "pure" form. This enables the phenomena under discussion to be understood and analysed more easily and gets around many of the problems of the complexity of phenomena which face the social scientist. Such forms are rarely found in practice and do not in any sense constitute an ideal in the moral or evaluative sense. Thus Weber's notion of the bureaucracy is an abstraction rarely if ever found in practice; but the notion of bureaucracy (to be examined again in Chapter 11) is an important guide to the kinds of question that can be asked in a study of a complex organization.

However, sociologists have faced considerable difficulties in applying the methods of science to social phenomena. A sociological study is a social phenomenon in its own right in which actors are playing parts and are aware of and react to this fact; thus individuals being questioned may give replies which do not represent the facts about their attitudes or beliefs but project instead a favourable image to the investigator. An investigator may choose a research project or take a particular line in an inquiry which reflects his own values. Although these difficulties can be guarded against (the sociologist can, as already suggested, make his values explicit from the outset), critics of the scientific approach stress the limitations of this methodology in understanding the subtleties and uniqueness of social interaction which may empty such interaction of real meaning. Thus Weber[9] stressed that the essential task of social sciences was the subjective understanding of the meaning attached by actors to interaction, and that the capacity to undertake this approach was, in fact, the great advantage that social scientists had over the physical or natural scientist.

But against this it is argued that such subjective or intuitive understanding is difficult to achieve since it allows for distortion on the part of the observer. Thus an intuitive understanding of how people define a situation is not enough; it must be accompanied by various methods and tools of social research, however difficult these are to administer.

## EMPIRICISM AND THEORY

Another related controversy is that between fact gathering and theory. Much of British sociology has been concerned with the observation of and the collection of facts about such questions as family life or poverty or the distribution of incomes. There have, for example, been a number of studies of the extended family in working-class areas. Again, an interest in the collection of data relating to poverty goes back to the early days of social investigation and is still a feature of research today. From such studies it is possible to know the extent and distribution of phenomena such as poverty or the distribution of income or wealth in general, which parallel in some way the understanding obtained in the nineteenth century of the main epidemic infections which from time to time decimated the urban population.

Although this descriptive approach is well developed, this fulfils only one aspect of a scientific approach. A more theoretical approach, in which hypotheses about such facts can be tested, has, certainly in Britain, been slower in coming.

Thus, to take the example of facts about income distribution, it is not clear what sociological significance can be attached to them.[8] Although such studies can indicate, for example, the distress and possible biological extinction which might result from very low incomes, it says little about the social relations which exist between individuals. Thus from the fact of knowing that different income levels exist it is impossible to say anything, or in particular to formulate and test hypotheses, about relationships between those on the same level (do they, for example, constitute a social group and if so of what kind?) or on different levels (are these co-operative or antagonistic?). Facts such as income differences thus provide the starting point for sociological analysis, which implies the formulation and testing of hypotheses about such facts. Thus income differences might be seen to reflect the power of one social group on another, or the rewards given for the performance of occupational roles to which are assigned different degrees of prestige.

The testing of hypotheses about observed phenomena is important, but the seeking of hypotheses is also a matter which requires considerable imaginative insight and original thought. C. Wright Mills[18] stresses the need for a highly developed sociological imagination and ably demonstrates his own capacities in this direction. Hypotheses may be derived in a variety of ways, as much by accident, idle thought, and speculation as by routine work. What distinguishes the imaginative thoughts of social scientists from, say, those of novelists, is that the hypotheses of the former must eventually be put to the most rigorous empirical tests and inquiries that can be designed, while the latter is often content with his original but unverified insight.

## SOCIOLOGICAL THEORY

The debate about empiricism and theory in sociology can be overstressed: in practice most sociologists adopt both approaches. The theoretical approach in sociology is sometimes difficult to understand because of the variety of levels at which theory is employed. As Merton[19] suggests, a "theoretical approach" can range from a general theoretical orientation in which the theorist points to the importance of one particular, and possibly hitherto ignored, variable in the study of some phenomenon (e.g. the influence of religion on birth rates) to the formulation of scientific theory in the shape of sociological laws; these are very rare, but one example would be Durkheim's[20] statement that suicide varies with the degree of integration of a social group. The kinds of concepts, such as role theory or reference group theory, which have been introduced so far belong essentially to what has been described as the middle range of sociological theorizing, i.e. theories which come in between the minor working hypotheses of everyday life and the large conceptual schemes which account for the growth and development of whole societies.

It is to a brief introduction to this latter type of speculation that discussion now turns.

One of the most fundamental questions posed by both philosopher and sociologist relates to the nature of social order; how is it that human societies cohere? Dahrendorf[21] has suggested that speculation about this question can be reduced to two major types (although these are not necessarily exclusive of the other)—the integration and the coercion theories of society. The integration theory of society, which has dominated sociological thought,

conceives of social relationships and social structure as based on the
following assumptions:

(1) every society is a relatively persistent, stable structure of
elements;
(2) every society is a well-integrated structure of elements;
(3) every element in society has a function, i.e. renders a contribution to its maintenance as a system;
(4) every functioning social structure is based on a consensus of
values among its members.

This approach is no more than an extension of the idea of a stable
social system suggested by the concepts of a shared set of norms and
values and a set of social relations in which co-operation rather than
conflict between participants is manifested.

The basic assumptions underlying the coercion theory of society
are:

(1) every society is at every point subject to processes of change;
(2) every society displays at every point dissensus and conflict;
(3) every element in society renders a contribution to its dis-
integration and change;
(4) every society is based on the coercion of some of its members
by another.

Again, this approach derives from suggestions already made
about conflict and the "definition of situations" and about the expectations surrounding social relationships and formalizes the ideas
of conflict which are implied in these earlier points.

Essentially, these models are not alternatives, but represent the
two faces of society; there are situations for which the integration
model provides the most adequate explanations, and others for
which coercion theory seems of greatest value. Clearly, the posing
of limitless conflict is as fruitless as the idea of complete consensus.
Conflict can only go on in the context of a system which has some
meaning for the participants. Again, the idea of integration has
little meaning unless it is recognized that there are different elements
to be integrated, which may be in a greater or a lesser degree of
harmony.

However, for the present purposes, certain implications emerge from the distinction between the two theories. Firstly, reference was made to the norms and values of a society, with the inference that a unitary culture existed about which there was consensus. Authority is thought to derive from such values and is exercised to further certain agreed goals. What emerges from this distinction is the possibility of different sets of values and norms being held by different social groups which may be in conflict. Rather than a common value system, there are a number of alternative systems of values, the dominant one being that of the group or class able to achieve authority over others. Such values are only legitimate in the sense that they are the values of the group who have power over others. Although in a sense a kind of equilibrium can be attained, this is constantly threatened by disruption and change because of competition for power between groups.

Secondly, in the integration theory deviance, or a rejection of the normative system, is seen as maladjustment or mal-adaptation resulting from defective socialization and which calls for responses in the form of social control and resocialization which serves to adjust the deviant individual to the social system and to restore equilibrium. In terms of role playing, the individual may or may not internalize role expectations; if he does he is adjusted, if he does not he is deviant. But, in term of coercion theory, the individual behaves in an adapted or adjusted way if he contributes to the conflict of contradictory interests rather than to the integration of a social system. Thus the same act can be interpreted in two entirely different ways.

These are illustrations of the differing insights these types of theory can give into the nature of social behaviour. In the past, the emphasis on integration theory in sociological analysis has been largely accepted by those practitioners who have been interested in applying a sociological perspective to human behaviour. This has led to a conception of practices such as social work in entirely integrationist terms, in which concepts like adjustment and equilibrium have been emphasized.

Again, it is important to stress that these approaches constitute models or ways of looking at society for the purpose of analysis rather than rigidly distinctive concepts of social reality.[22] In ths first place, the approaches are not entirely consistent in themselves; e.g. conflict can be distinguished from coercion and consensus from integration. Secondly, there is the assumption that if one element in the model is accepted, then acceptance of all others must follow. But it is possible to conceive of models of society which contain elements of both consensus and coercion; thus conflict and strain are inherent in most social systems, but there must be limits to this if the system is to operate at all. An emphasis on consensus and integration does not necessarily exclude change. It is important to move away, at some stage from the binary, or two-model, idea; however, for the purposes of analysis in some of what follows, one or other approach will be utilized as a theoretical framework. This should not, however, lead the reader away from a consideration of how such models might eventually be reconciled to produce some overall theory of society.

## NOTES AND REFERENCES

1. For a comparison of two very different approaches see S. Cotgrove, *Science of Society; An Introduction to Sociology*, Allen & Unwin, London, 1967; and P. Berger, *Invitation to Sociology; A Humanistic Perspective*, Penguin, 1963.

2. This framework is derived in general from Berger, *op. cit.*, chs. 4–6, which provides one of the most imaginative accounts of the nature of the sociological perspective of any current introductory book. Other introductory texts to which reference can also be made include G. Duncan Mitchell, *Sociology: The Study of Social Systems*, University Tutorial Press, London, 1959; A. Inkeles, *What is Sociology?*, Prentice-Hall, New Jersey, 1964; B. Green and E. Johns, *An Introduction to Sociology*, Pergamon, 1966; and S. Cotgrove, *op. cit.* See also G. Duncan Mitchell, *A Dictionary of Sociology*, Routledge & Kegan Paul, London, 1968.

3. E. Bott, *Family and Social Network*, Tavistock, London, 1957.

4. E. Durkheim, *Rules of Sociological Method*, Free Press, Glencoe, 1938.

5. W. I. Thomas, *The Un-adjusted Girl*, Little, Boston, 1923.

6. Texts on role include M. Banton, *Roles*, Tavistock, London, 1965; and E. Goffman, *Presentation of Self in Everyday Life*, Doubleday, New York, 1959.

7. G. H. Mead, *Mind, Self and Society*, Univ. of Chicago Press, 1934.

8. For a discussion see J. Rex, *Key Problems in Sociological Theory*, Routledge & Kegan Paul, London, 1963, ch. 3.

9. A selection of Weber's writing can be found in H. Gerth and C. Wright Mills, *From Max Weber*, Routledge & Kegan Paul, London, 1948.

10. For an account see E. Goffman, *Asylums*, Penguin, 1961.

11. For useful discussions of the various social sciences see N. McKenzie (ed.), *A Guide to the Social Sciences*, Weidenfeld & Nicholson, London, 1966; and D. Marsh, *The Social Sciences*, Routledge & Kegan Paul, London, 1965.

12. For a discussion of the relationship between psychology, social psychology, and sociology, see Inkeles, *op. cit.*

13. J. Rex and R. Moore, *Race, Community and Conflict*, O.U.P., 1967.

14. B. Rodgers *et al.*, *Comparative Social Administration*, Allen & Unwin, London, 1968.

15. Cited in D. Marsh, *An Introduction to Social Administration*, Routledge & Kegan Paul, London, 1965.

16. For a more detailed account see, for example, C. Moser, *Survey Methods in Social Investigation*, Heinemann, London, 1958.

17. M. Weber, *Methodology of the Social Sciences*, Free Press, New York, 1949.

18. C. Wright Mills, *The Sociological Imagination*, O.U.P., London, 1959.

19. R. K. Merton, *Social Theory and Social Structure*, Free Press, Glencoe, 1957.

20. E. Durkheim, *Suicide*, Routledge & Kegan Paul, London, 1952.

21. R. Dahrendorf, *Class and Class Conflict in Industrial Society*, Routledge & Kegan Paul, London, 1959.

22. P. Cohen, *Modern Social Theory*, Heinemann, London, 1968.

# PART II

## CHAPTER 3

# The Family and Kinship

## INTRODUCTION

The family is today the subject of much controversy. Attacks on the family, "with its narrow privacy and tawdry secrets . . . the source of all our discontent", are closely followed by equally strongly worded defences. It is difficult for the observer to know what to make of it all. Perhaps a sociological way of thinking can help. One immediate problem is that observers are involved in families themselves, through birth or by setting up another family on marriage, and therefore have difficulty in maintaining entirely objective positions. People are perhaps more personally involved with the family than with other institutions, and this makes a particularly difficult object of study.

What is the substance of the attacks on the family? The passage quoted above, taken from the Reith Lectures of 1967 by Dr. Leach,[1] referred to the psychological strain imposed by the family today, which stems from the isolation of the domestic household and the consequent intensification of the emotional ties between husband and wife, parents and children, a strain which "is greater than most of us can bear". This situation is seen as the result of changes stretching back into the previous century; the family was previously part of a wider community of kin and neighbours and relationships were not marked by such intensity. Bonds of neighbourhood, family, and occupation overlapped. Industrialization, which encouraged individual families of parents and children to move around in search of employment, destroyed this social system, split up the wider family group, and set families adrift in a mobile and changing world.

But it is possible to argue that this picture is an exaggerated one. There are those who deny that the present-day family is any worse than what has gone before.[2] Indeed, the family of the nineteenth century, in particular the working-class family, is pictured as suffering from cumulative evils, including poverty, poor housing, excessive work, drunkenness, and the domestic enslavement of women. Today's family, it is held, provides more adequately for its members and is protected by the State from the major crises which beset the family of the past.

Although such disagreements are puzzling, what is common to both arguments is a recognition that the family is an important unit both for individuals and for society. The family has certainly not been rejected as a means of child bearing and rearing, sexual satisfaction, and emotional relationships between the sexes, as a glance at the rising rate of marriage and the earlier age of marriage will tell.

## SOCIAL WORK AND THE FAMILY

Typically, the social worker is concerned with problems which derive from the family: the rebellious adolescent, the broken marriage. Some of the situations which face the social worker are the product of the greater intensity of family relationships and of the mobility experienced by many families today. Social work treatment is, apart from work with individuals, also organized around the goal of helping the family to function more adequately in the face of the various demands made upon it by modern society and the tasks it is asked to perform. The social worker may even, in certain circumstances, take on certain family roles in relation to clients; for example, the social worker may assume a parent role in relation to the treatment of certain kinds of clients, or again may be given statutory power in relation to children in need. Thus the social worker comes into close contact with the family, closer in fact than most other members of the helping professions.

The tasks of the social worker involve the exploration and assessment of the problems facing families. The process of diagnosis and treatment inevitably involves certain assumptions about the nature and functioning of the family. Goldberg[3] suggests that, despite claims to the contrary, social workers have a model of healthy family functioning based on certain beliefs about mental health derived from the child guidance–social casework progressive psychology ideal. Good parents are those who balance control of children with parental affection and acceptance. Conflicts between members of a family are seen as symptoms of malfunctioning. Marital relations are close, and there is a sharing of interests and tasks. Mothers who work, especially in the early years of their children's life, are also seen as contributing to family problems. The modern urban family is seen as a small nuclear family of parents and children which has become isolated from kin and other relationships and which is in part dependent on services rendered by the State. The socially healthy family is thus dominated by the ideals of maturity, democracy, and the integration of relationships.

A close dependency relationship between the nuclear family and the wider kin group (e.g. between a married daughter and her mother) has in particular been seen as an indication of immaturity by some social workers.[4]

Evidence that such views are actually held by social workers comes from Leichter and Mitchell's study[5] of family casework in a New York agency. Amongst other things, the kinship values of caseworkers and clients were compared. The former were found to be consistently less oriented in the direction of their extended families than were clients.

This model, and the work done on the basis of such assumptions, raise a number of problems. Although the family, as a type of small social group, shares certain common features, it is also highly differentiated in its functioning. This sometimes relates to distinctions of an ethnic or class nature. Thus judgements about the malfunctioning or immaturity of families are lacking because it is not stated what standards or norms are involved. There is an assumption of certain universal standards of social or mental health, but if these concepts are examined it is found that in reality "they are closely bound up with the social values of the society, the social class and the sub-culture to which we belong and that what we call social or mental health is not based on objective universal or objective criteria".[3] Thus the model Goldberg described bore a strong resemblance to the kind of family found in studies of North American middle-class communities.

A number of problems are suggested by this approach. One danger here is to assume that client situations which appear as problems to the social worker also constitute problems for the client or his family. They may, alternatively, be manifestations of differing norms or values. Problems may be perceived where no problems exist. If this is not taken into account then casework intervention may result in more losses than gains in family stability. Alternatively, differences in norms may be recognized, but for various reasons (considered in more detail later) are ignored. A third possibility is to assume that no problem exists when in fact it does. Thus from the extensive area of knowledge known as the sociology of the family, one important contribution that can be made to social work lies in the analysis of norms and values underlying family life and in the different forms which the family takes on in a modern society. If, for example, the social worker takes on parental roles, then it seems important to ask if such roles are defined in a similar way by all social groups.

One further difficulty relates to the full understanding by the social worker of the family as a small social group. Often, as Meyer suggests,[6] work is centred on the individual while the family as a whole is borne in mind. But terms like "the client" imply a "singularization" of a situation which is in many cases the inter-action of a number of persons, that is a "plurality".[7] One cause of this is that, in Britain at least, social work has developed in an *ad hoc* way on the basis of provision for individuals who have particular problems, such as the mentally ill or children in need, rather than for individuals who are members of families. This reflects in part the break up of old Poor Law practices where improvements in treatment for certain groups was only secured through separate administrative arrangements.[8] Thus a single department has been responsible since 1948 for the care of children. Again, the predominance in contemporary social work of theories drawn from psycho-analysis, with their focus on the individual or on certain "pair" relationships, has contributed to a neglect of the whole family, and in particular the wider group of kin (or the extended family) which are related to the nuclear family (the married couple and their children). One consideration here is that the problems of individual members of the family may have their source in the structure of the family as such; thus all small groups experience strains which are a function of the group as a whole, and the family is no exception to this. Thus the problem of the individual may be a function of the problems of the family as a whole. Sometimes, as the individual recovers, the problem of other members of the family worsen. Thus work undertaken with a single family member may run the risk of failure for these reasons.

Some social work agencies in Britain, such as the Family Service Units, have worked with the family as a unit for some time. The new plans suggested by the Seebohm Report for work with families may also result in the family being treated and understood as more of a unit. Thus another contribution that can be made from the sociology of the family relates to the understanding of the family, or of different types of family group, as a whole.

The difficulties which surround the understanding of the family derive partly from the elusiveness and peculiar nature of the institution. The fact that most adults are members of at least two families leads to the belief that all are experts on family life and that findings related to the family are obvious and require little further investigation. However, common assumptions about the family are often inaccurate. There is good reason why the family should be the object of academic study, and in the case of social workers the need is greater because they are involved in the family life of others and in "operationalizing" concepts related to the family.

## A SOCIOLOGICAL APPROACH TO THE FAMILY

The family can be approached at two levels; first the internal structure of the family can be explored; secondly, the family can be seen as part of a wider set of relationships in which the family and its constituent members become increasingly influenced by the wider social structure of which they form a part. In some societies, the family is so important that it dominates the lives and behaviour of its members; the fact of membership within a family is sufficient to determine entirely the behaviour towards an individual or members of other families. An individual spends his whole life fulfilling social obligations to family members; the family determines for the individual such matters as occupation, residence after marriage, religion, and so on.

In all societies, the family plays an important part in the lives of its members, but as societies become more complex and develop occupational and industrial systems and other institutions which are outside the purview of the family, the world outside the family takes on a greater significance for the individual. Although the family can effectively influence the child towards a particular interpretation of its attitude to society outside the family, and can control for a time the contacts he has with the outside world, there is no way of avoiding the eventual confrontation between the individual and society; as Cohen[9] puts it, even taking into account the power of the family over the child, "still the child, when he steps outside the home, like the high school graduate when he seeks his first job, must meet the world on its own terms".

The sociologist's approach to the family is quite different from that of the clinician and the psychologist. In attempting to account for problems of individual behaviour, the latter use a case study approach in which the relations between pairs, or within segments, of the family are described and analysed in great detail, with an emphasis on this or that aspect of these relationships. Here the behaviour of, for example, the child is accounted for in terms of the internal structure of this "little social system", but largely without reference to the wider social system outside the family. The "world outside" is rather treated as a theatre in which the role played and the attitudes shown by individuals have been formed entirely within the family and produced by interaction with family members.[9]

The sociologist suggests, on the other hand, that the world out-side can be likened rather to an arena in that it consists of facts and objects which the individual will meet which exist autonomously and outside the control of the family. These realities will leave their imprint on the personality as surely as the early experience within the family. One implication for this is that, for the sociologist, the study of the family leads on to a consideration of wider social processes and forms, in a sense, an introduction to the study of these processes.

One way of looking at the complex relationship between the family and society is to view the situation as a series of exchanges between the family and parts (or sub-systems) of society in which the family performs functions for and receives contributions from each sub-system.[10] The process could be likened to the import-export process. The major sub-systems involved include the economy, the community and the value system.

In the case of the economy the family contributes the labour of its members and receives economic and other rewards in return. For this to occur, the family must have prepared its members with certain minimum skills and the required motivation to use them. What is received in return is mainly wages but can also be non-monetary rewards such as recreation or help in times of crisis. The family has to adapt in various ways to the demands of the labour market. The internal routine of the family life may be in part determined by the dictates of shift working and the necessity to provide means for workers to recover and renew their energies. A wife may, particularly in the professional classes, be important in the successful performance of her husband's occupational role. Thus the economic sub-system will, through its demands, help to shape the character of family life irrespective of factors related to the family itself.

In order that the family can participate in these wider exchanges, certain activities must be performed within the family itself. External activities are not in themselves sufficient to guarantee the stability of the family. Thus the granting of wages and other services by the economy in return for labour involve the family in such internal activities as organization and leadership and the performance of certain key tasks which are unrelated to such external processes. Of all the tasks performed within the family, some of the most important relate to the welfare of dependent members of the family, including the very young, the sick and the old. Although such tasks have been in part taken over by agencies outside the family, responsibility for them is still vested largely in the family.

The family exists in an immediate context of the community, which can be referred to as a multiplicity of group relationships based on occupation, religion, common interests or physical proximity.[11] In an industrial society these form a number of different circles; thus membership in one circle does not imply membership in others, and, for example, a man's neighbours are usually different from his workmates. The community can be seen as providing the family with a specific status position and an "identity", together with more general support, in return for an adherence to certain norms and values. Relationships which family members have outside the family also help to define relationships within the family, and this will be illustrated later in terms of the conjugal (husband/wife) relationship. Further detailed discussion of the community is left until Chapter 4.

Finally, society is faced with the problem of the organization and control of behaviour. One solution is to seek acceptance of certain values by which behaviour is oriented (the value system). Values are transmitted to individuals by the family, as well as by such institutions as schools and social work agencies. The relationship between the family and the value system is a special one in that the family is the smallest and in some respects the most important unit which functions to preserve and transmit values. It is in the family that the human infant begins to learn about the demands of society and experiences in the family have important implications for personality development, and thus behaviour, throughout life.

Thus the process of socialization can be related to the entry of the child into other groups outside the family. Parsons[12] has likened the child to a pebble thrown by the fact of birth into the pond of life. Initially the point of impact is in the family, but as the child grows up he begins to make relationships in peer groups and at school. But the child is unable to participate fully in these wider circles until he has fulfilled the conditions of participation in the narrow and more intensive circle of the family.

The impact of the family on the child is also particularly powerful because of the length of time the child is dependent on this group, particularly in an industrial society. The process by which an individual acquires the values of a group or culture is referred to as socialization. Apart from the family, individuals are also socialized into professions, occupations, and a variety of other groups. When the values being transmitted become relatively stable elements in the personality, the process can be termed "primary socialization".

The exchange between the family and the value system takes place in two ways.[11] The system specifies standards and defines the kind of behaviour that is legitimate. The family accepts such standards and passes them on to children through the socialization process. In addition, the value system offers approval for conformity to these values. The family functions in part to provide such conformity and to receive approval. The family is seen as responsible to other sub-systems (e.g. the community) for the conformity of its members.

The interchange between the family and the value system is not one in which the child is moulded by an undifferentiated set of demands. Families are part of wider collectivities and this membership will make a difference to the way the child is reared.

It is increasingly being recognized that the kind of goals families seek for their children, and the strategies they adopt, relate to the ethnic, class, or other social situations of the parents. Thus only an aspect of the total value system is being transmitted which corresponds to the standards and values of, for example, the social class of the parents.

Further discussion of this issue is delayed until the subject of social class and social stratification has been introduced in Chapter 5.

The distinction between the family in its relation to society and in its internal functioning can be seen in terms of values. Although the family helps to transmit society's values, it is, as Timms[13] suggests, not a kind of "neutral conductor". Families are not highly organized and rational systems but are capable of variation. Families may develop their own values and allow areas of freedom to individuals which would not be possible in the wider society. As Timms suggests, the family "does not simply provide the proscenium arch beneath which the class war is enacted; it makes a difference to the way the forces and influences of the wider society are experienced within its boundaries". Not only may the family develop distinctive value systems but the values of individual members of the family may differ, a situation which centres, for example, on the generational relationship between parents and adolescent children, or on the grandparent–parent relationship.

## THE NUCLEAR FAMILY

The nuclear family (a man, a woman, and their children joined in a socially recognized union) is composed of a number of subsystems—the spouse system (the conjugal or marital relationship), the parent–child system (the generational relationship), and the sibling system (sibling relationship). Each sub-system can be seen as a functioning relationship between two or more people in which each acts as resources in terms of the needs of the other.[7] Thus a married couple will meet each other's needs for sexual and emotional satisfaction. Parents will meet their children's needs for physical and emotional support. Children may also take their parents as models of their own behaviour in later adult life. Siblings provide for one another models of behaviour different from those provided by adults because of the absence of an authoritarian element in the relationship.

Such relationships also change. A married couple must lessen the intensity of their relationship in order to incorporate children into the family. Although relationships in the family are initially dependent, in an industrial society parents and children have to establish a degree of independence from one another. This is finally expressed in the institution of a new family of procreation (in which a person has, or has had, the status of parent) separate from the family of origin or orientation (in which the person has, or has had, the status of child) and which incorporates members of an unrelated family. Thus each family experiences a cycle of change or adaptation in which relationships are periodically reconstituted and in which new adjustments have to be made to the *status quo*.

The family can, in this sense, be seen as a series of social roles, in which each individual is systematically related to others by culturally defined expectations.[14] As in all role systems, conflict and conflict resolution are features of the system. The individual owes duties to both his family of origin and the new family he has set up. The simultaneous roles of son, husband, and father may be highly conflictful and resolution usually implies a "retreat" from one or other of these roles. In spite of conflict, the family provides members with a consciousness which sets them apart from other kinds of group of which they may also claim membership.

One observed difference in the pattern of conjugal relationships is the degree to which such roles are segregated. In Bott's[15] study of twenty families in London it was found that in some families the spouses carry out their domestic activities separately and with little reference to one another, have their own friends and recreative pursuits. In others the spouses act jointly, plan things together, have the same friends, and go out together. The former situation can be termed a segregated conjugal role relationship, the latter a joint conjugal role relationship. Clearly, these are not distinctive types for elements of both are found in most families. It is possible, however, to suggest that families are characterized by a greater or lesser degree of conjugal role segregation. Bott, in seeking for explanations of such differences, considered but rejected social class[16] as the key variable. Husbands with the most segregated patterns were in manual occupations, but not all working-class families exhibited this pattern. In some families with non-manual husbands the degree of segregation was considerable. Instead attention was focused on the more immediate environment of friends, neighbours, and relations. This could be described as a "social network" rather than a form of organized group in which all members have relationships with one another. Thus each family is at the centre of a web of relationships with friends, neighbours, and kin. Some will know and have relations with one another, but others will not. The network does not, therefore, form a group with a defined boundary in which each member will have relationships with all others. Thus the network related to each family will differ in the extent to which it is connected, that is the extent to which its members know each other independently of the family. A close-knit network describes a situation in which there are many relationships between members; a loose-knit network describes a situation where there are few relationships between members. Bott suggests that the segregation of conjugal roles is related to the degree of connectedness in the family network. Families with a high degree of conjugal role segregation had close-knit networks but those with joint role relationships had loose-knit networks. What appears to happen, according to Bott, is that in close-knit networks, people are in close touch with one another and provide mutual assistance in times of crisis. When such individuals marry they continue to be influenced by such close relationships and demand correspondingly less from their spouse. Each marriage is superimposed on a series of such preexisting relationships, and the spouses will continue to be drawn into such a network and to obtain emotional satisfaction from it. This factor is, however, only one of a number of factors which might influence marital relationships.

A simpler explanation for the differences in conjugal relationships is advanced by Rosser and Harris[17] on the basis of larger scale study of the family in Swansea. They distinguish between a social network composed of friends and one composed of relatives and argue that there is no reason why a family whose marital relationship is a joint one should not have a close-knit social network of common friends. It is less likely that such a network would include relatives. The critical factor here is the degree of domestication of women, which will influence both the nature of the marital relationship and the type of social network. Domestication here refers to the performing of household tasks and the rearing of children. The greater the level of female domestication the more likely that marital roles will become segregated, and the greater the chance there will be of contact and mutual assistance amongst relatives, particularly female members of the extended family. Thus a "mothers' union" will be created into which females are drawn and from which males are partially excluded.

## THE FAMILY AND OCCUPATION

Segregation between the sexes has arisen in the past because of the unreliability of income from male employment at times of high unemployment. It also reflects the character of some forms of male employment, particularly extreme occupations such as deep-sea fishing or coal-mining.[18] Here males are absent for long periods or have work of a dangerous kind which makes for close companionship with the work group both in work and in leisure activities. In both cases this may lead to role segregation and a division of labour between man and wife.

Essentially such situations can be seen, as Hollowell[19] has shown, as a potential conflict between the two institutional areas of the family and the occupational system, or between the roles of husband–father and worker. These areas can be entirely integrated and the two roles may be compatible, as in situations where the occupational role does not in any way impede the functions of the family. Alternatively, various forms of adaptation may take place in which either work or family may be adjusted to suit the requirements of the other; for example the wife–mother may become totally dominant in the roles connected with domesticity and child rearing to the possible exclusion of the male (as in the mining community described by Dennis et al.[18]). Finally there are occupations which the family has great difficulty in adapting to and which are highly incompatible with family life. An example here is the deep-sea fisherman whose occupation takes him away for several weeks at a time and who becomes almost a stranger to his family. Here considerable tensions develop which are indicated by the very high divorce rate of the Hull fishermen.

In the case of lorry driving, the subject of Hollowell's inquiry, adaptations to the extreme nature of the lorry driver's occupation took the form of the acceptance or legitimation of the work by the driver's family because of the economic advantages of the work and compensation for long absences in the form of the wife's reliance on kin and children for company and the husband's intensive participation in family affairs when at home. However, drivers could not always fulfil their families' need for companionship, and the increased opportunities for sexual contacts resulting from long absences and the nature of the work led to conflict and the breakdown in the family life of some drivers. Thus the demands of the occupational role could not, in all circumstances, be adapted to the demands of role playing within the family.

However, as female employment outside the home has increased in recent years (due in part to the decline in the size of the family) it is possible that female domesticity and the segregation of marital relations may be on the decline as women become drawn increasingly into the occupational system and begin to share such experiences with their husbands. The effects of such changes include the possibility of conflict over changing marital roles and the declining significance of kin relationships in the social networks of such families. It is to the extended family that discussion now turns.

## THE EXTENDED FAMILY

A distinction is often made between the nuclear family (a man and woman and their children joined in a socially recognized union) and a wider group known as the extended family (any persistent grouping of persons related by descent, marriage, or adoption which is wider than the elementary family in that it characteristically spans three generations, from grandparents to grandchildren);[20] however, this distinction is often exaggerated for the purposes of analysis, for clearly each nuclear family and most individuals have relationships by blood or marriage. One variation is the extent to which each nuclear family is, in one way or another, in touch with the extended kin group. In some societies the distinction between the nuclear and the extended family is of little importance; thus the traditional extended family was a unit sharing the same residence, or in close geographical proximity, and extending over several generations.

One theory about the emergence of the smaller more compact nuclear family is that this group is better suited (or is more functional) for a modern industrial society, which puts priority on mobility and high levels of achievement, than the wider kin group in which external obligations may hinder mobility and the necessary motivation to achieve.[21] Thus a smaller and more compact family unit inevitably emerges in a modern industrialized society.

One of the features of contemporary British sociology has been research within the context of the extended family. By now several studies have been carried out in various parts of the country and, with certain variations, there is a measure of agreement about the structure and functions of the extended family; thus, according to the authors of one of the most recent studies, "it seems broadly correct to speak of a single form of extended family organization which is probably common to all urban areas in modern Britain".[17]

The authors of one of the first of these studies, Willmott and Young,[22] began their work in the belief that they would find the kind of families referred to above, that is isolated nuclear families with relatively few kin ties. To their surprise they found in Bethnal Green, the area of East London in which they carried out their work, nuclear families who lived in close proximity to their kin and with whom they interacted on an intensive day-to-day basis.

However, Bethnal Green was a small, densely populated area which facilitated such relationships and, partly in order to see whether this pattern of social relationships would be reproduced in a very different sort of area, Rosser and Harris undertook a far more extensive study in the much larger area of Swansea in which nearly 2000 people were interviewed about their kinship relationships and behaviour. Over two-thirds of married men and over three-quarters of married women had at least one parent living in Swansea. However, Swansea has an area of 41 square miles and these extended family members often lived in different localities, a situation which affected kinship solidarity. Thus three-quarters of married sons and over half of married daughters lived away from the localities in which their parents were living. But in spite of the dispersed nature of the town, the frequency of contact between kin (see Table 1) was remarkably high, being very similar to that found by Willmott and Young for Bethnal Green.

TABLE 1. FREQUENCY OF CONTACT WITH PARENTS (%)

| Last seen | Mothers | | Fathers | |
|---|---|---|---|---|
| | Married sons | Married daughters | Married sons | Married daughters |
| Within last 24 hours | 31 | 54 | 29 | 47 |
| Within last week | 40 | 27 | 41 | 30 |
| Week–month ago | 14 | 7 | 15 | 9 |
| Less frequently | 15 | 12 | 15 | 14 |
| % | 100 | 100 | 100 | 100 |
| Numbers | 345 | 348 | 237 | 254 |

*Source:* C. Rosser & C. Harris, *The Family and Social Change.*

Over half the married daughters had seen their mothers in the previous 24 hours and 81 per cent had seen them during the previous week. By contrast, 31 per cent of married sons had seen their mothers in the previous 24 hours and 71 per cent in the previous week.

Such intensity of contact between kin in an area as large as Swansea was only made possible by easy means of communication. The main reliance was on local bus services and in particular on the motor-car. More than a quarter of individual households had the use of a car and there were few extended families in which one of the constituent households did not possess a car. Apart from visits, contact between kin also took the form of letter writing and telephoning. Thus kin relationships did not simply take the form of weekly or daily visits. Kinship sentiment is based not only on physical proximity and the possibility of face-to-face communication.

Although there were few differences between the social classes in frequency of contact with kin, the middle class possessed more cars and telephones and wrote more letters than the working class, and this made kin contact easier.

Most studies have shown that the key relationship in the extended family is between married daughter and her mother. This partly reflects women's common functions of child bearing and rearing and the performance of domestic tasks. Here the younger woman is reliant to an extent on the advice and assistance of her mother, who may also act as a barrier between the outside world, particularly various welfare agencies, and the rest of the family. Thus in the triangular relationship between the married couple (the family of procreation) and their two respective families of origin, the balance is normally weighted in the direction of the wife's family, a situation which is, in the Swansea study, accepted by most families; "a fair balance", the authors comment, "is not necessarily an even one". But the relationships between married couples were intensified by the difficulty married couples had in finding separate housing immediately after marriage. In the majority of cases (Table 2) residence

TABLE 2. TYPE OF HOUSEHOLD COMPOSITION IMMEDIATELY
AFTER MARRIAGE (BY SOCIAL CLASS AND DATE OF MARRIAGE) (%)

| Date of marriage: | 1914–39 | | 1940–60 | |
|---|---|---|---|---|
| Class: | Middle | Working | Middle | Working |
| Type of household | | | | |
| With husband's parents | 11 | 12 | 20 | 22 |
| With wife's parents | 20 | 28 | 31 | 42 |
| With other relatives | 2 | 11 | 7 | 7 |
| On own | 67 | 49 | 42 | 29 |
| % | 100 | 100 | 100 | 100 |
| Total number | 119 | 511 | 118 | 502 |
| Percentage of those living with either parents | | | | |
| With husband's parents | 36 | 30 | 39 | 34 |
| With wife's parents | 64 | 70 | 61 | 66 |
| % | 100 | 100 | 100 | 100 |
| Total number | 37 | 205 | 60 | 323 |

Source: C. Rosser and C. Harris, The Family and Social Change.

was with parents or other relatives—in most cases with the wife's parents, a situation reflecting the continuing housing problem in the area of Swansea, which in this sense had worsened in the twentieth century.

Thus men tend to get drawn into the families of their wives sometimes at the expense of relationships with their other kin, and thus in some cases the balance of relationships in the extended family is disturbed. This can produce tensions, particularly between married couples. In Swansea men were less content than their wives to live with their mother-in-law and were more concerned with restoring the balance of family relationships. Independent residence on marriage was still the ideal. These tensions were even worse when residence was with the husband's parents, where problems arose over the sharing of domestic facilities by two women related only by marriage. Husbands who had experienced this preferred even to live with their wife's parents. The only advantage was where the wife's own parents were dead and the husband's kin acted as substitute for missing members of their own family. In their New York study, Leichter and Mitchell also found tensions greater between a married couple and the husband's parents. One explanation is that a wife's ties to her family are accepted by the husband, but a wife less readily accepts her husband's loyalty to his family because it constitutes a greater potential threat to the nuclear family. Thus there is strain in performing the two pairs of roles of son–brother and husband–father.

In Swansea the major difference in kin behaviour was that middle-class wives were less in contact with their mothers than their working-class counterparts. Here the dependence of mother on daughter declines partly as a result of the ability to obtain domestic assistance from outside the family.

The picture of the extended family presented so far suggests that even in dispersed urban areas kin ties are of considerable importance; the two major functions of the extended family appear to be that of social support and social identification. Kin are amongst the first people to be looked to as a source of support in a crisis. Again, extended family membership appears as part of the process by which stable elements of the personality are developed—membership of this group still appears an important primary identification in a mobile modern society.

But the nature of this group has clearly changed; in the absence of close physical proximity, social support cannot be given on a day-to-day basis, and therefore obligations are less easy to perform on an informal basis. Decreasing female domestication and the increasing employment of women may make it less easy to exchange services (e.g. between mother and married daughter) on a day-to-day basis. Contacts have taken on a more formal nature, and this appears one of the main results of the loosening of kinship ties which has occurred as a result of social changes. Rosser and Harris described the extended family in Swansea as:

> A variable, amorphous, vague social grouping within which circulate, often over great distances, strong sentiments of belonging and which is recognizable as a social entity of some significance . . . the wider kinship group is not so much decomposed by current social change but is rather modified to produce a looser, more adaptable structure.

Thus it is difficult to accept the view that the nuclear family has emerged as the only significant family group in modern societies. Although social changes have tended to isolate the nuclear family in a physical sense, this does not necessarily imply that support and communication cease to exist within the wider family. As Litwak[23] has suggested, a comparison of the classical extended family of the past with the nuclear family of the present is false. A third type, the modified extended family of the kind described above, is also important. Here the nuclear family may be physically isolated (although this is not universally the case) but continues to be part of a group which remains a focus for dependency and affectual relationships. Again, geographical and social mobility may not be disruptive, for such processes may be legitimized by the wider kin group and the mobile nuclear family given social and psychological support. What is required are more detailed studies of the kinds of function extended families still play.

## FAMILY NORMS

One common assumption about the family is that the social norms governing relations between family members are explicit and that there is a large measure of agreement about them. Again, it is sometimes thought that such norms are derived from and reflect the values of institutions such as the Church and the law.

However, as Bott[15] points out, such homogeneity is found (and then only in part) in small-scale societies where norms develop and are reinforced by constant social interaction and are known and accepted by most people. In a heterogeneous large-scale society in which there is a hierarchy of values and a range of sub-cultures, the situation is very different. In Bott's study not only was there little agreement about the norms governing family life but respondents found difficulty in making such norms explicit at all. Points of general agreement (or "norms of common consent") included the financial and physical independence of the nuclear family and a division of labour in which the husband played a mainly occupational role and the wife a mainly domestic role. Even these norms encompassed a considerable range of behaviour.

One type of variation was related to the "connectedness" of the social network. Families with closed networks tended to stress a rigid division of labour, the importance of relationships in the extended family, but did not consider the quality of sexual relationships as being important. In families with open networks there was less stress on a rigid division of labour and on kin relationships and more concern with the quality of sexual relationships.

However, few people were able to make definite statements about family norms, although there was little difficulty in describing norms governing other roles such as those in the occupational system. This may reflect the emotional involvements individuals have with their family life and, particularly in families with open networks, the lack of consensus resulting from low levels of group interaction in these contexts.

The most important source of family norms in Bott's study were parents, who constituted an important model for family life.

Friends, neighbours, and other relatives were also used as reference points, as well as other social groups. Thus the norms people think are common in some group or category (social norms), rather than legal or religious norms in the wider community, appear important in family behaviour. Again, the degree of "network connectedness" influenced the choice of reference groups. Those families with closed networks referred to groups composed of kin and neighbours, those with looser networks defined broader categories as reference groups, such as "people of our general class". In this case "personal norms" (or standards which were held privately) were more likely to be treated as social norms because it was usually possible to find at least one group with which to share such standards.

## THE WEST INDIAN FAMILY

Perhaps the most striking variation in the content of familial norms is that presented by the families of ethnic minorities. This pattern has been dictated by cultural influences which are not present in British society but which must be understood if this kind of family is to be helped to live in this society. Such families present, in the most extreme form, a challenge to the knowledge and skill of the practitioner.

As large-scale migration to this country is of comparatively recent origin, few studies of migrant family patterns exist. Probably most is known about the West Indian family situation.[24] Because of certain historical conditions specific to West Indian culture, the family is a more loosely structured unit than its British counterpart. Under conditions of slavery, marriage was scarcely possible. Thus today traditional Christian marriage, although an ideal, is not seen as the main basis for sexual relationships and the procreation and rearing of children. The basis for marriage is seen as the ability of the couple to achieve financial security and independence, a state which is impossible for many working-class individuals. An alternative is common law marriage (although the relationship is not recognized in law) where a couple set up home, procreate, and rear children, to which may be added children already born which are the products of other relationships. The couple act to all intents and purposes as a married couple. Apart from the lack of a legal basis, the main differences lie in the greater degree of independence for both partners (but particularly the male) who know that the "family" can break up at any time. Thus conjugal and parental roles are played out in a very different way than in British society. The father, in particular, plays a weak and in some cases almost non-existent role which, in the context of British society would be considered irresponsible, but is in fact fully accepted in West Indian culture. Women are left to perform the tasks of child rearing and socialization, and cannot count on economic support from the father or fathers of the children. As a result a woman may work, and for this reason a wide variety of kin and friends take a hand in child rearing. Thus whilst the West Indian nuclear family is weak the social network which surrounds it is correspondingly strong. Important individuals include the maternal grandmother—who will play a strong role when the mother is very young—a variety of other kin, and neighbours. Adoption is a well recognized practice. As motherhood carries high status there is no shortage of women to bring up a child, and parental rights and duties can be transferred in an easy and informal way. Children are encouraged to take on adult roles from an early age, including the care of younger children and domestic tasks. Fitzherbert sums up the situation of the child in the West Indian culture in the following way:

> Instability is a normal state of affairs and there are compensations for it built into the system. It would be most unusual to hear a West Indian complain about his childhood and feel sorry for himself for the sole reason that it had been unstable and his family broke up. The instability of the family in itself is not guaranteed to have serious after effects on a child.[25]

Although migrants make a number of adaptations to British society, many of the elements outlined above persist and often come into conflict with the norms of British family life, particularly when these are expressed in statutary forms surrounding child care or education. Some of the implications that this and other types of cultural variation have for the social worker will be explored later, but it should be stressed now that the West Indian family system, which is radically different from that obtaining in industrialized societies, can in its own context fulfil a large number of the functions performed by the family in our own society.

## FAMILY SOCIOLOGY AND SOCIAL WORK

It has been suggested that an important feature of the family in industrial societies is the variability and fluidity of its form and structure. Further stress has been laid on the necessity of understanding the family in its relationships with the wider society rather than as an isolated and self-contained unit. One way of understanding this is by seeing the nuclear family as involved, in various ways, with a social network and with the occupational and value systems. For example, nuclear families can have a variety of involvements with the social network of kin, neighbours, and friends ranging from loosely knit contacts, in which the nuclear family may form a relatively integrated joint unit, to close-knit contacts with the social network and a looser, more segregated, conjugal relationship.

It is important to view families as if ranged along this kind of continuum rather than bunched at one extreme or the other. A further way in which the complexity of the modern family becomes apparent is as a residential unit; thus the residential unit can vary from the one or two generation nuclear family to situations in which more than two generations of kin as well as unrelated individuals constitute the residential unit.

These points serve to illustrate the way in which the sociology of the family might help the social worker to understand problems which typically arise in work with families. One of these problems is that of the "cultural unrelatedness" of social worker and client.[7] In some circumstances client and social worker may share the same norms regarding the family, and clients may have some understanding for what the social worker and the agency are trying to do. In other situations, particularly where there is a statutory responsibility for the whole population (as in a Children's Department), client and worker are unlikely to share the same beliefs about institutions such as the family and may even have norms which conflict most sharply. In the introduction to this chapter it was found that in one American study the kinship values of caseworker and client were very different.[5] But in addition to this the two groups differed in their actual experiences. For example, clients' lived closer to their kin, maintained more intensive telephone contacts with them, and granted relatives freer access to their homes. When it came to the diagnosis of problems, clients rarely reported that problems with kin had led them to seek advice, but caseworkers frequently reported that problems relating to kin came up in treatment. Lastly, when analyses were made of the particular form that casework intervention in the family took, in 40 per cent of cases this was "restrictive", which involved the reduction of clients[2] involvement with kin and in particular the loosening of ties between clients and their parents (e.g. between a wife and her mother). In only 9 per cent of cases was intervention described as "expansionist" (an increase in involvement with kin), and in the remaining 50 per cent of cases family relationships were redefined, mainly in psychological terms.

Other work undertaken with families was consistent with the support by the caseworker for the greater independence of the nuclear family from its kin, involving greater independence in child rearing, marital relationships, economic, and financial functioning.

Here it appears that caseworkers, possibly without realizing this, have responded to differences in norms by emphasizing their own standards for, as the authors put it, "casework intervention involves altering the kinship values of clients".[5]

One of the most important variations in the norms of family life relate, as Bott has shown,[15] to the conjugal relationship. Married couples may vary in the extent to which they share activities and friends and consider sexual relationships important. Thus in some families husband and wife lead almost separate lives whilst in others there is a close relationship. Bott has suggested that this variation is related, amongst other things, to the type of social network in which the couple are involved.

In working with the family a frequent goal in casework (as Leichter and Mitchell have shown) is to attempt to strengthen the marital relationship and encourage an integrated or joint family structure, notably by attempting to change the nature of the relationships a couple have with their kin. Bott also notes that clinicians, doctors, and research workers seem to assume that the joint family is the normal form for family relationships to take.

But advice given on this basis will be bewildering for families with segregated relationships. It is not suggested that behaviour should be accepted as normal where it accords with the norms of certain types of families. What is important is to determine whether a situation is normal in relation to a particular family or group or is rather the result of the pathology of individual members or of the family as a whole. It is important to remember the immense variation in the playing out of conjugal roles and the necessity of exploring the meanings attached to these roles by the individuals involved. Again, to return to the question of kinship, it is possible that the holding of certain kinship values may legitimize relationships which appear from the outside to be highly conflictful. If, for example, importance is attached by the caseworker to the marital relationship and this is accompanied by attempts to lessen a wife's dependence on her mother, this may not make sense in terms of a family in which kin bonds are strong, for a close mother–daughter tie may not, in fact, disrupt the marital relationship.

Although cultural differences between social worker and client are not relevant in all circumstances, an important question relates to the choice between the cultural preferences of client or social worker. If the client's preferences are accepted, social work adopts the position of complete cultural relativity. If, on the other hand, the latter course is taken, this amounts to the use of social work and casework as a means of facilitating and directing certain social changes. Thus Pollak[7] suggests that "the helping process must assume a certain quality of aculturation in which the worker tries to help the client to move, at least somewhat, in the direction of the

mental health culture which the family service and child welfare
field in our society represent". Thus the move to reduce ties with
kin and to integrate and strengthen the conjugal relationship, which
characterized the caseworkers' efforts in the New York study,
would be explained by seeing such relationships with wider kin as
signs of "immaturity" or "unmet dependency needs", i.e. as
pathological. The caseworker has solved the problem of "cultural
unrelatedness" by taking his stand and basing his decisions on the
professional or "mental health culture". One problem raised by
this solution is that the social work professional or mental health
culture referred to may in practice bear a strong resemblance to
middle-class norms and standards.[26] Thus the whole process may
represent an attempt to substitute the values of one social class for
those of another. As already seen from the discussion of the extended family, relationships between the nuclear family and wider
kin (in particular married daughter–mother relations) appear
normal in certain contexts. Further discussion of this question will
be taken up in later chapters.

The material presented on the extended family suggests that if
social work is based on the assumption of a relatively isolated
nuclear family and a decomposed kin group, then not only are
valuable sources of support and assistance being neglected, but a
more subtle, but nevertheless important, source of identification is
being ignored. Thus Fellin[27] suggests that a modified form of the
extended family not only provides aid in times of crisis to the
nuclear unit, but serves to support its stability in a more general
sense, exerts pressure to keep it together, helps regulate the behaviour of children, and, not least, serves as a reference group for
behaviour. An important question is to determine when aid or
support can be provided from within the kin group or has to come
from a social work agency or other institution. Again, more study
is required of the kinds of situation in which nuclear families
become totally isolated from kin.

Rosser and Harris[17] suggest that while in Britain the Welfare
State has taken over responsibility from the wider family for the
major crises (such as shortage of housing, unemployment, etc.), the

kin group is the most appropriate unit to provide for minor crises which occur in all families, such as childbirth and rearing, illness, and old age. Assistance can range from minor domestic help, such as baby sitting, to financial loan for house purchase. Here not only is it too costly for this to be provided by the State, it is also likely that more effective support comes from a group in which there are strong emotional ties. This kind of support, affective support, is likely to continue irrespective of changes in the circumstances (e.g. the physical dispersion) of the wider family. Effective care is dependent on physical proximity and the level of female domestication, but affective care is dependent in part on social and cultural proximity. Thus, it is argued, mobility of a social or geographical kind might limit affective care and, because of this, the mobility of individuals in an extended family may be limited. Here the most severe problem is that the need for care of old people is greatest at a time when children may have experienced greatest social or geographical mobility, making both effective and affective care difficult. The lowering of the age of marriage could, in the future, exacerbate this problem. So important are communications (bus services, telephones, etc.) in maintaining the dispersed extended family that Rosser and Harris suggest that they should be regarded as social services in their own right.

Although the kin group is, in many cases, amorphous and scattered, it can often be reconstituted. But this depends on a prior acceptance that such relationships have retained their importance. An illustration of the difficulties and rewards of accepting the extended family as the primary source of support comes from Fitzherbert's study of West Indian family life,[25] in which it might be supposed that the experience of migration would have led to an extreme degree of isolation among nuclear families. After intensive work on 22 cases in which children had been admitted to the care of a Children's Department, it was found that in 20 of these relatives or friends existed who would have been able to provide care for the children. Thus admission to care was in some instances unnecessary and was due, in part, to the social workers' primary concern for the child to the exclusion of the family as a whole. But explicit consideration of the kinship and network structure, in particular of this ethnic group, although it would have involved considerably more work, might have resulted in the lessening of the number of these children in care.

On the other hand it must not, as Pollak points out,[28] be assumed that because kin exist, or individuals share households, that they will necessarily see themselves or be seen as resources in time of need. The family cannot be artificially extended to include individuals who are not willing to be drawn into such a circle or are not accepted in it. What is important is to accept that for each individual there may be groups in which are located potential sources of aid whose actual utility can then be explored.

When this group is described as "the family" Pollak suggests that it can be defined as existing "when people related to one another by blood or sharing of a home consider themselves resources for one another on a more comprehensive basis and at a higher degree of intensity than they consider other people".

This warning is a timely one when assumptions are being made about the capacity of "the community" (which means in many cases the nuclear or wider family group) to care for mentally or physically sick individuals or the aged, and a drive is being mounted to keep such dependants out of institutions for most of the time.

Thus, although effective and affective support may be available in the wider kin group, it is important to treat this as a hypothesis to be tested, rather than as an assumption which can be accepted.

Again, consideration of the extended family is also important in view of the likelihood that members of the social network, particularly kin, may influence attitudes to and use of social services. Thus the influence of social workers must be seen in the context of advice from individuals outside the nuclear family. Thus Willmott[29] comments (of Bethnal Green) that "all along the advice of doctors, midwives, health visitors, children's officers and the rest is sifted, filtered and evaluated by mum". Klein[30] comments that this has both positive and negative repercussions. "Mum" mediates in an important way between the family and the outside world; she has more experience and authority and can help to manage the problems of a young family, whilst her more deferential manner eases the relationship between families and those agencies which may have an authoritarian caste. On the other hand, her influence is mostly conservative and she functions as a regulator of outside influences only allowing in those which she approves and which have been tried and tested by traditional means. American research[31] has shown that the views of significant individuals in the client's social network about the efficacy of casework treatment are important determinants of whether the client continues with the agency. The spectrum can be widened still further, for advice must also be seen in the context of the growing influence of the mass media of communication (television, radio, literature) which will clearly mediate, in various ways, the influence of professional counsellors. More needs to be known about the interplay of such forces.

Finally, if the extended family or some other wider unit is seen as the relevant unit, then proposed and actual changes in one set of relationships will have implications for other relationships in this unit. For example, the reduction of the strength of the mother–daughter relationship in favour of the strengthening of conjugal ties will have repercussions not only for both these sets of relationships, but for others in the extended family, such as those between the husband and his kin.

One problem in choosing the three generation family as the appropriate unit is that of social differences which separate the social worker and oldest generation in the family. Here there is likely to be the maximum difference, and therefore of potential conflict, between the norms of the social worker and of the aged, third generation in an extended family, irrespective of who is, in fact, the client.

The idea that the extended family (and the social network in general) should be the appropriate unit for treatment is, as Leitcher and Mitchell suggest, the logical extension of treating the nuclear family rather than the individual. So far little attention has been given to the membership of this network beyond the extended family. But family members spend a large proportion of their time in situations outside the family, such as work or education, which have important implications for inner family relationships. In all cases the problem is to choose the segment of the social network which appears relevant to the problems of the family whilst recognizing that the total network is an area of potential significance for the client. It seems clear, as Leitcher and Mitchell put it, that social work with families "should neither begin nor end with the nuclear family".

However, the full significance in practice of the nuclear family is also difficult to grasp. Pollak[7] has suggested that diagnostic understanding in social work should begin with the readiness of the worker to accept the family as the client rather than the individual. This is necessary not only to counteract the negative repercussions of treatment on other members, but because members of the family serve as models for each other's behaviour and development.

One way of looking at individual families is in terms of the life cycle. Thus each family has to deal with conflicts which relate to changes in the family life cycle and to the role relationships of its members as well as those which may result from the personalities of individual members. One way of looking at the family is to see the individual as becoming enmeshed in an increasing number of role obligations as he approaches adult life which reach a peak on marriage and the founding of a new family. Here the individual is related not only to his newly founded family of procreation but to his own family of origin and that of his wife's own family. Within this wider circle of relationships, a traditional pattern is that of the continuing attachment of the wife to her own family and the drawing of the husband into this same circle. Here the husband may find it difficult to meet the requirements of two sets of role obligations, to his family of origin, and to the new family of procreation. Thus one of the most difficult life-cycle changes is the balancing of affective involvement between the various families in which the individual is involved. It is important to note that such life-cycle changes may proceed at different rates, depending on the type of family structure. Expectations derived from families in which the pace of such changes is rapid are not necessarily valid for families in different situations; in some circumstances the "disengagement" of individuals from their families of origin on marriage may be quite slow and related to kinship values which legitimize this. Thus the extent to which this situation is a problem for families will depend on the values actually held.

Strains of a structural nature may also arise in the conjugal relationship itself, one of which relates as illustrated to the effects of the occupational situation of the male. Another source of strain arises where the social networks of married couples change. When families in close-knit networks with segregated relationships move to new social situations, as are frequently found in housing estates or new towns, a change to a more open network structure often results. The couple are drawn less intensely into a circle of kin and friends and, as a result, have to adjust to a greater closeness in their own relationship. Sometimes the social skills to manage this new type of network, as well as a changing marital relationship, are lacking. It is important to recognize that certain strains or problems in the family have structural sources rather than resulting necessarily from the personalities of individuals. The evidence of studies such as that of Leichter and Mitchell in New York suggests that caseworkers tend to see most problems in the family in psychodynamic terms; an extra dimension is added to casework if strains are also seen as resulting, for example, from life-cycle changes and from other structural features. The Seebohm Committee[32] recognized, in their recommendations for a new administrative structure for the personal social services, the importance of understanding problems in the context of the family and the community rather than as the isolated symptoms of individuals. Their recommendations for a new service which avoids the compartmentalization of problems and which meets the needs of individuals, families, and communities implies, if put into practice, that social workers will have to rethink their approach to such problems. A sociological approach to the family appears one of the most promising aids to this process.

## NOTES AND REFERENCES

1. E. Leach, *A Runaway World*, B.B.C. Publications, 1968.
2. R. Fletcher, *Britain in the Sixties: The Family and Marriage*, Penguin, 1962.
3. E. Goldberg, The normal family—myth and reality, in E. Younghusband (ed.), *Social Work with Families*, Allen & Unwin, London, 1965.
4. P. Leonard, Depression and family failure, *Br. J. Psychiat. Soc. Wk.* **7** (4) (1964).
5. H. Leichter and W. Mitchell, *Kinship and Casework*, Russell Sage Foundation, New York, 1967. See Chapter 1, p. 7, for more details of these findings.
6. C. H. Meyer, The quest for a broader base for family diagnosis, *Social Casework*, **40** (7), July 1959; cited in Leonard, *Sociology in Social Work*, Routledge & Kegan Paul, London, 1966.
7. O. Pollak, A family diagnosis model (1960), in Younghusband, *op. cit.*
8. *Report of the committee on Local Authority and Allied Personal Social Services* (Seebohm Report), Cmnd 3703, H.M.S.O., London, 1968.
9. A. K. Cohen, *Delinquent Boys*, Free Press, Glencoe, 1956.
10. For an outline of this approach to the family see N. Bell and E. Vogel (eds.) *A Modern Introduction to the Family*, Free Press, New York, 1968; another introductory text is W. J. Goode, *The Family*, Prentice-Hall, New Jersey, 1964.
11. N. Bell and E. Vogel (eds.), *A Modern Introduction to the Family*, Free Press, New York, 1968.
12. T. Parsons and R. Bales, *Family, Socialisation and Interaction Process*, Routledge & Kegan Paul, London, 1956.
13. N. Timms, *A Sociological Approach to Social Problems*, Routledge & Kegan Paul, London, 1967.
14. For an analysis of the family in terms of role theory see Leonard, *op. cit.*
15. E. Bott, *Family and Social Network*, Tavistock, London, 1957 (a comment on this study can be found in Chapter 12).
16. The concept of social class will be examined in more detail in a later chapter; the term "middle class" will be taken to refer to non-manual workers and the term "working class" will refer to manual workers.
17. C. Rosser and C. Harris, *The Family and Social Change*, Routledge & Kegan Paul, London, 1965.
18. See J. Tunstall, *The Fisherman*, Eyre & Spottiswoode, London, 1956, and N. Dennis *et al.*, *Coal is Our Life*, Eyre & Spottiswoode, London 1957.
19. See P. Hollowell, *The Lorry Driver*, Routledge & Kegan Paul, London, 1968.
20. For a discussion of different definitions of the extended family see Rosse and Harris, *op. cit.*

21. See, for example, T. Parsons, The social structure of the family, in Anshen (ed.), *The Family, its Functions and Destiny*, Harper, 1959.

22. P. Willmott and M. Young, *Family and Kinship in East London*, Routledge & Kegan Paul, London, 1957.

23. E. Litwak, Occupational mobility and extended family cohesion anp geographic mobility and extended family cohesion, *Amer. Sociol. Rev.* **25** (1960); cited in Rosser and Harris, *op. cit.*

24. See K. Fitzherbert, *The West Indian Child in London*, Occasional Papers in Social Administration, Bell, 1967, and S. Patterson, *Dark Strangers*, Penguin, 1965.

25. K. Fitzherbert, *The West Indian Child in London*, Occasional Papers in Social Administration, Bell, 1967.

26. K. Davis, Mental Hygiene and the Class Structure, *Psychiatry*, **1** (1), 1938.

27. P. Fellin, A reappraisal of changes in American family patterns, in E Thomas (ed.), *Behavioural Science for Social Workers*, Free Press, New York, 1967.

28. O. Pollak, Social determinants of family behaviour (1963), in Young-husband (ed.), *Social Work with Families*, Allen & Unwin, London, 1965.

29. P. Willmott, Social administration and social class, *Case Conference*, **4** (7) (1958).

30. J. Klein, *Samples from English Cultures*, Routledge & Kegan Paul, London, 1965.

31. See J. Mayer and A. Rosenblatt, Client disengagement and alternative treatment resources, *Social Casework*, **47,** Jan. 1966.

32. Seebohm Report, chaps. vii and xix.

## CHAPTER 4

# *The Analysis of the Community*

### INTRODUCTION

Apart from work with individuals and families, social workers are also involved in various ways with what is loosely termed the community, an involvement which appears to be increasing in its importance.[1] One reason for this has been the new emphasis on care outside residential institutions for groups such as the mentally and physically ill, which has meant a greater awareness amongst the social workers involved of the dependence of their clients on others in the community. The concern of the social worker with individuals and families has sometimes meant that the immediate social environment has escaped the detailed analysis to which the interior of the family has been subjected.

Another reason for the growing concern with the community arises from a lack of success in the treatment of certain problems in terms of the individual client. One limitation to work undertaken with the individual is that it often fails to modify the environment which in many cases appears to be a factor contributing to the situation in which the individual client finds himself. Thus adjustments to the environment or work with the community are an important alternative to work with the individual.

For these and other reasons social workers are becoming more aware of the situation in which the client and the family find themselves and, in particular, are faced with the political implications of community work. One complicating factor is that many social workers find themselves in their work situation in bureaucratic roles in local authorities or other institutions which are in many cases the targets of those groups in the community who wish to work for change and to alter their environment. In Part III of this book the potential conflict between the bureaucratic and the professional role of the social worker is taken up in more detail.

Interest in the idea of community has grown in a number of other ways. Since the Second World War the development of new housing estates and new towns has involved much discussion amongst planners and architects of the desirability and feasibility of promoting community or neighbourly feelings. Amongst social scientists there has also been a revival of interest in such issues. An Institute of Community Studies has been founded in which one of the aims has been research into social relationships in particular localities. There have been a number of other studies of different localities, ranging from small villages and medium-sized towns to urban housing estates.[2]

Recognition of the importance for social workers and others of the many issues surrounding community work is not new but has recently been given a new impetus and is now coming to the attention of those who are professionally engaged in the organization of services and the training of future practitioners. The recent reports of the Seebohm Committee[3] and the Gulbenkian Study Group on training for community work[4] are illustrations of the growing importance of this field.

The purpose of this chapter will not be to essay a systematic discussion of the whole field but to attempt to clarify something of the nature of the contribution that a sociological study of the community can make to community work. Although the contribution of the various social sciences (particularly sociology) to community work was recognized by the Gulbenkian Report, the account given of the nature of this contribution suffered from being presented in the form of fragmented extracts from the views of a number of contributors.

Here a brief reference will be made to some of the many meanings of community work, and this is followed by a discussion of the contribution of the sociologist in the analysis of the community and of the many difficulties surrounding the use of the term. Finally, the feasibility of using the community as a way of obtaining certain ends is discussed, and some account is given of the reasons for the current popularity of the community idea.

There are many unquestioned assumptions made when terms like "community" are used in such contexts as community work, and one of the tasks of the sociological contribution is to examine such assumptions in the light of what is actually known about the nature of social relationships and of social interaction.

## COMMUNITY WORK

Community work can be discussed mainly in terms of a distinction between community organization, and community development.[5] Community organization, a term which is used to describe most forms of community work in the United States, involves the mobilization of local resources within the community to support various services, health, welfare, or education, which already exist. Community development involves the principle of helping people to help themselves either by mobilizing people to make better use of existing services or by pressing for changes in services, or by developing systems of self-help, with the assistance of outside agencies. Initially this term applied to work in underdeveloped countries, but it is recognized that industrialized countries like Britain and the United States also have areas with special needs, such as housing estates and the twilight areas of cities, to which the idea has been applied.

A common element in community development which distinguishes it from other forms of community work is its grass-roots approach in which the focus is on people's own appreciation of their needs and formulation of plans about such needs. Community organization, on the other hand, is based on institutions and services which have already been established by others.

Finally, the term "community care" can also be distinguished in the literature on social policy and social work.[6] This is not so much concerned with work with groups as with the care outside various institutional settings (such as mental hospitals) of individuals by their family or kin or by domiciliary services. It also includes the rehabilitation of individuals who had previously been removed from the community. In this sense the community is seen as a source of identity, support, and therapy.

These distinctions are partly distinctions in the use of the term in Britain and the United States. Thus one sense in which community work is utilized in the United States is in situations where the kin group is not utilized by social workers as a source of support and identification for the individual nuclear family. Instead, other forms of social relationship are utilized, and community work is one important way in which these are mobilized or organized. In Britain, on the other hand, such policies as community care are more likely to include the kin group as a means of social support.

A common element in most usages of the term in these contexts is that work is undertaken with a group or groups of people, usually in a defined physical area such as a neighbourhood, and in pursuance of certain goals which are accepted to a greater or lesser degree by those concerned.

It will be clear that community work is the concern of a number of groups besides social workers, including the teacher, the doctor, and the local authority administrator, each of whom may make a variety of different contributions at a number of levels.

Community work is thus part of the process of influencing and controlling social change. The wider aims and values of community work relate to certain general social values such as democracy, and there is a particular concern with the encouragement of democratic processes at the local level. There are also more specific counselling or social work values involved; these, together with the general relationship between social work and social change, are discussed much more fully in Part III, Chapters 8 and 9, and the present chapter can profitably be read in conjunction with these sections.

## THE MEANING OF COMMUNITY

Many difficulties have surrounded the meaning and use of the term "community", not least of which has been the reluctance of sociologists to refine the term in ways which would make it more useful either for the concerns of social policy[6] or for actual sociological analysis. The term has reached a "high level of use but a low level of meaning".[7]

Two general levels of meaning can be distinguished, both of which raise problems of various kinds.[8]

Community is used in the sense of social relations in a defined geographic area (residence community) and in the sense of belonging to a group with shared values or beliefs (a feeling or moral community). Often a sense of belonging is associated with residence in a defined area, but a distinction between the two meanings can usually be made. The size of the geographic area, which is the basis of community, varies from writer to writer, from the local area and the immediate environment to the society or nation as a whole. Two forms of residence, or locality community, can be distinguished. In one sense the term has been used to describe a situation in which all the elements of a common life exist—a kind of small-scale social system or society in miniature. Thus McIver [9] describes a community as "a social unity whose members recognize as common a sufficiency of interests to allow of the interactivities of common life . . . the completest type of community is the nation". Secondly, and this is possibly the most popular use of the term, the idea of community is seen as involving social interaction of a certain degree and kind. It is thought that a place is more like a community if the people who live near each other also mix and interact in specific ways.

Those who have used community in the feeling or moral sense have described such situations as a community of interests amongst people of a certain kind (academics, social workers) or as synonymous with relationships outside a particular institution, such as the State or Government. A geographic element has returned in the description of certain closed institutions, such as prisons or hospitals, as communities of one sort or another.

A number of difficulties are raised by such usages.[8] For example, referring to the residence or locality community, no system of social relations can be said to have a specific geographic boundary.

Local areas are composed of particular social institutions or groups such as the factory, the school, the neighbourhood, or kin groups, none of which may necessarily be based exclusively on the local area. Again, the institutions present in any one area may be so shaped by influences external to that area (such as social policy or political decisions taken elsewhere) that the fact that they are located in a particular area may have little or no significance.

Thus the term "community" has been used in a variety of ways and at a variety of levels by sociologists. One way out of the confusion is to make clear in what sense the term is in fact being used, e.g. by a prefix denoting whether it is the locality or moral community which is being referred to.

But there is doubt in the minds of some sociologists as to whether the community is in any sense a useful starting point for the main task of sociological analysis, the study of social institutions, and social relationships. It has been argued[10] that studies of the community become involved with the meaningless trivialities of everyday life and that the proper task of the sociologist lies outside the community, e.g. in the analysis of class relationships and other institutions which dictate the character of community life.

The deficiencies of the sociological analysis of the community for the critical development of social policy can be seen in the enthusiasm with which the community care policy (which involved the attempt to provide in the community for the mentally and physically handicapped who had previously been in institutions) was received. Thus very little thought was given to the possibility of care being given in the community to those who had in many cases been rejected by it. Thus assumptions of various kinds were made about the community, that it gave off, as Titmus[11] has suggested, "a sense of warmth and human kindness, essentially personal and comforting, as loving as the wild flowers so enchantingly described by Lawrence in *Lady Chatterley's Lover*", which were largely unquestioned.

## COMMUNITY STUDIES

The greatest manifestation of sociological interest in the community has been in the form of studies of particular localities. These are of two kinds. Firstly, those concerned with studies of particular institutions, such as the family, in a particular local context, such as the studies of Swansea and Bethnal Green referred to in the previous chapter, and, secondly, those concerned with the interrelationships of institutions within a locality and which attempt to show the pattern of social relationships which result. Examples include the study of the village of Gosforth by W. M. Williams and the town of Banbury by M. Stacey. One concern of students of the community has been to attempt to trace and understand the development of industrial society and the change from rural to urban settlement, and community studies are particularly valuable in this respect. Frankenburg[12] has arranged a series of community studies, from the most rural to the most urban, on a continuum and, in linking this with the concept of role, has provided a useful approach to these changes. In small-scale face-to-face communities, individuals play many of their roles to the same people or set of people, and in addition play most of these out in public. It is difficult to insulate the playing out of one set of role relationships (e.g. in the family) from another (work relationships) because of the small-scale nature of the community and the fact that people are constantly interacting with one another in a variety of ways. Role relationships here can be described as multiple or many stranded, i.e. there are a variety of cross-cutting ties which bind individuals together. Because of this closeness, conflict is never far from the surface in such communities.

In urban communities, where the scale of population is much greater, role relationships take on a different character; people play out their different roles to different audiences and there is a considerable degree of insulation between the segments within which roles are played. Each person plays many parts but to many different audiences. Role relationships are overlapping or single-stranded. Conflict, although it occurs, has not got the same implications as in small-scale situations, for there is little chance of it spreading from one series of role relationships (say at work) to another (e.g. in the home). Frankenburg suggests that small community life is characterized by complexity, as against the complication of city life, and that complexity changes to complication with technological and other developments.

To term one locality a community and another not on this or any other basis is as fruitless an operation as deciding which occupation is or is not a profession. What is more important is to ask certain questions in any area which may give some idea of the character of the social relationships which are found. Size of population is certainly not the only criterion to be considered.[12] Thus Bethnal Green (pop. 54,000) was found to be in some respects a community because of strong cross-cutting links of kinship and neighbourliness, but Banbury (pop. 19,000) was not a community, mainly because of the extent of ties with social groups outside the town. Again, community life of a special kind grows up in areas which have particular class or ethnic character and which are subjected to particular pressures. Thus the kind of community structure which developed in the ethnically mixed twilight area of Sparkbrook (Birmingham)[13] depended on such factors as the state of the housing market, the opportunities for people to leave the area, and the nature of the resolution of the conflicts between the different social groups living in the area and the extent to which they could be reconciled to each other's presence. Thus communities essentially are composed of groups who have something in common, whether this is in the economic and work sphere, in values or beliefs or interests, or in ethnic origin. Although the community may be described as a simple form of society, the character of the interrelationships which have been described suggests great complexity.

In view of the many criticisms of any approach based on the idea of community, it is important to justify the study of particular communities or localities. Stacey,[8] in a recent defence of such studies, argues that studies of social relations in localities provide a unique means of understanding which social institutions are related to each other and in what ways, although it does not matter particularly whether such localities are isolated or not. Again, such studies provide the means by which the influence of the two dimensions of time and space can be studied, influences which are very important in determining the nature of social institutions. Thus local social systems have developed over considerable time periods of the order of 50–80 years, and all the components of social life are to be found within their boundaries. Therefore the aim should be to study part of the wider social system, or a set of inter-related institutions, in a local context, although in some circumstances a local social system will not exist or exist only partially. Clearly there are no social systems in which all the parts are inter-related, although this idea can be considered as some form of ideal type. Thus a local social system may have some component missing, e.g. there may be no extended kin connections or family system at all, as in some closed institutions such as prisons. The concept of the local social system involves not only institutions but also social processes, which must be studied over time if their full meaning is to be appreciated. Locality studies provide the setting in which such studies can be made and also have an important place in the study of more total social systems, such as whole societies. Apart from the sociological justification for the continuance of such studies, these points are also of importance to the practitioner, for they offer some refinement of the nebulous concept community.

## SOCIAL WORK AND THE COMMUNITY

From the account given so far in this chapter it will be clear that the concern of the social worker and the sociologist with the community is of rather a different nature; however, it is also clear that the revival of interest in the many issues surrounding the subject is shared by both. The important issue now arises[14] as to why, in view of the difficulties and doubts raised by the subject of the community, such an idea should succeed in gaining such prominence in a particular society at a particular time?

Before outlining an answer to this question it is necessary to consider some of the implications of the foregoing arguments for the practice of community work. Two issues arise; in what sense can the sociological analysis of the community illuminate the way in which community problems arise? Again, distinguishing between the desirability and the feasibility of work involving the community and accepting that community work is desirable, what is the likelihood that such problems can be solved at the level of the community? Is the regeneration of the community which is assumed by much that is written about community work actually possible?

One of the most important points to have emerged from the various community studies is the changing nature of the social situation in which people find themselves as life in small-scale face-to-face communities gives way to large-scale urban existence. This problem, which is current in most industrialized or industrializing societies, has many facets, and an important one is the change from many-stranded to single-stranded role relationships. In an urban context, as individuals develop role relationships (e.g. at work) which are not linked by common kinship or residence to other relationships (in the family or locality), the individual and his family lose the fabric of a close community and become increasingly exposed to certain elements of a total society. As Bott[15] suggests, "in a small scale relatively closed society the local group and the kin group mediate between the family and the total society; in an urban industrial society there is no single encapsulating group which mediates between the family and the total society". Because social status in the community is now not clear, one influence is the pressure to consume as a means to social status. Social workers are familiar with situations in which families accumulate hire purchase and other commitments with apparently little power to resist such pressures. Another effect is that norms of behaviour become less clear in such situations and because people are uncertain about how to react to and what to expect from others,[16] a withdrawal into a more privatized existence takes place and the capacity of such a community to provide for dependence is considerably diminished.

Again, the control of deviant behaviour in face-to-face communities was accomplished informally and was effective because, with a close community fabric, much activity was of a public nature and the consequences of deviant acts would immediately be felt by the miscreant. In a more complex situation, where roles are played out to different audiences, behaviour in each role thus becomes more private and the individual can escape from the implications of a deviant act and from the control exerted by kin and neighbours in small-scale situations.

Finally, as Stein[17] has suggested from an appraisal of American community studies, a problem of the nature of individual identity is raised by the nature of social life on urban estates and in suburbs. In more stable small-scale communities, individuals were evaluated by others on the basis of "who they were". Identification was based on family, kin and community relationships built up over time. In the new residential areas of modern cities this kind of identification is impossible and is replaced by evaluations based on occupational status and patterns of consumption. This, Stein argues, may provide only partially for the support of the adult and in particular the adolescent personality. Identity may sometimes be sought through the services of professional counsellors who discharge the same function as members of the previous close-knit community. This is an interesting illustration of the way in which the location of emotional or personal problems can be sought in the social structure of the locality and provides yet another justification for the revival of the local community. It also offers an opportunity for linking the approaches of those social workers mainly interested in problems as they manifest themselves in the individual to those who are more concerned with changing the immediate environment of the individual.

But can the community, however defined, be regenerated in the way which is implied by much of the discussion of community work? What are the limitations suggested by the foregoing analysis to some of the ambitious schemes for community organization and development now being discussed? Using community in the sense of small-scale social system in which all the elements of a common life were present, it has already been suggested that large-scale urbanization implies the geographical specialization of services and activities to an extent that they are rarely found in any one area.

For example, even if certain social services operate at a local level, their control and administration is almost invariably located outside the area and is not linked to other services or institutions at that level. In particular, the persons who run such services—school teachers and social workers, for example—almost invariably reside away from those areas in which they work. The urban housing estate is in particular an area in which there is a low level of community in this sense, for control over it is often exercised by a distant city authority which conveniently exported its surplus population to other areas, but continues to exercise administrative control.

Thus the possibility of regenerating community in this sense appears to have considerable limitations. The fact that over four-fifths of the population of England and Wales live in areas which can be described as urban, and that one characteristic of urban areas is the specialization of activities and services and the segregation of different social groups in different areas, appears to constitute formidable barriers to this end. [18] It is also important to recognize the dimension of power in this situation and to recognize that the changes that may result from even a small-scale reconstitution of the social system community may not be in the interests of those holding power in the existing and more centralized system.

The possibility of reconstituting community in the sense of inter-action within the locality depends on the carrying on of activities which provide the basis for interaction such as common work, leisure, or recreational activities. [14] Linked to this sharing of common experiences is a sharing of common memories, of attending the same schools, workplaces, and leisure associations. This is the temporal element stressed by Stacey. Again, these experiences are at their height in immobile one-class areas, and, at the other end of the continuum, the housing estate, are least likely.

This form of social interaction may give rise to the social system community, but it is far more likely that social interaction will result from the existence of a social system community. Thus it is possible to have people co-operating in a social system without this giving rise to social interaction.

Finally, to what extent can the locality community be reconstituted so as to provide for the control of deviant behaviour?[14]
First it would be necessary to establish that in fact control would be
possible because of what others in the locality think or do and that
in fact this kind of control was exercised in small-scale communities.
In an urban situation the fact that the individual is taken up into the
social system of the city as a whole is of the greatest significance;
thus control may be effectively exercised by influences within this
wider system. The influences of the locality can also certainly be
escaped by the simple device of remaining away from the neighbourhood of residence for long periods of time; for city dwellers
the locality can mean as much or as little as the individual chooses.
The notion of the community as a means of more effective social
control is thus probably one of the weakest arguments for the
regeneration of the community.

In assessing the feasibility (but not the desirability) of the community as a basis for the attainment of certain ends, the sharpened
perspectives which have been given to the notion of the community
by these commentators seem of great importance. Thus if the
community is thought of as a local social system made up of a
number of components which may be related in particular ways, it
may be possible to construct a check-list of the most important
components (key social institutions, the possibility of common
activities leading to a shared culture, and so on), in the absence of
which it would be difficult to envisage a local social system. The
next step would be to identify the missing components of a system
and to decide, within the limits of the resources available to community development, whether these can be replaced by outside
intervention or whether other components can be substituted.
Clearly, from the evidence presented above, replacement and substitution may be very difficult tasks; thus in certain situations the
question would arise as to whether intervention of the community
work kind would or would not constitute a waste of scarce resources of manpower and finance.

In the light of the many obstacles in the way of the emergence of
community (however defined) in the mid-twentieth century, in

particular the irreversible tide of urbanization and its various implications for social relationships, it is all the more puzzling that the subject should have reappeared. Community does not die easily and its continued life has been officially blessed by the Seebohm and Gulbenkian reports. Although the fate of these reports is still not clear, it is likely that "community" will become an established part of the language of social welfare in the next decade.

Historically, belief in the principle of the locality emerged at a time of intense industrialization and when large masses of working people were coming together in towns.[10] This, to some observers, constituted a significant threat to society and its values.[19] One way of countering this threat was the penetration of the working masses with middle-class and "civilized" values, and, indeed, the objects of the early settlement movement were of this kind. The idea of breaking up the threatening mass into communities with an admixture of middle-class people and middle-class values was also a principle by which new model settlements were planned. It later became a principle adopted in the policy for new towns after the Second World War, although here the rationale was the belief that the socially balanced communities it was hoped to create would foster an atmosphere where the classes could mix and gain from each other's presence.[20]

Thus one way of interpreting the vogue for the community is as a way of taming the political extremist and the trouble-maker by involving them in local issues and in the tedium of administration;[14] clearly this is not the manifest function of such a policy, but it seems important to show that such fears did at one time exist and that there were particular consequences of such beliefs. It is significant that the community movement, both in this country and in the United States, has gained momentum and in some cases received official sanction at a time when the amount of radical and even violent protest and conflict is sharply on the increase.

Again, the idea of the locality community as a factor in the causation of personal and social problems and the belief that these can be ameliorated by an adjustment of the community environment, diverts attention to issues which lie outside the community in

the social structure. Rarely do studies of communities direct attention to such wider issues, and thus support for such studies and for
therapeutic work with the community comes readily to hand. A
more intensive examination of these issues than has hitherto been
mounted appears an important task for community work in the
future.

Thus the aim to link the individual with the decisions which are
being taken about him, to generate local interest in and action about
social services, can be interpreted as attempts to insert meaning into
the democratic process, to fight political apathy, and to humanize
bureaucracies. Yet the uncomfortable feeling persists when reports
such as Seebohm and Gulbenkian are read alongside discussions of
the ideology of social movements, that the mixture is as before and
only the wrapping is different. Thus the attempt to involve people
in decisions occurs at a stage too far removed from the positions
where power is actually held and that, once more, the appeal to the
community only results in the avoidance of real issues, that in
concentrating on social situations a means is found whereby attention can be diverted from social structures.[21]

The dilemma into which many social workers have been thrown
by the prospect of involvement in political action may not be so
real as it appears for, interpreted in this way, community work
does not contain the basis for a real confrontation with authority or
any major threat to established institutions.

## NOTES AND REFERENCES

1. For a discussion of this and other current developments in social work in
   Britain, see A. Forder and S. Kay, Recent developments in social work,
   *Soc. and Econ. Administration*, **3** (2), April 1969.
2. See, for example, W. M. Williams, *The Sociology of an English Village*,
   Routledge & Kegan Paul, London, 1956; A. M. Stacey, *Tradition and
   Change—A Study of Banbury*, O.U.P., London, 1960; and J. Mogey,
   *Family and Neighbourhood*, O.U.P., London, 1956.
3. *Report of the Committee on Local Authority and Allied Personal Services*
   Cmnd. 3703, H.M.S.O., 1968, chap. xvi.
4. *Community Work and Social Change*, Longmans, London, 1968.

5. For a discussion see Gulbenkian Report; R. A. Leaper, *Community Work*. N.C.S.S., London, 1968; and D. Groves, Community self help groups, *Case Conference*, **16** (4), Aug. 1969.

6. For a discussion of this and other meanings of community see S. Elkan, The different meanings of community, *Case Conference*, **14** (8), Dec. 1967,

7. P. Mann, *An Approach to Urban Sociology*, Routledge & Kegan Paul, London, 1965, chaps. 6 and 7. These chapters also contain an analysis of the community based on the ideal-type approach.

8. M. Stacey, The myth of community studies, *Brit. J. Sociol.* **20** (2), June 1969; this also contains a critical account of the community in sociological terms.

9. R. M. McIver, *Community*, Macmillan, London, 1924.

10. R. Glass, Trend report in urban sociology, *Current Sociology*, **4** (4), 1955 (also in R. Pahl, (ed.), *Readings in Urban Sociology*, Pergamon Press, 1968).

11. R. Titmus, Community care; fact or fiction, in Titmus, *Commitment to Welfare*, Allen & Unwin, 1968.

12. R. Frankenburg, *Communities in Britain*, Pelican, 1966.

13. J. Rex and R. Moore, *Race, Community and Conflict*, O.U.P., London, 1967.

14. N. Dennis, The popularity of the neighbourhood community idea, in R. Pahl, *op. cit.*

15. E. Bott, *Family and Social Network*, Tavistock, London, 1957.

16. This situation can be described as "anomie", and is discussed more fully in Chapter 7, Social Deviance.

17. M. Stein, *The Eclipse of Community*, Harper & Row, 1964.

18. For a general discussion of urbanization see R. Pahl, *Patterns of Urban Life* Longmans, London, 1970.

19. Thus an observer passing through Manchester in 1842 could not "contemplate those crowded hives without feelings of anxiety and apprehension almost amounting to dismay . . . it is an aggregate of masses. . . . We speak of them as of the slow rising and gradual swelling of the ocean which must, at some future and no distant time, bear all the elements of society aloft upon its bosom and float them—Heaven knows whither"; quoted in Glass, *op. cit.* (W. Cooke Taylor, *Notes of a Tour in the Manufacturing Districts*).

20. For a brief account see B. Heraud, Social class and the new towns, *Urban Studies*, **5** (1), Feb. 1968.

21. For a further discussion of this issue see C. Wright Mills, The ideology of social pathologists, *Amer. J. Sociol.*, **49** (1943).

# CHAPTER 5

## Social Stratification

### INTRODUCTION

It is frequently suggested that the whole question of social differences, particularly distinctions of social class, is no longer of any importance in a modern welfare state and is the product of a society long since dead. There is a strong emotional belief in equality and a dislike of the implication that some are "better" or "worse" than others. Phrases such as "class has lost its importance" or "we are all middle class now" are frequently echoed. Social scientists in particular are sometimes accused of helping to keep alive, by their insistent interest in such issues, a class-based society.

This chapter and the one following are based on the assumption that social differences, in the sense of people who think, speak, and act differently, do still exist, and that such individuals also form aggregates on the basis of factors such as occupation and income and, under certain circumstances, form groups based on common interests for the purpose of common action. In particular it will be suggested that such differences are of great importance in understanding the interaction between social workers and individuals, groups, and communities.

So far terms such as "social stratification", "social differences" and "class" have been used in both the previous paragraphs and in preceding chapters. The variety of terms in use gives some idea of the differences in approach and of the difficulties met with in this field. In the next section of this chapter some attempt will be made to explore some of these difficulties before the terms are put to further use in the following chapter, where specific topics of importance to the social worker are dealt with, including child rearing, language, and changes in the class system. In the intervening paragraphs the terms "working class" and "middle class" will be treated as meaning manual and non-manual worker.

In Britain, social work can be seen in part as a service rendered by members of one social class to those of another. Thus social workers, who can be termed middle class in origin or in education, training, or status in the community,[1] spend much of their time in the context of the working-class community and function in the main with working-class clients and their families.

This raises certain difficult problems. One way of looking at the social classes is as groups who are distinguished by different styles of life or cultures, i.e. different ways of thinking and acting about such activities as child rearing, education, and work. Here the social worker may apply a set of middle-class assumptions about behaviour to working-class clients and their families. For example, the diagnostic concept of maturity, which is often used by social workers rests, as Leonard[2] has pointed out, to a large extent on assumptions of a class nature. Thus maturity is seen as based on such qualities as ambition, self-reliance, toleration of frustration, and control of physical violence. However, such a concept becomes diagnostically useless if applied to individuals without taking into account its essentially class-based nature. Thus the concept of maturity, with its often unacknowledged basis in the culture of the middle class, may have little relevance for certain parts of the working class. If the values of another class are adopted, these may be vaguely conceptualized or misunderstood through constant contact with the abnormal in that social group.

Related to these differences is the fact that members of different classes may see their problems and also the solutions of them in a number of different ways. For example, as Stein and Cloward[3] suggest, working-class individuals may locate the source of their problems in the external and possibly unchangeable environment, while in the middle-class problems are seen as the product of the personality and of certain inner states. The professional culture of the social worker, which emphasizes the solubility of problems on the basis of long-term assessment and treatment, may run contrary to the more fatalistic and passive elements in the working-class culture by which certain states are seen as the inevitable lot of man. This point has relevance for diagnosis as well as for treatment, for there is also likely for the same reasons to be disagreement about the definition of certain situations as problems at all. Again, the professional model of the helping process by which problems are seen in intra-psychic rather than material terms and in which the emotional make-up of the client is explored may also run contrary to the expectations of working-class individuals. As increasing numbers of social workers become trained and internalize such ideas, the gulf between their professional culture and that of the working class widens.

Thus social work stands at the meeting point of a number of groups which have up to now been mostly categorized under the familiar term of social classes. What is important now is to refine such categories in order that such distinctions can be made more useful. Clearly, however formulated, the notion of social class is an extremely useful way of looking at the different ways in which the social services—including the services of the social worker—are perceived and used. Until recently, as Timms[4] suggests, attention has been concentrated on the different norms and values of the classes or on class cultures. What is also important is to widen the concept of class to include such factors as communication between different classes based on language and perception, differing educational experiences, and the definition of the helping situation in terms of power or authority. This will provide a useful framework for future discussion in this chapter.

This general picture of the relationship between social work and social class is changing in a number of important ways both in Britain and America. As the social services, including social work, become more of an accepted part of the life of industrialized societies and the stigma attached to their use declines, a wider range of clientele become available to social work agencies, in particular members of the middle and professional classes. At the same time, as sections of the working class become more economically self-sufficient, the disorganized lower strata of this class, which was previously concealed by the poverty of the working class in general, are revealed and (particularly in the United States) are increasingly becoming the focus of social work. Thus a polarization of the clientele of social work agencies may be occurring in which the professional and middle class and the lower working class become increasingly predominant.[1]

Whilst this is occurring, the social origins of social workers appear themselves to be changing, partly as a result of the rapid development of training schemes, and recruits to the profession appear to be coming from much wider social origins than before. Thus, as Wilensky and Lebeaux[1] point out, the old question "Can a professional, teacher, social worker, minister, etc., of middle-class status and origin break through the cultural barriers of class?" may give way to the new question "Can a professional of working-class origin, but newly won middle-class status, deal comfortably with the personal problems of clients of higher social background?"

The challenge of this new question centres in part around the kind of problems and questions middle-class individuals might bring to social work agencies. These, as Rapoport[5] points out, are often related to problems of *anomie* and identity, situations in which the norms and values which guide behaviour have become blurred. Such questions are ones, however, to which the social worker may also, possibly unsuccessfully, be seeking answers. Moreover, the close identification between the client and worker may produce strain and a feeling of helplessness which is, for the social worker, a greater problem than the material needs of the working-class client.

## INTRODUCTION TO SOCIAL STRATIFICATION

### Social Differences

The subject of social stratification can be introduced by returning to the subject of the family and the relationship between the family and the wider society.

The family essentially confers a certain position or status upon its members in the wider society;[6] most people in any community, say a village or small town, would be able to arrange in order of social standing or rank the families in that community. Some will be of high standing, others will count for less, and yet others will count for nothing. It is likely that some families will have a similar ranking and come to occupy the same position in the social scale. This social scale is one way of expressing the idea of social stratification.

How are these evaluations which place families and individuals in a different social order actually made? Although all individuals are different one from another, some of these differences are considered to be of greater importance than others in evaluating people and allocating to them superior or inferior status; in some societies age and sex differences are important ways in which people are ranked. Thus to be elderly is in some cases a sufficient reason for high status; in other cases males are accorded greater prestige than females. Neither of these qualities are of particular importance in Britain today. There is some general agreement that the characteristic which is seen as of greatest importance in the ranking of individuals is that of occupation. An individual's full-time job and its relative importance to society appear, certainly in modern industrial societies, to take on the greatest weight. A family's position or status in the community is often evaluated by reference to the occupation of the male head of household, and the respect which attaches to his job will also attach to other family members. Occupation is also important because it is related to other social differences such as income and way of life. Thus occupations which have high prestige often command high incomes. Occupation has also become an important "social difference" because it is relatively easier to find out an individual's occupation than other less tangible social factors, and thus is often used in research. For example, the population is divided up every 10 years according to occupation by the Government Census of Population. Table 3 shows the percentages of the population in each of the five occupational groups which are used (1961 Census).

TABLE 3. PERCENTAGE OF OCCUPIED
AND RETIRED MALES BY SOCIAL CLASS
IN ENGLAND AND WALES—1961 CNESUS

| Social class | % |
|---|---|
| I. Professional | 4 |
| II. Semi-professional | 15 |
| III. Unskilled non-manual and skilled manual | 51 |
| IV. Semi-skilled manual | 21 |
| V. Unskilled manual | 9 |
| | 100 |

Source: Census 1961;
    Occupation tables (H.M.S.O.).

*Socio-Economic Aggregates*

It is not difficult to demonstrate the existence of a number of aggregates of differing socio-economic character. For example, both property and income are unevenly distributed over the population. One recent estimate[7] is that in 1960 the top 5 per cent of the population owned 75 per cent of all personal property, while 1 per cent owned 42 per cent of all personal property. Again, such inequalities have not shown any marked change in the preceding two decades. Although some income redistribution has occurred, research has shown that the inequalities of income distribution have taken certain new forms. Again, if wealth has accumulated at one extreme than it is also likely that poverty will exist at the other. This is in fact what recent research has shown. Taking the National Assistance Board's (now Ministry of Social Security) scale rates as a defined poverty line, Abel Smith and Townsend[8] found that, in 1960, 18 per cent of households representing $7\frac{1}{2}$ million people were living below such a level. The largest groups were dependent on earnings followed by those on pension and others primarily dependent on State benefits.

## Social Stratification

So far we have referred to a series of objective ways in which individuals and families are distinguished—including prestige, occupation, and income. In one sense what is being suggested is no more than a series of statistical aggregates based on such differences. But when there are clear-cut and consistent differences of this kind in a society a series of strata emerge which consist of a hierarchy of layers marked off by differences of status. One example of a stratum would be the slaves of ancient society. Again, there are various types of stratification of which the class system of modern societies is but one.[9] One way in which these systems could be distinguished is by the ease of movement from one level to another, or the fluidity of the system.

In the caste system, which was found in most developed form in India, membership of different castes was based on birth; there was a rigid hierarchy and individual movement from caste to caste was impossible. Within each caste rules governed all aspects of life, including dress, speech, occupation, and marriage. In the estate system strata were also distinguished from each other by law and custom, and the whole system—which distinguished nobility, clergy, merchants, and peasants—was considered divinely ordained. Birth largely determined membership, but individuals could move within their lifetime by performing outstanding service or by entering the priesthood.

The class system differs from other forms of stratification because it does not imply legal or religious distinctions. Often class is found in association with beliefs in equality (or citizenship as Marshall[10] has termed it), but because various qualities are evaluated as of greater or lesser desirability, and because each strata can perpetuate itself, a tendency to inequality is still found. Barriers to mobility are largely related to differences in the opportunities which exist at different social levels. Thus to an extent, even in a modern class system, the various strata are partially self-perpetuating in the sense that parents already in high positions are able to give their children a good chance of remaining in the same stratum through access to *élite* or specialized education and training.

Although the class system is more fluid than other systems of stratification it still makes itself felt in the course of everyday life in a number of ways. One aspect is the physical segregation of different social groups in residential areas. Typically, the social classes tend to occupy different parts of towns and cities. In some areas where housing for different social groups is built close together, physical barriers have been erected to separate the groups from one another. In the Cutteslowe area of Oxford[11] a wall 7 feet high topped with iron spikes stretching across a road and a footpath was erected in order to separate a private group of houses from a council housing estate which was built in close proximity. The wall succeeded in physically and socially isolating one group from another, and it took over 20 years of legal argument before it was finally demolished.

## Social Class and Social Status

The existence of a variety of strata or aggregates with similar status and sharing similar conditions does not necessarily imply the existence of a class in the sense of a situation in which the members are conscious of their own existence and act together in their own interests. A number of writers, including Marx, have distinguished between the two situations of a "class in itself" and a "class for itself", and the transformation from the former to the latter situation. The elements in this process include the consciousness of identity, of belonging to a group with common characteristics and a common fate, the emergence of shared beliefs, attitudes and values (a culture), increasing interaction between the members of such emerging groups, and the pursuit of common interests through associations such as political parties.[12]

For the present it seems important to concentrate on the evidence relating to the emergence of cultural patterns within broad strata such as manual and non-manual workers as well as interaction within these strata. Not only can cultural differences between the strata be distinguished, but a distinction can also be drawn between traditional and non-traditional orientations in each strata. Klein[13] brings together a number of studies of the situation of the traditional manual and non-manual worker and stresses the following points. Amongst manual workers society is seen very much in terms of a "them" and "us" distinction, where "them" are the bosses, people who order you about and dictate your lives, at least in the context of work. In the face of this, a tightly knit community develops based on kinship and a similarity of working environments, in which neighbourliness and practical assistance in times of crises are highly valued, and in which there is a desire to show "them" the respectability of honest working-class life. Again, time perspectives are short. Money is often spent on a periodic "splash" at week-ends, weddings, or funerals, and there is little evidence of long-term planning. This can be seen in particular in the lack of development of a formal associational life. Instead of developing formal associations, with their commitment to a future orientation, the instant sociability of street and pub is preferred in which no investment in the future is necessary.

The contrast here with certain aspects of middle-class life is apparent. Associational life plays an important part in the social life of the middle class and is part of the future orientation associated with this class. Such associations are seen as having an ongoing and enduring character, and are in themselves part of the orderly progression towards certain future goals. As Klein comments: "To book a date in a diary for an appointment six weeks ahead is a middle class act." Amongst the traditional working class, on the other hand, people will know each other and where to find each other because of the close-knit character of the local community. There will be little need to plan out meetings in advance and to order in this rational style the functioning of social life. Again, while the traditional working class take life as it comes and accept in a stoical way the blows of fate, the middle class are more likely to see problems as a challenge to ingenuity or resource and to use formal means of solving them.

One important distinction within the traditional working class is that between the so-called rough and respectable elements. Although the "splash" is an accepted form of behaviour, it does not preclude emphasis on thrift, cleanliness, and self-respect at other times which characterize the so-called "respectable group". By contrast, the "rough" element do not emphasize such norms, and at all times live from hand to mouth with an excessively present oriented approach which constantly brings them in contact with the social services. This group include the category known as problem families which will be discussed in Chapter 7 on Social Deviance.

The culture of the traditional manual worker is undergoing considerable change, particularly as the tight-knit one-industry communities are broken up by rehousing in new estates and towns. There is inevitably less reliance on kin and neighbours and a greater emphasis on individual self-reliance. Changes in the class structure will be discussed in more detail in the following chapter.

Reviewing the evidence relating to such processes, Cotgrove[12] concludes that "there seems little doubt that classes exist in a more solidary form than mere statistical aggregates of individuals of similar income, occupation or prestige. There is consciousness of kind, of belonging to perceived and definable groups marked off by differences in beliefs and values and styles of life." However, Cotgrove argues that it is differences of status which are at the basis of these distinctions rather than the broader and more pervasive distinctions of social class, and that the most important distinctions are between the manual worker and the higher status white-collar jobs.

The distinction between social status and social class is an important one in sociology[14] and is based on the distinction between the evaluation of the individual by others, defined in particular by the playing of roles in the system of consumption, and the individual's membership of social classes based on the system of economic production and in particular on the ownership of property and wealth. Another distinction is between the competitiveness of statuses and the actual or potential conflict situation which exists between classes.

Statuses and classes are related in the sense that economic wealth often implies high status, but this is not always the case. The two forms of stratification must be thought of as distinct though related entities, emphasizing once again the complexities and many dimensions of modern systems of stratification.

A number of sociologists have suggested that more weight should be given to the notion of status groups than to economic class, as there appears little real conflict over inequalities of wealth but a good deal of status striving and competition involving symbols of status.

These differing notions of social stratification imply differing ideas about the functioning of society as a whole and it is to certain major theoretical formulations and the theories of stratification which derive from them that discussion in this introductory section finally turns.

### Theories of Stratification

Several theories of stratification exist which help to organize and explain the many facts about social stratification which could be presented. One way of looking at such theories is to see them as deriving from the two major types of theoretical speculation about the nature of the social order outlined briefly in the introductory chapter on sociology. Broadly, an integration or consensus theory of society was compared with conflict or coercion theory. In the same way two types of theory relating to social stratification can be distinguished, an "hierarchical" and a "dichotomous" model. In these distinctions the two general theories of society, the integrative and the coercive, reappear.[15]

The hierarchical model of stratification suggests order and integration; the idea of a dichotomy or division between groups suggests conflict, dissensus, and coercion.

The hierarchical model approximates to the idea of a number of strata arranged in some order of rank or prestige. Dahrendorf suggests that this view of the social order is most often adopted by dominant groups who express, in ideological terms, their satisfaction with the *status quo* in which they have a fortunate place. The notion may also be derived from a bureaucratic hierarchy in which everybody has a defined place or position.

Associated with this idea is the theory that an hierarchical structure inevitably occurs in an industrial society and serves important functions in that society. This theory, the functionalist theory of social stratification,[16] states that in a society in which there is a considerable division of labour and where tasks are specialized, some occupational positions require greater degrees of skill and knowledge than others. These can only be performed by highly trained individuals. In order to foster the necessary motivation for such tasks, for which a lengthy training and education is also required, it is necessary for these positions to be highly rewarded and to carry high status. Thus a series of strata will inevitably develop which have considerable wealth, status, and power and make contributions to the social system of a high order. Given also that the human family exists, these strata are likely to perpetuate themselves through inheritance and socialization, although a certain amount of movement from strata to strata will be possible. This system is seen as important for the survival and development of society and is thus accepted and accorded legitimacy by most groups. Conflicts within the system are seen as personal or individual, and rarely involve the entire social structure.

The dichotomous model of society, and the theory of conflict which underlies it, is best expressed initially in the language of people who hold this view of society; it need scarcely be emphasized that this view is most often held by subordinate rather than dominant groups, who view society from below rather than above. As suggested a distinction between "them" and "us" emerges as characteristic of the two sides of the dichotomy; Hoggart[17] has summarized this attitude in a collection of illuminating statements: " 'they' are 'the people at the top', 'the high ups', the people who give you your dole, call you up, tell you to go to war, fine you . . . 'get yer in the end', 'aren't really to be trusted', 'talk posh', 'are all twisters really' . . . 'are all in a clique together', 'treat y' like muck'."

Dahrendorf suggests, from an analysis of the above study and others, various ways in which the dichotomy between the two groups can be distinguished. There is the distinction between the power and authority of "them" by contrast to the weakness and impotence of "us"; there are those who work (us) and those whose work is invisible or who do not work. Manual and non-manual, wage earning or salary earning are other typical ways in which the groups are contrasted in people's minds; but the distinguishing criteria are not sufficiently exact to be entirely clear about the two groups—where "they" begin and "us" end differs from group to group. But there is sufficient evidence from this general view to suggest that the idea of a dichotomy into two broad social groups is a powerful social fact which challenges fundamentally the idea of a harmonious and integrated society.

The most important name to be linked with this idea is that of Marx.[18] In Marxist thinking there are in every industrial society two major contending classes defined by their ownership or non-ownership of the means of production. This distinction had developed during industrialization when certain groups had achieved power over and possession of land, machines, and the right to dispose of products and to control labour; by contrast other groups had lost any control they might have had over such resources and were left with nothing but their labour to sell. Thus for Marx and the theorists that have come after him, the division of labour did not simply mean that people did different jobs to which were attached differences in prestige, but meant a distinction between two groups based on differing relationships to capital and property which overshadowed all other distinctions.

One of the consequences of this system was that this basic economic division meant the unequal division of other privileges. Given power in the organization of economic activities, the bourgeoisie also acquired political power and control over other spheres including arts, science, and law. Another consequence of the exploitation of one class by another and the resulting conflict over goals was the development of class consciousness; thus the proletariat are a "class in themselves" in the sense of being an aggregate of individuals who share the same economic position, but in certain circumstances become a "class for themselves" in the sense of becoming aware of their common interests. Providing these circumstances, such as the concentration of industry and the development of communications, existed a major social upheaval would ensue and the classes would become locked in overt conflict.

The capitalist system was, to Marx, the fundamental fact of economic life; an important assumption made was that the economic system of capitalism also had significance for social relations, thus giving rise to the notion of capitalist society. Here the assumption was that social relations, social values, and institutions were a superstructure which developed on the basis of the economic conditions of capitalism. Basic to the idea of capitalism is the private ownership of the means of production, mechanized factory production, the propertied and the propertyless classes, acquisitiveness, and economic rationality. The "culture of capitalism" centres in part around the notion of individualism which points, in particular, to the kind of industrial organization found in the most developed of capitalist societies, the United States of America.[1] Here there is great emphasis on the rational, acquisitive, and self-interested individual; this reflects the selling of labour on an open and competitive market. Individualism is based on the idea that man pursues self-interest because of a need to acquire goods and that the good of society will best be served if he is left alone to do this. A doctrine of "equality of opportunity" exists, and everyone has a moral duty to strive for success; failure is seen as the fault of the individual, which should be accompanied by guilt. These beliefs can be seen in the socialization of children in which the desire to succeed is implanted by parents from an early age. Individualism is fostered by more general democratic values which stress the individual's unique value and right to determine his own life.

It is also argued that the capitalist system is not unique but has features which are central to any industrial society, whatever its political or cultural context. Capitalism is merely one form of industrial society, and most of its features, e.g. a labour market and an emphasis on economic individualism, are universal to highly developed economies. Thus the problems faced by industrial societies are, in general, very similar.

## Stratification and Community Studies

It is important to gain some idea of how such theories have been used to interpret actual social relationships and the community studies, already introduced in Chapter 4, provide useful illustrations of class relationships in a local context. In the study by Williams[19] of the village of Gosforth in the north of England, the system of stratification was composed of classes in the economic sense of the word and of status groups. There were three economic classes in the village—those who lived either on capital or rent, farmers who owned or rented land, and the rest who worked for wages. The situation was complicated by differences of prestige in the community. People in Gosforth recognized two main divisions—the upper and the lower, and Williams went on to divide these into seven categories which can be described as status groups.[20] The first group, the "gentry", had all been to public or boarding schools and, although not all were wealthy, none of them appeared to work for their living; they had little to do with the social life of the village although they were much in demand as patrons of village associations. The second group, the "lower upper", is the small group of businessmen found in most small towns who aspire to be accepted by the upper class but also attempt to make themselves acceptable to village people. The third group, the "intermediates", are professional people (such as teachers) who are present in the village by virtue of their jobs but who have few local ties. The "upper medials" are villagers and farmers who are distinguished by their desire to "get on" or improve themselves. The two largest groups are the "medial" and "lower medial"; these are farmers and other agricultural workers who form the basis of the social life of the village. Finally, the "lower" (or "submerged tenth") status group is a small group who ate the "roughs" of Gosforth. These seven groups have distinctive styles of life and also tend within each group to interact socially and to intermarry.

In Gosforth, as well as in other communities which have been studied, there has been little evidence of the tendency to conflict suggested by Marx.[20] Although there were situations which implied conflict, such as the existence of the two groups of farmers and farm labourers, conflict is rarely met and takes place in situations removed from the immediate locality, e.g. in politics or the trades unions. The kinds of conflict which have been described in small face-to-face communities relate to conflicts entailed by multiple role relationships and the conflicting obligations which arise from these.

In the studies of larger towns, conflict between classes becomes more overt, but again can be mediated by avoidance or formal group processes. Conflict becomes most noticeable in situations where there is competition for scarce resources. Thus in the twilight areas of Sparkbrook (Birmingham),[21] where housing is the scarce resource, three "housing" classes can be delineated—the outright owners of dwellings, council tenants, and private tenants. Membership of these classes determines much else in life, including social relationships, style of life, and the position of the individual in the social structure of the city, and entry to each class is also based on particular qualifications such as economic and work situations and colour. There is competition to move from the less to the more-favoured class. This is one example of conflict and the formation of class interests in relation to the ownership of domestic property rather than the means of industrial production.

## NOTES AND REFERENCES

1. H. Wilensky and C. Lebeaux, *Industrial Society and Social Welfare*, Russell Sage Foundation, New York, 1958.
2. P. Leonard, Casework and Social Class, *Case Conference*, 8 (7), Jan. 1962.
3. H. Stein and R. Cloward, *Social Perspectives on Behaviour*, Free Press, Glencoe, 1961.
4. N. Timms, *Social Casework—Principles and Practice*, Routledge & Kegan Paul, London, 1964.
5. L. Rapoport, In defense of social work, *Social Work (U.S.)*, April 1962.

6. A. Cohen, *Delinquent Boys*, Free Press, Glencoe, 1956; see also C. Owen, *Social Stratification*, Routledge & Kegan Paul, London, 1968.

7. Cited by R. Blackburn, The unequal society, in Blackburn and Cockburn (eds.), *The Incompatibles*, Penguin Books, 1967.

8. B. Abel Smith and P. Townsend, *The Poor and the Poorest*, Occasional Papers in Social Administration, Bell, London, 1965.

9. For an account see Owen, *op. cit.*, and T. Bottomore, *Classes in Modern Society*, Allen & Unwin, London, 1965.

10. T. H. Marshall, Citizenship and social class, in Marshall, *Sociology at the Crossroads*, Heinemann, London, 1963.

11. P. Collison, *The Cutteslowe Walls*, Faber & Faber, London, 1963; see also *The Cutteslowe Saga*, New Society 25 April 1963.

12. S. Cotgrove, *Science of Society*, Allen & Unwin, London, 1967.

13. J. Klein, *Samples from English Cultures*, vol. 1, Routledge & Kegan Paul, London, 1965. For a further discussion of the middle and working classes see J. Raynor, *The Middle Class*, and G. Rose, *The Working Class*, Longmans, London, 1969 and 1968.

14. For a further account see Bottomore, *op. cit.*

15. R. Dahrendorf, *Class and Class Conflict in Industrial Society*, Routledge & Kegan Paul, London, 1959.

16. K. Davis and W. Moore, Some principles of stratification, *Amer. Sociol. Rev.* **10** (2), April 1945.

17. R. Hoggart, *The Uses of Literacy*, Chatto & Windus, London, 1957.

18. For an account see T. Bottomore and M. Rubel, *Karl Marx: Selected Writings*, Penguin, 1956; see also Bottomore and Dahrendorf, *op. cit.*

19. W. M. Williams, *Sociology of an English Village*, Gosforth, Routledge & Kegan Paul, London, 1956.

20. R. Frankenburg, *Communities in Britain*, Penguin Books, London, 1966.

21. J. Rex and R. Moore, *Race, Community and Conflict*, O.U.P., London, 1967.

CHAPTER 6

# Child Rearing, Language, and Social Class

## INTRODUCTION

The subject of child rearing has already been introduced in general terms in Chapter 3 on The Family, but discussion was postponed until now because of the importance of social class in the understanding of this process. Although there are certain features in the rearing of children which are common among all families, what is important in the present context is to trace certain features in the socialization process which may give rise, at a later stage in the development of the adult personality, to particular attitudes and values which may have implications for the use of the social services, including the services of the social worker. Sociologists and psychologists have for some time been concerned to outline variations in basic personality types which may have resulted from early experiences, and recent research, which bridges sociology and psychology, has been useful in this respect. Thus, early childhood has important implications for the later development of personality, and one way in which the class differences noted in the last chapter are preserved is through the internalization of class values in childhood. Thus, as a result of their study of the rearing of one-year-old children, the Newson's[1] comment that "men may be born equal but within its first month in the world the baby will be adapting to a climate of experience that varies according to his family's social class".

Clearly class is not the only variable in the process of child rearing. Strategies adopted by parents vary in relation to other factors, such as the age of the child. There are a variety of differences in child-rearing practices in different geographical areas and amongst different social groups. Instead of treating all these differences separately, most observers have decided that in order to simplify matters the concept of social class adequately summarizes most of these differences.

One complication in using this approach is that because of the changes in the class system already mentioned, certain differences in child rearing have become of less importance than in the past, whilst others have retained or increased their importance. Here, amongst other things, an attempt will be made to summarize those differences which have retained their importance, in particular for the development of personality in adult life, and to say something about the character of the socialization process in different class situations.

## CHILDHOOD AS A
## PREPARATION FOR CLASS MEMBERSHIP

Taking into account both British and American studies, Cohen[2] suggests that "middle class socialization, in comparison with working class socialization, is conscious, rational, deliberate, and demanding". There is a concern amongst the middle class for the child's future, and the child is likely to be made aware of what is expected of him. Concern is thus with the future rather than the present, and parents will deliberately structure a child's physical and social environment to hasten the preparation for a middle-class way of life by, for example, surrounding the child with "educational" toys, supervising friends, and emphasizing order and punctuality. This lays the foundation for the principal task of socialization in the middle class, that the child (and later the adult) should learn to commit himself to activities which are not immediately rewarding.

The life of the working-class boy is relatively easy-going and will be more governed by the present inclination or convenience of himself and his parents and less governed by factors which are seen as leading to some future goals. In many ways the working-class child is allowed more freedom than his middle-class counterpart, in particular freedom to explore the world outside the home in the company of a group of peers. However, as the working-class child grows up he is likely to be subjected to sudden changes in social routines. In infancy children are often indulged to the extent of becoming a kind of family "pet" and frequently share the daily routine of adults. However, as the child grows older this is replaced by a stricter routine which minimizes the amount of attention adults have to give to the child; at a later stage there may be an attempt to make the child independent of the mother, and relations with peers or members of the extended family will replace those with the nuclear family. One explanation[3] suggests that these sudden changes in attitude to children are a reflection of working-class conditions of housing and work routines, and result from rapid changes in family size. In a crowded house in which there may be a number of shift workers on irregular routines of sleeping and working, a baby has to be kept quiet and is therefore indulged. However, as the child grows up, and with the birth of other children, he becomes abruptly subject to a stricter control of impulses, and is at a still later stage encouraged to seek the independence of the street. The discontinuity of this type of upbringing, to which can also be added the variability of day-to-day control in which both rewards and punishments may be meted out at different times for the same act, is an important feature of working-class life, and carries implications for future personality development. As Klein[4] suggests, such a pattern is close to that of some traditional societies in which children are not given a specialized upbringing because of the narrowness and unchanging routine of the values that have to be imparted and where socialization can safely be left to sources outside the family.

Types of control exercised by parents also have important implications for the socialization process. These include corporal punishment, withdrawal of privileges, the isolation of the offender, and a number of sanctions of a psychological nature, including the threat to withdraw love. Different selections will be made by parents in relation to cultural or sub-cultural norms. Again, intentions which parents have in mind when controlling children differ. Klein[4] suggests a distinction between disciplines in which the intention is to control children's behaviour in the present and that which aims at more long-term goals, including the development of an approved adult character. The former type is continued in adult life in the form of social control in which response is to approval or disapproval in others. Offences would be accompanied by embarrassment or shame. The latter encourages self-control which is largely concerned with the consequences of actions and inner feelings of right and wrong. Offenders would feel guilt rather than embarrassment or shame. One American study[5] suggested that the development of self-control was highly related to techniques such as praise or reasoning but not to deprivation of privileges or corporal punishment. Corporal punishment implies, on the other hand, the resort to short-term methods of control and to the intention of controlling behaviour in the short term. Although the use of this method is, according to British evidence, sparing, the Newsons[1] found that its incidence was greater among the working class than among the middle class. Deprivation of privileges was a more typical method of short-term sanctions. Amongst the upper middle class, isolation was an important technique. This emphasizes self-control and the independent learning of what is correct. Children who are unable to behave are sent away until they can regain control; but this is done in the child's own time and on his own volition. Boarding schools are also an important means of solving disciplinary problems in this class. Here a hierarchy of peer groups, masters and headmasters, backed by the force of the school code, remove the sole focus of control from the parent. At the furthest extreme from physical control is control by reasoning, an essentially verbal process.

Recent research by the Newsons,[6] who are following a sample of 700 children from all classes through childhood, on children who have reached the age of 4 years, suggest that one of the most important differences in child rearing relates to the quality of control which mothers exercise over their children. One important difference lay in the greater use of verbal reasoning by middle-class mothers; thus if a child broke a rule which required some response from the mother, this would (in the middle class) mainly involve lengthy reasoning and rational argument. Working-class mothers were less likely to enter on a verbal explanation of the rules to which the child is supposed to be adhering. This difference is shown by the fact that middle-class mothers are more likely to intervene in children's quarrels than working-class mothers, and thus to indulge in verbal arguments with children over their actions; this would have the effect of encouraging middle-class children to respond verbally and increasingly rationally to questions and arguments, whereas the working-class child is more likely to be left to settle his own battles, and thus is not encouraged to indulge in verbal interaction with adults.

The process of child rearing was regarded by most mothers as a serious, long-term training which would have a lasting effect on the character of the child. Thus punishments and rewards were not just responses to particular situations but were part of a more general programme related to quite specific ends in the future lives of children. While this was true of all mothers, middle-class mothers were more concerned to stress the generality and fairness of the principles they were trying to instil by emphasizing the child's duties towards the adult as well as the adult's duties towards the child. By comparison, the working-class mother felt less of a need to justify principles of behaviour in terms of their fairness, but leant more heavily on the natural authority of adults and parents.

Perhaps the greatest differences between the two groups lay in the avoidance of subjects and questions, e.g. of a sexual nature, which commonly cause problems to parents. Thus a far greater number of "lies" were told about such subjects by working-class than by middle-class parents, illustrating not only different attitudes to questions of sex but also to truthfulness. Such distortions went far further than the mild teasing of children which is commonplace in most families. Thus 75 per cent of unskilled mothers, compared to

12 per cent in the professional classes, would not tell the four-year-old where babies came from if asked. Other distortions of truth, such as threats of abandonment or of calling a policeman, are also more liable to be found in the manual classes.

Thus one important general distinction between the classes is one of the use of language in child rearing; the middle-class mother is more likely to put a high valuation on words as agents of truth and rationality, whereas the working-class mother, although in most cases none the less verbal, is less likely to use language as a rational tool and more likely to use it as simply a means of controlling the child in the short run.

## SOME RESULTING PERSONALITY DIFFERENCES

It should not be assumed that childhood experiences necessarily imply particular kinds of adult personality, or that socialization within a particular class will produce individuals with identical class characteristics.

One of the few attempts to study the personality development of members of different social classes was that of Spinley;[7] she compared the upbringing and personalities of two contrasted groups of boys and girls—one from a London slum environment and the other from public schools. It should be noted that these two groups, the "deprived" and the "privileged", represent extremes which are probably found in only a minority of cases in the working class or the middle class; in between there is a continuum with the basic personality tending toward one or other of these extremes.

Members of the slum group were insecure in their relationships, mainly as a result of the discontinuous nature of upbringing by which the infant was first indulged and then put aside in favour of a new baby or as a result of growing up. There was a dislike and a distrust of authority, since authority figures in the family had been weak and variable in their behaviour. There was little ability to defer gratification or to tackle difficult or long-term problems.

The public school group provided an almost total contrast. They were secure in their lives and were able to adjust to relationships with their own and with the opposite sex. There was both a respect for and a balanced criticism of authority, which enabled them to negotiate successfully school and occupational life in which they began to assume authority positions themselves. There was the ability to work for rewards which were not immediately forthcoming.

In short the personality traits of these two groups were broadly what would be expected from the extreme differences in the patterns of child rearing noted in very young children by the Newsons. But the patterns that have given rise to these characteristics and the way they have been interpreted are complicated by a number of factors. Thus if the differences in child rearing between classes are interpreted in terms of a distinction between permissiveness and strictness, this is complicated by the fact that most parents of either class are strict or permissive about different things at different times. Thus in the middle class there is a permissiveness surrounding, for example, the sexual curiosity of the child or the exercise of discipline. But this permissiveness is also discriminatory and becomes mixed with certain demands about children's behaviour—in particular that there should be an increase in self-control and a willingness to please and make an effort. These demands can be reinforced by such techniques as early bedtimes and an early start to toilet training—as the Newsons found, the middle class achieve earlier and more successful toilet training and impose earlier bedtimes than the working class. This would assist in the development of the kind of characteristics found at a later stage by Spinley.

At the other extreme, in the lower stratum of the working class, there is a pattern of extreme indulgence and an absence of training for long-term goals which is quite different from the calculating permissiveness of the middle class. This contributes to the unsocialized personality of the kind described above. However, an extreme and a quite different picture is presented by the working-class "respectables" who, like the middle class, take the job of child rearing seriously.[8] The degree of difference which is still found by comparison to the middle-class pattern relates again to the use of language, the practical and economic difficulties in which most working-class families find themselves and other factors. It is to language that the discussion now turns.

## SOCIAL CLASS, COMMUNICATION, AND LANGUAGE

Differences in class cultures outlined in Chapter 5 are further highlighted when the classes come into contact and begin to communicate, e.g. in the context of the social services. Doctors, teachers, and social workers interact and communicate in mainly linguistic terms with members of different cultures. Here the analysis of differing norms and values can be broadened into a discussion of language and the relationship between language and social structure—a hitherto neglected aspect of social analysis. As Bernstein[9] has shown, language is a social process in the sense that it is related to social interaction between individuals and is a consequence of this interaction. Each relationship involves the use of a particular speech system (adjectives, adverbs, pronouns, and so on) which stems from and symbolizes the social character of this relationship. For example, when the adult talks to a child a particular kind of speech form will be used which has a limited vocabulary and a simple arrangement of words. Here the type of social relationship generates a certain speech form or the selection of a certain sort of verbal content. Different forms of social relationship or interaction will then generate different speech systems which will in themselves condition the social relationship. Thus a speech system becomes a consequence of a social relationship and is a particular quality of the social structure. For example, a child will learn his place in the social structure through the process of communication. Whenever a child speaks or listens he becomes aware of the social structure of which he is a part, and the requirements of this structure become reinforced in him. In terms of role theory, each role relationship an individual enters into is transformed into linguistic terms. Language then becomes a crucial if hitherto unrecognized variable through which social relationships are channelled and defined. Bernstein distinguishes two types of speech systems or codes—a restricted and an elaborated code. In one type of restricted code all the words used are determined in advance and are outside the control of the individuals using them. The content of communication is highly predictable. This occurs, for example, in religious services where priest and audience communicate through given responses. Individual differences cannot be expressed verbally although they may be expressed non-verbally by facial expressions or by changes in pitch or rhythm or in the use of words. In some circumstances (such as a cocktail party) a social routine develops (small talk) which is highly predictable and highly impersonal. People know little about each other in a verbal sense and can only signal individual differences by extra verbal signals. The second type of restricted code is one in which the syntax of the language, i.e. the arrangement of words, is drawn from a narrow range. This code is found in situations where social relationships are based on common identification or expectation, as in closed social systems such as prisons, army units, or adolescent peer groups. Individuals will have little need to verbalize their intention which has already been defined by the social system and by the social situation, and their speech will thus consist mainly of descriptive and narrative elements rather than analytical or abstract ones. Such restricted codes are not used simply by certain sections of the population in particular social situations, but are used from time to time by all members of society, e.g. in a relationship between two close friends. Here a code develops by which communication, although limited, is meaningful. This limitation is mainly in the signalling of individual experiences and differences.

However, for some sections of the population an elaborated code is also available. Here meanings are signalled explicitly by the use of a variety of verbal selections which have a low predictability. This code enables the expression of the individual's unique experiences and intentions. Here, as in the restricted code, the condition of the listener is not taken for granted. The speaker orients himself sensitively to the listener, and thus recognizes individual differences between himself and the listener. "Speech", in Bernstein's words, "becomes a voyage from one person to another." Thus the initial restricted code of the cocktail party may give way to an elaborated code in which individuals begin to sensitize themselves to their own and other people's differences. Thus the way people relate to one another, or the ability to vary the way in which roles are played, relate to language, which in its turn expresses and regulates such relationships.

Certain aspects of working-class life, e.g. a close community and kin structure which becomes the basis of social identity, are likely to give rise to restricted codes and to inhibit the learning of elaborate codes. Aspects of middle-class life, on the other hand, are likely to be favourable to the development of an elaborate code. A more specific distinction between language codes relates to the form of parental authority they imply. Status-oriented and person-oriented ways of controlling children can be distinguished. In the former the behaviour of the child is related to status-based rules which regulate conduct ("don't talk to your father like that"). Person-oriented control allows the child to communicate with the parent or regulator, in particular to verbalize intention and motivation. Status-oriented control, which is perhaps a particular feature of the working-class family's authority structure, involves simply the power inherent in status and does not allow further discussion of the motivation for the consequence of actions. Thus in the one situation the child is encouraged to explore relationships and causes through the use of language, in the other the development of relationships and exploration of causality are abruptly shut off. This is a further important way in which expectations surrounding the parent–child relationship may be developed.

Another interpretation of the impoverishment of language at the lower end of the social scale is advanced by the Newsons.[6] Rather than the lack of verbal skill suggested by Bernstein, they suggest that other factors, of attitude, emotion, or situation, are also inhibiting factors. For example, while parents may be able to communicate adequately with children, such situations as hospitals and schools where there is contact with an alien middle-class culture, may in themselves be sufficient to raise barriers to communication.

## CHANGES IN THE STRATIFICATION SYSTEM

Changes in a number of aspects of traditional working-class life have become a major basis for discussion. The basis of such changes are economic in that there has been some diminution in economic differentials between the classes, e.g. between the incomes of manual and non-manual workers. The inference here is that this change has led on to the adoption of middle-class culture, life styles, and norms and to the progressive breaking down of distinctions and barriers between classes. One further factor here is the development of the welfare services themselves, which, according to Marshall,[10] have established a basis of citizenship in which all stand on the same footing and have common experiences within the structure of the welfare services. Again, class differences can be seen as operating in only certain spheres of life but of minor importance within others. Such statements as "I'm working class only in the works. Outside I'm like anyone else" suggest the distinction in the minds of some between traditional areas of class differences which have changed little and the breaking down of such differences in particular situations.

Such hypotheses have been subjected to considerable discussion, and inquiries have been launched to test out such statements. Already it has been suggested that the economic basis of this argument must be challenged. Although income differentials between different occupations have declined, differences have emerged which are not fully taken into account by the available statistics on incomes.[11] Again, the increased spending power of the working classes has rested partly on full employment and the increasing employment of women, both of which are variable factors. Again, there is little evidence that middle-class norms have been taken on in relation to the work process. The working class still retain a traditionally subordinate and powerless position in the authority structure of employing institutions. In a recent study of factories employing affluent workers,[12] work was viewed as little more than the selling of labour and was conceived in instrumental terms, i.e. as a means to a high standard of living. The majority of workers found their jobs monotonous and did not give them their full attention. Less than half felt that there were chances of advancement or promotion. By comparison, white-collar workers were unlikely to view their jobs solely in terms of economic rewards, and a majority believed that chances of promotion were good. Thus in spite of a money income which, although based partly on overtime, was sufficient to warrant a middle-class standard of life, few of the other concomitants of the middle-class work situation were present. Where changes within the traditional working class are most in evidence is in the family and in the decline in aspects of family life based on the previous experience of economic insecurity. Thus the traditional organization of the working-class family with an extended, female-based structure in which the male plays a marginal economic role, has given way to a more balanced and nuclear family structure particularly in areas where the traditional basis of working-class life has changed. A lengthening time perspective and a decline in short-term hedonism are also characteristic of the new style working-class life—again reflections of greater economic security. However, as Cotgrove[13] points out, these aspects of working-class life have always existed within what has been called the labour aristocracy. This group, in relation to the economically insecure "rough" group, have grown by comparison, but this is a long way from justifying the assertion that because of this the working class has taken on middle-class norms and a middle-class culture.

The process of change can rather be looked at in terms of a number of stages as Lockwood and Goldthorpe[14] suggest. First, there is a decline in involvement with traditional working-class communities and norms. The family life of the working class becomes home-centred and privatized, and there is a progressive withdrawal from involvement with the wider community. At this stage, however, there is no aspiration to take on middle-class norms. Secondly, there is identification with the middle class and the middle-class culture; and, thirdly, there is the acceptance of working-class families by members of the middle class. Such evidence as exists suggests that the process has gone little further than the first stage.

In the study of Luton previously referred to, large numbers of workers were not members of traditional working-class community life based on residential stability and extended kin ties. However, little support came for the view that a middle-class set of norms had taken the place of this traditional working-class life. For those who were isolated from kin, the way in which this was compensated for was chiefly by association with immediate neighbours. Amongst white-collar workers, however, neighbours did not figure as important contacts. Here there was more contact with friends and kin than with neighbours, and a much wider social circle existed. Perhaps most important of all was the extent to which white-collar workers figured in the lives of manual workers. Here a considerable degree of status segregation was noted. Seventy-five per cent of those named by manual workers as people with whom spare time was spent were also in the manual category. Participation in formal organizations emphasizes this division. Few working-class people were members of organizations in which they might meet members of other social classes, and for the most part belonged to traditionally working-class associations such as angling or dart clubs in which they made few contacts outside the working class. Thus although there has been change in the traditional pattern of working-class life, in particular the move to a more privatized mode of living in contrast to the communal and often kin-based life of the traditional working class, specifically middle-class styles of life have not emerged. Rather there has been a convergence between the norms of the classes. In particular it is unlikely that the "us–them" dichotomy or the traditional power model that some of the working class hold of society, has been changed in any marked degree. Certainly it appears that most of the working class have not taken on the middle-class model of society which sees the society in terms of a hierarchy of status positions up which the individual can climb by his own efforts.

## SOCIAL CLASS AND SOCIAL WORK

In order to bring the foregoing discussion into focus it is useful to consider class differentials in the use of the social services and the possible reasons for such differences. Class differentials in education are perhaps the best known of all such differences. Using a sample of 5000 children representing the population of Britain as a whole, Douglas[15] demonstrated that proportions of boys gaining entry to grammar school fell from 32·9 per cent in the professional middle class to 13·0 per cent in the manual working class. The same group of children was also studied at an earlier stage where class differences in the use of child welfare centres by mothers was also revealed.[16] The greater use was made by black-coated workers of whom 18 per cent used the centres regularly. This figure fell to 15 per cent for semi-skilled and 9 per cent for unskilled workers. Professional workers used the services less than the black-coated group because they were able to make use of private medical care. Again, Hollingshead and Redlich[17] have shown in an American study how the use of psychotherapy in the treatment of mental illness declined from 73 per cent for professional workers to 16 per cent for the unskilled workers.

One explanation for such differences is that the social services involved a process of interaction between groups holding differing values and norms. The services and those who run them exhibit a culture very different from the majority of users. Whereas in many cases the classes exist independently of each other because of the prevailing pattern of residential and social segregation in most urban areas, within the context of the social services they interact and because of cultural differences come into conflict. Such conflict may result in a withdrawal from or infrequent use of the service. In the case of the counselling professions, including social work, such conflicts may be exacerbated by the professional culture of the counsellor with its distinctive techniques and principles.

Conflict may even be two-sided. In the American study referred to above, not only did working-class neurotics not get on with their psychiatrists, but the psychiatrists also express dislike of their patients. Here the norms of the two groups were so different that conflict was almost inevitable.

More information is becoming available in Britain about attitudes to the social services, such as education and social work. Willmott[18] comments that in Bethnal Green social service agencies were so far outside the common experience of the population that they resembled embassies in foreign countries, staffed by strangers who administered a service few understood. More particularly, "the social worker is often regarded as a foreigner; she is a stranger come from outside to help and advise local people. The help she gives, where it is of obvious practical value, is graciously accepted. To what she says, the Bethnal Greener is seldom responsive."

Here the working-class population of the area appear as culturally aliented from such agencies and the workers themselves as they are from schools and teachers. Both represent values largely external to this culture purveyed by individuals also seen as foreign and external. The dilemma of the social worker faced with this situation is not unlike that of the teacher in the working-class secondary modern school. Here the teacher encounters class-linked attitudes to education which are largely divergent from the way education is viewed and understood by most teachers and middle-class people.[19]

This is in part due to class differences in child rearing for the educational system. Contrasting, again, children reared in deprived and privileged situations, as a result of a slum upbringing the child is likely to see the teacher as an authority figure who is trying to impose an alien code of behaviour. The world of the school and of the home are different and even opposed. What is learnt as the "correct" response in one situation is labelled "deviant" in the other. By contrast, for the child with the privileged public school upbringing, the worlds of the school coincide and reinforce one another.

One illustration of the difference between the classes is where working-class aggression becomes middle-class initiative; thus the same aggressive drive could result in a working-class boy actually striking a teacher and in a middle-class boy working hard at a difficult task and pleasing the teacher.[19] These differences, as noted, have repercussions throughout the whole educational system and influence entry to selective secondary schools.

The problems created for teachers, schools, and for the educational system by class differences in child rearing suggest that similar problems may be created for social workers and social work agencies.

Clearly the difference in techniques and aims of parental control need to be taken into account when working with parents and children. Thus social workers who enter the situation with a set of middle-class norms about child rearing will have difficulties; Leonard[20] quotes the case of a social worker who was upset because a working-class mother had beaten her young son because of his sexual curiosity, thus failing to recognize that physical control was an acceptable form of control in this situation.

One practice which is increasingly recognized in social work is that the caseworker should assume an overtly parental role with certain kinds of immature or deprived clients, thus providing a substitute parental role, with the expectation that the client will take on the child role. But because of the different ways in which parent and child roles are defined, it is possible that expectations of what is the appropriate content of such roles may differ. Thus the caseworker who sets limits and structures authority on the basis of middle-class child-rearing norms, runs the risk of being misunderstood by a working-class client, with a consequent risk that the process, and the goals it is supposed to achieve for the client, will fail.

Again, there appear to be considerable differences in the way interpersonal problems are conceptualized amongst working-class people and professional counsellors.

A recent study[21] of family casework in the Family Welfare Association in England showed that working-class clients did not always receive the treatment they expected or wanted. Some expected to be told what to do on the basis of the social worker's greater experience or knowledge, or thought they could enlist the help of the social worker in settling a problem of interpersonal relationships. However, clients were often nonplussed by the help they were offered. For example, the social worker often attempted to widen the perspective of the problem and to shift the focus on to individuals who often appeared to the client to have little to do with the problem in hand. Again, techniques for eliciting material from clients such as pauses, long silences, nods, and smiles were misunderstood by the client, and seen either as a lack of interest in the problem on the part of the social worker or of agreement with what the client was saying. The psychological frame of reference adopted by the caseworker which attributed certain feelings such as guilt to the client was also misunderstood. A woman, for example,[22] felt angry because it was assumed she would feel guilty about the death of her husband (killed on a building site), a matter for which she felt in no way responsible. The authors concluded that: "We were not dealing with a minor difference in outlook but a very basic cleavage between workers and clients. We were dealing with two different cultural systems when it came to coping with problems, the worker system and the client system."

The authors suggest that although both caseworker and client are interested in the same general ends, e.g. preventing the recurrence of unpleasant behaviour, each will use very different means to achieve this. Many social workers, and middle-class people in general, have a causal approach to problems and are interested in knowing *why* difficulties have come about. Treatment is sometimes centred on the causes of problems such as marital disharmony rather than on the actual behaviour involved. Causal thinking of this kind is a central but often unacknowledged part of middle-class thinking, but is found infrequently in working-class culture. The working class are not interested in causes, primarily because nothing can be done about them. Problems of interpersonal relationships relate to such immutable factors as "human nature", "moral weakness", or "inheritance"; this emphasizes the fatalistic attitude previously described as a feature of working-class culture. The techniques adopted instead are mainly of a "suppressive" kind which deal in various ways with the behaviour which is offensive rather than with its causes; this attitude is also consistent with the behaviour of working-class people in other areas, e.g. in relation to deviant behaviour or child rearing. Here little interest is shown in the causes of problems but, instead, measures are approved of or taken which suppress problematic behaviour.

The differences between these views sometimes leads to a breakdown in the casework situation for the client expects his views and general cultural orientation to be shared by the case-worker.

Although the findings of this study are similar to those in previous inquiries (such as that by Hollingshead and Redlich), the authors do go a step further by suggesting that the way in which working-class people approach their problems derives from the social system of which they are part and is in fact given support by this system. Thus their orientation to problems is explicable and reasonable in this context, although this is not the case if it is viewed from a middle-class standpoint. Social workers appeared unaware that such working-class clients entered the casework situation with different attitudes to problem solving. It was thought that clients' difficulties and behaviour during interviews, as well as discontinuance from treatment, was attributable to anxieties aroused by treatment, but there was little realization of the fact that such difficulties also had their source in location of the worker and the client in two differing social systems. As the authors comment: "viewed from a distance the worker/client interactions have the aura of a Kaffka scene: two persons ostensibly playing the same game but actually adhering to rules that are private."[23]

Apart from the psycho-dynamic approach of the social worker, these difficulties stem also from the fact that there is little precise knowledge about the differing ways people have of conceptualizing and coping with interpersonal problems. Again, there is little evidence as to whether the orientations of clients in this study were different from those of the working class as a whole. Certainly what emerges from these orientations to treatment fits in well with what has been said previously about working-class life. For example, the shortened time scale and the "present" orientation already noted would appear to result in a resistance to the long-term exploration of problems without immediate rewards of some kind. The fact that little can be done about the causes of problems also suggests and reflects the sense of powerlessness expressed in the "us–them" dichotomy.

But to what extent are techniques such as "self-understanding" and "insight promotion" in fact part of the equipment of social workers by contrast to such approaches as support, guidance, or the provision of services? Bernstein[24] suggests that various types of psychotherapeutic techniques are of increasing importance in the training and work of social workers and other counsellors, but that such techniques raise special problems for sections of the population who do not share in a belief that "just talking about something" will be of any use in the solution of problems and who also possess what has been described as a "restricted speech code".

Amongst other things the therapeutic relationship involves a client in a conscious restructuring of his experiences in verbal form. Reference is made to the motivational processes of the client. The relationship implies a differentiation of the individual from the social group with which he is identified, for without this the perception of self by the individual is hindered. Again, such techniques involve the suspension of authority relationships traditionally expressed in other professional roles such as that of doctor, lawyer, or teacher. Therapeutic techniques involve a reordering of the distribution of this authority and a temporary suspension of authority based on distinctive areas of knowledge not possessed by the client. As Bernstein points out: "The shape of the relationship is not defined in any detail. Differences in social status which serve as an orientation for behaviour outside the therapy relationship do not serve to indicate appropriate behaviour within it."[24] Finally, the basic belief in the efficacy of psychotherapy rests on the view that the client's problems may be ameliorated by participation in a social relationship of which the essence is communication through speech. Bernstein argues that the use of language in this process is in itself a major stumbling block to the application of this technique to the lower working class (about 30 per cent of the labour force). Those members of this group who are limited to a particular speech system will find the above requirements hard to meet, and so may benefit less from therapy or break off treatment early. In the main such clients will have difficulty in verbalizing personal experiences and feelings about this. These difficulties do not necessarily stem from low intelligence but from speech systems learned by the child in its culture. The implications of a restricted code are, for example, that the intent or motivation of others is taken for granted, and that this sharing of the common intent or purpose removes the need to elaborate experiences in verbal terms. Thus social identity is created at the expense of personal identity. Self is rarely explored verbally and speech is not used as a means for sensitive communication. Often non-verbal means take the place of speech. Such restrictions serve to strengthen the solidarity of the group. Such observations would seem to fit in with a great deal of what has already been said about traditional working-class culture in which the individual is embedded in a close community network of kin and neighbours. Thus the psychotherapeutic relationship involves some individuals in situations in which they are not able to "play the game" of the therapist. Individuals are forced into a language code which is foreign to them and are involved in a loss of identity which the restricted code has generated. Bernstein suggests that if therapy is to be successful, then a change in the patient's code will be necessary. Here there is no suggestion that one language is better than another, for each has its own aesthetic, but in relation to specific institutions such as schools and social work agencies and the goals of these institutions, the possession of a restricted code only may be a severe disadvantage.

In the face of this situation the social worker is faced with two possible alternatives. It may be thought possible that the client will take on the practitioner's way of looking at the helping process—either through direct re-education by the practitioner or simply because the client realizes the beneficial results of the whole process. Alternatively, the social worker may accept the client's own orientation. Thus using language again as an example, Nursten[25] suggests that the social worker faces the choice of attempting to change the speech code of the client, and therefore the client's behaviour, or of reinforcing the restricted code. The former course implies extensive re-education; the latter may lead to important consequences for the client–worker relationship, including a greater understanding of the client's view of the worker as an authority figure and of the implications of the introduction of an elaborated code (e.g. the raising of defences).

The problem of the selection of the cultural preferences of social worker or client is not a new one, but the material presented by Mayer, Timms, and Bernstein does put in a fresh light the difficulties of altering patterns of conduct, or of assuming that such alteration will, in fact, occur. Yet the client's assumptions are rooted in a total social system into which the individual has been socialized at an early age and in which coping patterns are part of and are supported by other aspects of working-class culture.[23] Similarly, the conceptions of practitioners are likewise part of their "world view" which has developed over the course of years, initially on the basis of middle-class membership but latterly, and probably more importantly, on the basis of professional education and socialization. Again, even if it is assumed that changes in working-class patterns of behaviour can be effected in the context of the social work agency, it is not clear what further repercussions this would have on other aspects of working-class life.

Certainly it would appear important, as Hellenbrand[26] suggests, that social work "treatment styles" take into account in a sensitive way certain important cultural features of working-class life. This need not imply the "deification" of cultural relativity, for there may be situations in which social workers are justified in contributing to changes in the social system. Thus society may be changing at a faster rate than some of its sub-groups, and thus social workers may function to adjust this rate of change by work with individuals and families. Again, it is important for social workers to continue to explore the ways in which the goals of social work (such as "self-determination") are rendered inappropriate by the social situations of working-class individuals and to understand the kinds of changes in the institutional arrangements of the wider society which would be necessary for such goals to take on some significance for such groups.

Finally, it is important to make clear that attitudes to the social services and the social worker relate not simply to differences in cultural norms but to the authority of one group over another and to the legitimacy of that authority. As Timms[27] has commented:

"people may feel that in coming to a social service they are in the power of others considered to be their superiors and the applicant's power can be exercised only in implicit or explicit refusal of the service." Thus the working–class client may feel coerced or bullied into something which is not understood by the representative of what is considered to be an alien class. It is in fact scarcely surprising that social workers, with their power to remove children from parents under some circumstances, and to bring probationers before the court, are regarded as holding authoritarian positions (although not necessarily being authoritarian figures). These positions may be viewed as more authoritarian than the teacher, whose jurisdiction is confined to the school and the classroom, situations which are in many cases defined as irrelevant and unimportant. Thus in the eyes of clients, social workers may appear as part of a range of undifferentiated bureaucratic figures who, because of their power over financial and material sources of aid, have displaced the boss as the authoritarian figure in traditional working-class life. Again, such authority, because it is less easily understood, may appear more subtle and pervasive and thus less easy to counter than the power of the old style boss.[28]

It is important to understand that the sources of such attitudes may lie in the early experiences of the child and may be very deep-rooted. This is revealed in the studies of child rearing, particularly in the recent evidence about the differences between the social classes in the distortion of truth during child rearing and the possible link between this and later attitudes to authority.[6]

The mother is the child's first experience of a person in authority and when, as appears customary amongst lower working–class mothers, authority is upheld by a series of threats (that the mother will put him in a home, call a policeman, pack her bags and leave) which are never realized, it is possible that the discovery of the unreliability of the first and possibly most important model of authority will colour future attitudes to authority in other guises, such as the school, the employer, and the social work agency. As the Newsons[6] put it, the child "learns at an early age that authority in the person of his mother, despite pretensions to having his own welfare at heart, is yet not averse to using trickery whenever this suits her purpose of controlling him".

Amongst the unskilled working class the most widely used deception, apart from stories about where babies come from, was the threat of authority from outside the home in the shape of the policeman, the doctor, or teacher. Just as the child learns that the mother has used these figures as an idle threat, so also will these figures be seen as conspiring with or in league with the parents.

Apart from challenging and undermining, in the eyes of the child and later the adult, the authority held by such figures as teachers and social workers, this attitude may also prepare the way for a view of society as divided into two social groups, "them" and "us". "They" are people who seek to control you, usually by unfair means; "we" are those who are controlled but who really know "what the game is". Thus an unbridgeable dichotomy is created between two sides or camps in what comes to resemble a battle. As a character from Sillitoe's *Loneliness of the Long Distance Runner* says: "Whether I pinch another thing in my life again or not, I know who my enemies are and what war is."[29]

The possibility of conflict between the classes is often insufficiently stressed in the discussion of processes such as social work and education, and instead there is a ready acceptance of consensus or equilibrium theory and an adoption of a set of attitudes to society which stems from this. Thus if the social system is viewed as one in which there is basic agreement about values which then take on a unitary character, problems such as deviance or disorganization can be viewed as soluble by the redirection or resocialization of the individual along paths which it is assumed are agreed by all. Society, as Timms[30] points out, is often seen as a sort of "personified mother figure" who sets up services to reclaim the deviant and help the maladjusted. Thus social workers often find themselves standing for elements of social solidarity in society, and the aim of social work is sometimes expressed as the achievement of "personal and social equilibrium", but it is sometimes not clear what elements are to be brought into balance, and it is assumed that such an equilibrium is somehow a natural state.

This is certainly one way of interpreting the situation, but it is also important to consider in more detail the possibility that society is composed of opposing groups and that equilibrium is attained by the coercive power of one group over another. Thus, "it is important for social workers to appreciate that the social services are the meeting point of two or more groups whose interests may be, partially at any rate, in conflict".[30]

Thus, taking up once more the disjunction in the attitudes of clients and social workers to the casework process, while one interpretation of this derives from the differing cultural systems of the working-class client and the middle-class social worker, it is doubtful if this would be resolved totally even if the social worker could bridge the gap between the cultures. An alternative interpretation[31] is that such differences relate more to the inequality of power in the relationship, to the differing positions in the class structure of social worker and client, and to the fact that the social worker can have little appreciation of the desperate nature of the situation in which many clients find themselves.

One explanation for the emphasis in social work thinking on the consensus and equilibrium view of society might lie in the development of social work in America and of the influence on social work of certain tendencies in American sociology.

As Stein and Cloward[32] point out, there is a great difference between American and European approaches to social stratification. The more traditional social systems of Europe, with their basis in status ascription, leads to an emphasis on the economic forces underlying social differences, and a class system based on conflict and change. American society is seen as less divided by differences of social origin, but based on status achievement. Here old class allegiances are broken down by the substitution of a common value system where hard work, striving, and independence are legitimately rewarded by differential status. Thus American theories of stratification are based more on consensus models, and they, in turn, have influenced social-work theory to adopt implicitly a consensus model of society which leads in its turn to a particular view of the class system. This kind of social work theory has been exported to societies like Britain and has had wide influence amongst British social workers.

Critics of the "hierarchical" picture of the class system, a picture which derives from the consensus model of society, suggest that this theory may represent a defence of the *status quo* and may mask the real circumstances of social inequality. For example, stratification is supposed to promote the efficiency of the social system and is therefore found in all developed societies. But efficiency may in fact be hindered by stratification because it ensures that members of an already privileged strata obtain the most important positions rather than those who are most qualified. Again, the need for large income differentials as a way of attracting the most talented to the most important positions is challenged by the view that such positions are so intrinsically satisfying that such high rewards are not required. Thus the existence of social classes is based more on the possession of superior power or authority, which is also of a coercive nature, rather than on the needs of any particular society. A classless society is, in theory, possible providing there also exists a value system favourable to the idea of equality. At the moment, however, the inheritance of privilege and power prevents such a system from emerging.

Clearly these two approaches suggest very different accounts of the position of social work and the social services in an industrial society, and a further exploration of these issues will be made in Chapters 8 and 9 on The Social Functions of Social Work.

The concept of authority also helps to clarify something of the new problem of the relationship between the social worker and the middle-class client. One way of looking at this is to see the traditional authority relationship between the social worker and the working-class client as one of status "ascription" in which the worker is seen as representing an undifferentiated "them" category. Where the middle class are concerned the social worker may be seen not as a traditional status carrying figure but increasingly in terms of status "achievement", in which acceptance by the client is based on the worker's professional skills and knowledge which may be evaluated by the client. In a profession in which there are large numbers of partially trained or untrained workers, this may be a particular source of strain. Again, if one reason for the social worker's choice of profession is the chance of exercising authority over the weak and the inadequate,[33] then the removal of the security which comes from this (in working with the middle class) and from the dependency of working-class clients, may be an additional strain.

It is sometimes suggested that widespread changes in society have made differences in culture, language, or authority between the classes unimportant and that middle-class norms and values have become the "modal" pattern in society. In particular, it is held that differences in the material circumstances of people in different classes have narrowed to such an extent that little further significance need be attached to this aspect of social class. As a result of this evening out in material differences, it has even been suggested that social workers can now concentrate on the personal and emotional rather than the material difficulties of their clients.[34] Another implication is that cultural differences in attitudes to and use of social services between the working and the middle classes may be on the decline, particularly in the younger age groups.

The evidence so far presented, which mainly relates to the position of the economically affluent worker, suggests at the most a retreat from a working-class style of life based on economic insecurity and the stable working-class community of the past. But there is little evidence of an acceptance of specifically middle-class norms. In particular there appears little broadening of social relationships between classes, and even affluent workers have few contacts with middle-class people. Thus the type of social relationships in which most working-class people are involved, which would function as reference groups and as social supports, may not have altered very much. The detailed studies of working-class attitudes to social work by Mayer and Timms illustrate afresh the differences in cultural orientations and perceptions of working- and middle-class people. Thus the sweeping assumptions that have been made about changes in the class structure are difficult to justify. Even the changes which are apparent (e.g. of an economic nature) may proceed at different rates in different groups and have consequences which are difficult to forecast.

Evidence about the continued existence of income and property differentials also makes it hard to accept that the social worker of today is now in a position to relegate such differences to a low level of importance.

The research on "affluent workers" suggests, in particular, that there has been little change in the position of the manual worker in the authority structure of the modern industrial enterprise. Thus the manual worker still occupies an almost entirely subordinate position within the productive process in which there is little opportunity to exercise initiative, responsibility, or authority.

But the requirements surrounding the worker's position in industry differ markedly from those attaching to his position in the family as husband or parent. Thus within the family and the community the individual is expected to accept responsibility and to use initiative and authority on behalf of himself and his dependants. Yet the influence of the work situation, which may be so powerful that it is carried over into family life, may effectively prevent the worker from developing such qualities.[35] This has important implications for the child-rearing process.

Stress has in the past been laid on the mother figure as the major influence in the rearing and socialization of the child. More recently the importance of the father in this process has increased as a result of the greater participation of males in the domestic process. This is true not only of the middle class, but increasingly in working-class families where there is evidence of some decline in the degree of segregation in family life. Thus the father not only brings into the home experiences of the "outside" world and expectations for the future of his children, but functions as an important figure in the actual process of child rearing.[1] It has been suggested that the punitiveness and severity of working-class child rearing patterns reflects the lack of status in the occupational situations of working-class fathers, which is compensated for by a display of authority in the home.[36] This illustrates the way family life is shaped by situations outside the family; thus if change is desired in family be-

140 SOCIOLOGY AND SOCIAL WORK

haviour, these external situations must also be taken into account, as well as the immediate family situation.

The discrepancy between the requirements of work and of the community may be increased by the goals of self-responsibility and self-determination which social workers sometimes set for their clients. This highlights a series of dilemmas in which social workers find themselves involved and which derives from their general relationship with society and from the demands of society. This will be the subject of Chapters 8 and 9.

## NOTES AND REFERENCES

1. J. and E. Newson, *Infant Care in an Urban Community*, Allen & Unwin, London, 1963.
2. A. Cohen, *Delinquent Boys*, Free Press, Glencoe, Ill., 1956.
3. J. Robb, *The Working Class Anti-semite*, Tavistock, London, 1954.
4. J. Klein, *Samples from English Cultures*, Routledge & Kegan Paul, London, 1965 (vol. II).
5. R. Sears, E. Maccoby, and H. Levin, *Patterns of Child Rearing*, Row, Peterson, Evanston, Ill., 1957; cited in Klein, *op. cit.*
6. J. and E. Newson, *Four Years Old in an Urban Community*, Allan & Unwin, London, 1968; see also "Some social differences in the process of child rearing" in *Penguin Social Sciences Survey*, 1968 (ed. Gould).
7. B. Spinley, *The Deprived and the Privileged*, Routledge & Kegan Paul, London, 1954.
8. For a recent account see G. Rose, *The Working Class*, Longmans, London, 1969.
9. From a variety of articles on this subject by the same author see B. Bernstein, Language and social class, *Br. J. Sociol.* **40** (3) (1960); Social class, speech systems and psychotherapy, *ibid.* **45** (1) (1964); and A sociol-linguistic approach to social learning, in *Penguin Social Sciences Survey*, 1965 (ed. Gould).
10. T. H. Marshall, *Sociology at the Cross Roads*, Heinemann, London, 1963.
11. R. Titmus, *Income Distribution and Social Change*, Allen & Unwin, London, 1962.
12. J. Goldthorpe *et al.*, *The Affluent Worker; Industrial Attitudes and Behaviour*, Cambridge Univ. Press, 1968; see also J. Goldthorpe The Affluent worker. *Sociology* **1** (1) (Jan 1967), and J. Goldthorpe *et al.*, *The Affluent Worker in the Class System*, Cambridge Univ. Press, 1969.
13. S. Cotgrove, *Science of Society*, Allen & Unwin, London, 1967.
14. D. Lockwood and J. Goldthorpe, Affluence and the British class structure *Sociol. Rev.* **7** (1963). For a comprehensive account see J. Westergaard,

The withering away of class; in Anderson (ed.), *Towards Socialism*, Fontana, 1966.

15. J. W. B. Douglas, *The Home and the School*, McGibbon & Kee, London, 1964.
16. J. Douglas and J. Blomfield, *Children Under Five*, Allen & Unwin, London, 1958.
17. A. Hollingshead and F. Redlich, *Social Class and Mental Illness*, Wiley New York, 1958.
18. P. Willmott, Social administration and social class, *Case Conference*, **4** (7) (Jan. 1958).
19. P. Musgrave, *The Sociology of Education*, Methuen, London, 1965.
20. P. Leonard, *Sociology in Social Work*, Routledge & Kegan Paul, London, 1966.
21. J. Mayer and N. Timms, Clash in perspective between worker and client, *Social Casework* **50** (1) (Jan. 1969); see also id., *The Client Speaks; Working-class Impressions of Casework*, Routledge & Kegan Paul, London (to be published).
22. J. Mayer and N. Timms, *Working Class People's Reactions to Casework Treatment*, unpublished, 1968.
23. J. Mayer and N. Timms, Clash in perspective between worker and client, *Social Casework* **50** (1) (Jan. 1969).
24. B. Bernstein, Social class, speech systems and psychotherapy, *Br. J. Sociol.* **45** (1) (1964).
25. J. Nursten, Social work, social class and speech systems, *Social Work* **22** (4) (Oct. 1965).
26. S. Hellenbrand, Client value orientations; implications for treatment, *Social Casework* **42** (4) (April 1961).
27. N. Timms, *Social Casework—Principles and Practice*, Routledge & Kegan Paul, London, 1964; see also J. Handler, The coercive children's officer, *New Society*, 3 Oct. 1968, and R. Foren and R. Bailey, *Authority in Social Casework*, Pergamon, 1969.
28. E. Bott, *Family and Social Network*, Tavistock, London, 1957.
29. A. Sillitoe, *The Loneliness of the Long Distance Runner*, Allen, London, 1959.
30. N. Timms, *op. cit. Casework.*
31. A. Sinfield, *Which way for Social Work?*, Fabian Tract 393, 1969.
32. H. Stein and R. Cloward (eds.) *Social Perspectives on Behaviour*, Free Press, Glencoe, 1961.
33. B. Kent, The social worker's cultural pattern as it affects casework with immigrants, *Social Work*, **22** (4) (Oct. 1965).
34. K. McDougall, Implication of social change for the social worker, *Case Conference* **4** (1) (May 1957).
35. R. Titmus, *Essays on the Welfare State*, Allen & Unwin, London, 1963.
36. D. McKinley, *Social Class and Family Life*, Free Press, Glencoe, Ill., 1964.

# CHAPTER 7

# *Social Deviance*

## INTRODUCTION

The social system has so far been understood as constituting behaviour which is governed by a series of rules (or norms). So far, although variations in rules of conduct have been discussed (e.g. between different cultures or social groups), departures from them have been suggested only in outline. In this chapter such departures, known in sociological terms as social deviance, will be discussed in more detail, although it will only be possible to introduce a few of the approaches that have been taken.

It is appropriate that this should follow discussions of some of the major social institutions and processes, such as the family and socialization, because the idea of deviance (and of disorganization) implies prior consideration of conformity to rules and of organization. The twin concepts of conformity and deviance thus help to clarify our understanding of the social order. Again, discussion of deviance also raises the question of the recognition and control of deviance, or of society's reactions to deviant behaviour. Deviance and control, then, constitute a single field for discussion; thus some analysis of the relationship between social work and social control will take place in Part III, and the two areas can be seen as forming part of the same field.

Social workers are one of the professional groups, and social work one of the major institutions, involved in the definition, recognition, and control of deviant behaviour. Other parts of this institutional complex include the other mental health professions, the police force, the law, and the courts. One important way in which the social worker becomes involved with deviant behaviour is through holding an official or statutory position in an organization in which part of the function is the recognition and control of deviant behaviour. Examples of social workers in this position include the probation officer (an officer of the court) and the child care officer (an official of the local authority). However, social work has distinctive ways of looking at deviance which to an extent conflict with the ideology of these kinds of organizations and with the social system of which they form a part. Generally, social work appears to view the treatment of the deviant in mainly therapeutic terms, seeking where possible to reintegrate or resocialize the rule breaker into the society which, by his deviance, he has rejected and which has rejected him. In the face of this social work has evolved an attitude to deviants which, in the characteristic words of one of its leading philosophers,[1] constitutes "a bridge function . . . on which the social worker crosses from society to them and tries to bring them back into ordinary social relationships". Against this, society tends to isolate and ostracize the deviant, who is seen as dangerous and unnatural. Yet, according to Younghusband, one test of the degree of civilization and "health" of a society is the extent to which it can accept the deviant and the social failure. Social work has an important role to play in helping society to accept its non-conforming members and, by involving itself with deviants, helps to bridge the gap between them and society.

Apart from the insight which these passages give into the ideology of social work, with its humanistic and religious overtones, it is important to note the kind of perspective used to describe deviance and reactions to it. Deviance is classified as "social pathology" and society is seen as preserving its own "health" by sealing off (through inflammation) poisons that would otherwise invade it; various kinds of deviants "stick up like sore thumbs".[1] In other words, the model of deviance used is closely analogous to the medical model used to describe physical illness. Thus society and the individual are seen as manifesting the symptoms of the ill or diseased body; social illness becomes equated with physical illness. Social workers are not alone in holding this view of deviant behaviour, and part of what follows will illustrate some of the implications and limitations of this kind of approach.

## INTRODUCTION TO SOCIAL DEVIANCE

Deviance has so far been defined in a preliminary way as departures from the rules of conduct which govern social relationships. The person who has broken one or a number of these rules is defined as "deviant", or, more usually, "abnormal", "delinquent", or "ill", depending on the type of rules broken. He is seen as an "outsider",[2] not to be trusted to live by the rules accepted in society. But what kind of rules are being considered here? Rules vary from formal ones which are enforced officially to informal agreements to act in certain ways sanctioned by custom. A vast number of rules are not enforced and are broken frequently and without fear of punishment; for this reason some are forgotten or put to one side. Here the main concern will be with rules which are enforced and which are of importance in everyday life.

Perhaps the simplest view of deviance is that of the statistician. Deviance is defined as anything that varies very much from some average; to be left-handed is in this sense deviant because the majority of people are right-handed. This approach may seem of little value because deviance, in this sense, includes the left-handed, excessively fat or thin people, and murderers. This definition is of little use because obviously these categories of deviance are viewed very differently. But this approach has its use because it makes clear that questions of value arise in the definition of deviance; some kinds of deviants are seen as committing morally wrong acts. Consideration of morality forms no part of this discussion as such; the deviant will be discussed objectively as if in fact deviating from some average, but which is for the purpose of the present discussion outside the realm of morality.

A second approach to deviance is the medical or pathological approach already mentioned. Here social behaviour is defined as healthy or unhealthy in the same way as doctors view the body; thus to recognized illnesses such as fevers or fractures have been added such conditions as neuroses or depressions; even homosexuality and divorce are seen as "illnesses" because they offend certain kinds of social norms.[3] But while it is relatively easy to define a state of bodily health, there is no general agreement about what constitutes the social health of individuals or societies. Thus the state of health towards which Younghusband feels that social work can direct society would be rejected by some, and perhaps many, as unhealthy. One limitation to this approach is that it locates the source of deviance in the individual and so ignores response to and interpretation of individual actions; this, as will be shown, is one important way of understanding deviance.

The medical model is also the basis for a sociological approach to deviance based on the ideas of function and dysfunction. The features of a society which promote order and stability are said to be functional, by contrast to dysfunctional elements which disrupt stability. Some of the difficulties of the functionalist approach include, for example, the fact that it is difficult to say in what way features are functional or dysfunctional as such without taking into account such factors as the interests of different social groups. Thus a situation may be dysfunctional (or deviant) in the light of the interests of one group, but not for another.

Another sociological approach accepts that different groups have distinctive rules and that deviance is the failure to obey such rules. There are a variety of groups in any society (e.g. of a class or ethnic variety) and, although there is agreement or consensus about a great many rules, groups do not for a variety of reasons all share the same rules. Thus ethnic minority groups may differ culturally from the rest of British society because of their history or culture. Rules of different groups may conflict and there will be disagreement about proper behaviour.[4] Thus deviance can occur if one group infringes the rules that another holds important and feels are applicable to all. The offenders are labelled outsiders; however, it is quite possible that those labelled in this way may disagree with this judgement, or question its legitimacy (or rightness) and themselves look upon the group which has affixed the label as outsiders. The homosexual may feel that his critics are misguided and unjustified in their views; the juvenile delinquent may feel that teachers or social workers do not see the world properly; consequently they may be labelled as "outsiders" or "squares". However, one group is often in a position to force its version of the rules on to others through greater political or economic power; alternatively, there is often power invested in particular social positions through custom, tradition, or convention. For example, the old and middle-aged make rules which they expect the young to obey; men make rules for women; and the middle class makes rules for the working class. Power is thus an important element in any social relationship, and is important in understanding rule making and rule breaking.

## THEORIES OF DEVIANT BEHAVIOUR

An individual may break a rule unintentionally because he is not aware of its existence or does not apply it in particular circumstances; for example, a member of an ethnic group may be unaware that others do not share the social norms of his group. In cases of intended nonconformity it is customary to ask what caused the individual to act in the way he did. In the past many factors have been suggested to account for the motivation to deviant behaviour; psychological theories stress the importance of early experiences of an unsatisfactory kind which lay the foundations in the individual for deviant acts at a later stage in his development. Social theories stress the importance of factors such as income, bad housing, or broken homes which, acting together or separately, produce a strain which provides the delinquent with his motivation, and provides the solution to his problem. It is theories of this latter kind which are now discussed in more detail.

### Anomie Theory

One of the most important theoretical approaches to the subject of deviance is that of anomie theory, initially developed in sociological form by Durkheim.[5] Anomie develops in societies or groups when aspirations rise and come to dominate men's minds; traditional rules lose their authority and there is a breakdown in the regulative norms which govern behaviour. Anomie, or "normlessness", ensues.

The American sociologist Merton,[6] in developing Durkheim's approach, was concerned to suggest a framework for the sociological analysis of deviance. His theory comprises three main elements. In the first place there exist in all societies certain cultural goals which individuals are encouraged to regard as worth striving for; secondly, there are various prescribed ways in which such goals may be obtained, which can be termed institutionalized means. In some circumstances there may be a very considerable stress on goals and little concern with the prescribed means to attain them; the motivation to obtain certain goals may be so strong that the most effective, rather than the prescribed, means may be adopted, including the use of illegitimate means. There occurs a dis-equilibrium between goals and means which is close to the meaning Durkheim attached to anomie. For example, an athlete whose aim is to win at all costs rather than adhering to the rules of the game has implicitly accepted the use of illegitimate means.

Merton suggests that in American society the goal which is elevated above all others is achievement, measured chiefly by accumulated wealth. Thus money has importance in itself and has become a symbol of prestige; this value is transmitted by family, school, and workplace. Merton's assumption was that substantial numbers of people at all social levels had accepted, or internalized, this goal.

A third element in the situation derives from the social structure; whilst cultural goals and institutionalized means exist in any society there also exists a pattern of social or group relationships in which individuals are involved, e.g. of a class or ethnic kind. This social structure implies differences between groups in the extent to which access to means is legitimately possible; e.g. different groups have different educational experiences and therefore different chances of obtaining access to means and goals. Therefore in some circumstances there is a conflict between what is expected by the culture and what is possible under the existing social arrangements for access to cultural goals and means; in Merton's words:

> The social structure strains the cultural values, making action in accord with them readily possible for those occupying certain statuses within the society and difficult or impossible for others. The social structure acts as a barrier or as an open door to the acting out of cultural mandates. When the cultural and the social structure are malintegrated, the first calling for behaviour and attitudes which the second precludes, there is a strain towards the breakdown of the norms, towards normlessness.[6]

Merton then defines anomie as "a breakdown in the cultural structure occurring particularly when there is an acute disjunction between the cultural norms and goals and the socially structured capacities of members of the group to act in accord with them".

Merton set out various types of possible response or adaptations to this state of anomie in relation to the two elements of cultural goals and institutionalized means. Adaptation involves the acceptance (+) or rejection (−) of either of them; rejection may be passive (−) or may involve the active substitution of new values (±) (Table 4).

TABLE 4. TYPES OF ADAPTATION

| Cultural goals (ends) | Institutional means | Type of adaptation |
|:---:|:---:|:---|
| + | + | Conformity |
| + | − | Innovation |
| − | + | Ritualism |
| − | − | Retreatism |
| ± | ± | Rebellion |

*Source:* R. K. Merton, *Social Theory and Social Structure*[6]

The most common reaction to such strain in stable societies is conformity. Without conformity to certain expectations and values the social system as such would break down. The remaining adaptations constitute deviance of one form or another. Innovation implies the acceptance of major cultural goals but a rejection of prescribed means of obtaining them. Business practice, in which the legality of certain methods is doubtful, is one example of the desire to be successful at all costs. Pressures to abandon legitimate means may be greatest for groups in the lowest social strata where cultural goals are accepted but, despite the ideology of equal opportunity, opportunities to achieve these, to get "in the money", are severely restricted. In these situations the pressure towards deviant means is very powerful, in particular because the internalization of legitimate means may not have taken place or may have had only a partial effect on the personality; thus crime is almost a "normal" activity for the population of certain working-class areas. Here there is a "disjunction" between goals and opportunities, for the social structure prevents sizeable numbers of individuals from obtaining access to ends they are taught to believe are desirable and obtainable.

Adaptation III, ritualism, involves the scaling down or abandoning of goals in favour of an excessive concern with means, or the ritual of everyday life. Whether such behaviour constitutes a social problem in the same way as "innovation" is in doubt, but it does represent a departure from the striving characteristic of industrial societies. The ritualist is defined by others as being "in a rut"; whereas the innovator is found mainly in the disadvantaged sections of the working class, the ritualist is characteristic of the lower middle class, where there is pressure to abide by rules and norms coupled with a restriction on the likelihood of success, by comparison with other social groups.

As the most common form of deviance is innovation so the least common is "retreatism". Retreatists are the furthest removed from conformity in the sense that they have rejected both cultural goals and means; in this group Merton includes vagrants, tramps, alcoholics, and drug addicts.

Here the goals shared by others in society have been given up and behaviour is far outside that considered normal in society. This is most likely to occur where both cultural goals and the legitimate means to achieve them have been thoroughly assimilated by the individual and are valued highly by him; yet access to them is restricted and does not result in successful attainment. Conflict then results from pressure to keep to legitimate means in the presence of the illegitimate paths which others follow with success. But so strong has been the commitment to legitimate means and so thoroughly have these been internalized that the individual is prevented from using illegitimate means. To eliminate this conflict both goals and means are relinquished and the individual escapes from the requirements of society. This constitutes the most extreme form of deviance, for the innovator at least shares cultural goals and the ritualist cultural norms with the conformist. The retreatist has repudiated both, and in its turn society relentlessly pursues him for his rejection of such basic values.

Rebellion represents the final and very different response to structural strain; here, instead of adapting within the existing system, support is removed from it—the rebel seeks, often through political means, to substitute for existing goals and standards a new social order which he sees as being of greater worth.

In this famous essay Merton has sketched out a theoretical approach which locates the sources of deviance in the relation between culture and social structure. The cultural goals cited by Merton were, for the sake of simplicity, those of American society; goals of other societies may be substituted for the theory to be applied elsewhere. The importance of the theory in the present context lies in the way in which attention is directed away from the individual or biological bases of deviance, towards explanations of a sociological nature.

## The Problem Family

Anomie theory has provided the framework for a considerable amount of research into deviance; of greatest interest in the present context is an approach to the type of deviance known as the "problem family", i.e. the family with multiple problems which distinguish it markedly from the rest of the population. This research, by Baldamus and Timms,[7] is also of interest as it represents one of the few examples of research jointly carried out by a sociologist and a social worker in Britain. Previously, attempts to explain the problem family had been mainly of a biological nature, which viewed such families in terms of poor heredity, in which "defects" of one kind or another were transmitted from generation to generation. But observation also suggested that such families were characterized by sets of beliefs and values at variance with the established culture; it therefore seemed important to understand such families as constituting a group with a cultural life different from that of the rest of society, that is a separate sub-culture. To do this it was necessary to adopt some theoretical approach which would take into account deviance from accepted goals and standards. Here Merton's typology, particularly his concept of retreatism, appeared the most suitable. The most promising line of approach appeared to be the study of the goals and means, in particular the norms or standards, actually held by such families. A small group of families from a social casework agency were selected and ranked by social workers in order of their degree of social inefficiency, based on such criteria as child neglect, standards of cleanliness of home, etc. They varied from a near normal family to an extreme of inefficiency; thus some comparison was possible between near "normal" and "problem" families. In answers to questions on goals, mostly about plans for the future, there was a sharp contrast between families at the upper and lower ends of the scale; only families at the upper level of the scale of performance could think in terms of future expectations such as a new house or education for their children. Others had virtually relinquished conformity to goals, in some cases showing a hopeless and defeatist attitude—one woman's greatest wish was "to be under 6 feet of turf". Few families had entirely abandoned standards or norms of behaviour, but in some cases conformity lacked conviction and was of a nominal kind which hid "real" deviant standards. Thus lip service was paid to certain rules (mainly because of the fear of what other people, such as social workers, would say), but such standards were rarely kept.

The authors concluded that although personality and other individual factors appeared to play a part in the orientation towards deviance,

the evidence of deviant beliefs and orientations as a separate determinant is still sufficient to warrant a more elaborate enquiry into the nature and importance of this factor. Thus it appeared that, with certain qualifications, the more extreme cases of disorganization and inefficiency in problem families approach a situation of retreatism ... conformity to established values is virtually relinquished especially in respect of standards of behaviour.

This was a small pilot study from which it was difficult to make generalizations, but it is important because it represents one of the few attempts to introduce a sociological perspective into a problem hitherto viewed in largely individual terms.

## Illegitimate Opportunities

Merton's great achievement lay in the spelling out of the ways in which the social structure exerted strains on cultural goals and norms because of differential access of social groups to such goals. However, although he dealt with differential access to *legitimate* means, he left out of account the possibility that access to illegitimate means might also be differentially distributed over the population. The implication of Merton's theory was that, in the face of the frustration of goal attainment by legitimate means, illegitimate means would be freely available. But, as Cloward[8] points out, motivation to deviant behaviour is not sufficient to account for its existence unless opportunities to commit deviant acts also exist: if legitimate means are differentially distributed it is also likely that illegitimate means will have a similar distribution. There are, for example, the appropriate learning environments for the acquisition of values and skills associated with illegitimate means; secondly, there are the opportunities to discharge a deviant role once the necessary skills have been learnt. Thus, while the opportunities to learn such roles may exist there may be a lack of opportunities to practise such skills. Again, individuals may be exposed to opportunities to learn the ways of deviance in situations where they come into close contact with other rule breakers in delinquent neighbourhoods, in hostels or prisons, and through such contacts learn how to play the "game" of rule breaking. By adding the concept of differential distribution of delinquent opportunity to Merton's anomie theory, Cloward brings together the "cultural transmission" approach of earlier writers in which deviant norms and values are passed on from generation to generation, with that of anomie theory, so providing a more coherent framework for the analysis of deviance.

Cloward's point has implications, for example, for the response known as "retreatism". The factor encouraging retreatism in Merton's formulation was internalized restraint against the use of illegitimate means to achievement. If one could not "win" through accepted means, then alternative channels were not available and the "game" was lost; in the absence of this restraint, innovation became the appropriate response and illegitimate means were used. However, Cloward points out that "retreatism" could also occur if individuals failed not only to use legitimate but also illegitimate means. The "double failure" which resulted would serve to make the form of deviance all the more severe, and an escape from reality of an extreme kind would result. Although retreatism can occur in the way Merton specifies, failure to use illegitimate means, or lack of access to these, are explanations for retreatist adaptations amongst individuals who have not internalized restraints on the use of illegitimate means. Thus individuals can "fail" in both conventional and unconventional terms. Retreatism resulting from failure to use legitimate means is more likely to occur amongst the middle class where restraints against use of illegitimate means are strong—such individuals are failed conformists. Lower classes are more likely to have failed in the use of both legitimate and illegitimate means— they are "failed innovators".[9] This may account for the severity of the withdrawal of problem families who cannot "get by" even with the use of illegitimate means, or are not able to gain access to such means; the past criminal records of some working-class retreatists is further evidence for this point. Clearly it would be important to clarify the process by which retreatism of the problem family type has become stabilized and to establish whether such intervening events have played an important part in this type of response.

*Sub-cultural Theories*

Anomie theory and its developments represent one important level at which deviance can be discussed. But it leaves unanswered a number of important questions which require further discussion. While Merton concentrates on the sources of strain and possible responses to this, another question concerns the character of different kinds of response; in particular, to what extent do these responses depend upon the support and approval of other individuals? Some possible answers to such questions are suggested by a variety of approaches known collectively as "sub-cultural theory". The idea of a sub-culture is briefly that of a set of norms and values arising from participation and interaction in a social group and which is distinctive from the wider culture; this may be based on age, work, or other common experiences, including deviance. One particular theory of this kind, that of Cohen,[10] derives from the class structure and continues the discussion of the cultural aspects of social classes begun in the previous chapter. Cohen follows Merton in suggesting that certain strains arise out of the social structure, in particular the class system. Such strains are particularly severe at certain stages in the life cycle, particularly on the young adult male. The way in which young people see themselves depends in part on how others see and evaluate them; in American society this happens in situations and through individuals largely middle class in character, e.g. in schools and through school teachers. Here middle-class standards, such as verbal fluency, achievement, ability to defer gratification, are used to measure success and, because of the democratic ethos, are applied to people of *all* classes. Thus individuals of different class or social origin are judged by the *same* standards and have the *same* goals held up to them and compete for them under the *same* set of rules. But, primarily because of the different ways in which the classes are socialized, the middle-class child is far better equipped to succeed in this and the lower-class child is often exposed to failure and humiliation. One way of responding or "adjusting" to such strain is by withdrawing from this situation and competing in situations in which success *is* possible. But so powerful have been the previous unattainable middle-class values that rejection of them is only possible if it is of an extreme kind; thus values are adopted which not only go against the middle-class pattern but which symbolize complete hostility to it and which lead to a reaction of violent destructive behaviour in relation to such middle-class institutions as property.

However, in part because the problem against which this reaction occurs is one of status and frustration of status, a successful "solution" to it requires the presence of others, a collective response in which it is possible to agree on new criteria for "success" and to be able to apply it to others. Thus a group will develop of people "in the same boat" which seeks a collective solution to a shared problem; the coherence of the group will depend on the ability of individuals so placed to locate and communicate with others. If this occurs a new deviant sub-culture may emerge in which individuals derive support from the group; thus it is the sub-culture itself which allows for a successful substitution of delinquent for legitimate activities. This allows for a new self-respect to develop through the evaluation of others similarly placed which could not develop in legitimate spheres (e.g. school and work). Thus the sub-cultural nature of the response to strain is of crucial importance to the success of the response. Cohen also argues that the non-utilitarian nature of much delinquency, where goods and property are destroyed rather than acquired, is not explicable in terms of Merton's theory (which stresses success through acquisition of material wealth), but can be taken account of by the theory of status frustration.

## Developments in Sub-cultural Theory

This kind of theorization has been subject to criticism of various kinds; it has been argued that Cohen greatly oversimplifies the relationship between class and values by wrongly reducing the value system of society to that of the middle class, while ignoring also the complexity of the middle-class value system. Cohen's theory has been influential among practitioners, and it is important to view it against the background of English experience. Although in America the sociology of crime has been relatively well developed, in Britain with some exceptions[11] it has been neglected in favour of other approaches. However, the recent work of Downes[12] suggests that while American sub-cultural theories may throw considerable light on certain forms of deviance of the adolescent delinquent kind, it is important to reinterpret this approach in the light of British findings.

Cohen's thesis was that the status frustrations of the working-class adolescent, who had internalized middle-class aspirations but had little chance of fulfilling them legitimately, led to a "problem of adjustment" to which the solution was a collective form of delinquency. In considering this idea in the English context, Downes asks whether the working-class adolescent in this society faces a problem of "adjustment" at all. The few studies undertaken of adolescent delinquency and the adolescent situation suggest that the problem is not one of conflict with the wider culture. For example, job aspirations of working-class adolescents are rarely in terms of the whole range of occupations but are scaled down to a realistically low level where the important criterion is money rather than status. This also reflects the legitimation of manual employment in the more traditional British working-class situation, and the small income differential between manual and certain routine non-manual occupations. Rather the working-class boy becomes "dissociated" from the sphere of work which does not take on for him the importance attached to it in the American situation; the middle-class norms of status striving in work have in general not been internalized—rather the ideologies of the two classes are in conflict; therefore the status frustration characteristic of the American situation is not present. Another important factor in the "dissociated" nature of the working-class adolescent is the school. In Britain the lower working-class adolescent has, through the operation of the formal system of selection at 11 years and through informal selection as early as 7 or 8 years, been prepared for "failure" in educational and occupational terms. Orientation towards a subordinate status is so powerful that individuals are in some cases scarcely motivated to compete for a grammar school place and a chance for "success" in middle-class terms. At the same time, the working-class boy who is able to compete in middle-class terms is starting his journey up the status ladder and out of the working class. Thus for the British boy the "educational contest" is over by the age of 11, or even earlier, and those who have "failed" become dissociated from the school, from teachers, and from any further association with formal education. In the American situation, however, the operation of a more "open" educational system, where final selection is delayed to as late as 17 years, encourages ambitions and aspirations which may at this late stage still be doomed. Thus a very real frustration of status can occur in a situation where individuals are unprepared for failure, thus producing a "problem of adjustment" to such failure. The English boy does not encounter, therefore, the kind of problem which faces his American counterpart and which results, in the American context, in widespread delinquency on an organized scale. Instead, he successfully negotiates the failure and humiliation of the school and job situations by reaffirming working-class values in these spheres and by displacing his search for achievement from school and work on to non-work activities. At the same time, the working-class job status does not present much of an economic problem because of the absence of widespread unemployment in the large urban centres. The problem of adjustment that the English lower working-class adolescent faces occurs, according to Downes, in the leisure context. Here the desire for excitement, for status, and for achievement outside the context of school and work cannot be met by the traditional working-class leisure pursuits of pub and working men's club. Thus the "corner boy" drifts into a pattern of leisure activities divorced from this tradition and which carries with it a high potential for delinquent activity. Downes vividly describes, from his own study in the East End of London, the corner boys' often fruitless search for excitement and "laughs" through riding "bikes" and by gathering in groups in "caffs"; delinquency becomes a diversion from the boredom of "caff" life and often took the form of rowdyism and affrays. Thus a delinquent sub-culture developed to provide an outlet for the dissatisfactions of leisure. The groups involved shared a more general adolescent culture with others of their age in the community, but because of their dissociation from work and the school, laid greater stress on the attainment of leisure goals. But, because of the cultural poverty of their areas, the chances of obtaining satisfactory goals legitimately were considerably less than for adolescents elsewhere; hence the greater likelihood of a resort to a delinquent, although not necessarily a violent, reaction.

### The Interaction Approach: Reactions to Rule Breaking

In sharp distinction to these theories, which define deviance as the breaking of some recognized rules and which set out to understand in what ways the social situations of deviants may cause this, is an approach which takes the reaction to a so-called "deviant" act as the starting point for analysis. In previous approaches deviance was seen as a quality of some rule breaking act and took as a starting point definitions of acts as "deviant" made by official agencies (e.g. the police). But deviant acts are not homogeneous in this sense because the responses to them vary considerably; some rule breaking, although it has taken place, is ignored, while other acts elicit a response which results in individuals being labelled "deviant". Thus deviance is not a quality of the act a person commits "but rather a consequence of the application by others of rules and sanctions to an 'offender'. The deviant is one to whom that label has successfully been applied; deviant behaviour is behaviour that people so label."[2] Thus the concern in this approach is less with the personal and social characteristics of the deviant than with the process by which some come to be labelled as "outsiders" and the way in which individuals react to this judgement. Thus whether or not an act is "deviant" depends on how others react to it; the fact that a rule has been broken does not by itself mean that others will respond as if this has happened. There may even be occasions where no rule breaking has occurred, yet the label of deviant is successfully applied.

The responses of others to rule breaking may vary in a number of ways; there may, from time to time, be drives mounted against one form of deviance or another which would make the risk of being labelled greater at some times than at others. Variations also depend on who has committed the act and who feels he has suffered from it; thus rules are applied to some rather than to others. Studies of juvenile delinquency show that middle-class boys are not likely to progress so far in the legal process if they are caught than working-class boys, in spite of the fact that they have broken the same rule. Similar variations occur in relation to the colour of the miscreant; again crimes committed by business corporations are treated differently from those committed by individuals. The outcome of rule breaking also influences the response; illicit sexual activity is unlikely to bring punishment on to the heads of the individuals involved, yet if this leads to a girl becoming pregnant it is more likely to elicit a disapproving response.

Thus deviance is not a simple quality, but is the result of complex processes which involve the responses of others; the same behaviour may be treated as an infraction of rules at one time but not at another. Thus an important distinction can be made between behaviour defined as deviant without reference to reactions to it, which can be termed "rule breaking", and rule breaking which is actually labelled as deviant by some segment of society; this can be termed "deviance".

## SOCIOLOGICAL APPROACHES TO MENTAL ILLNESS

"Interactionist" approaches have been used in recent studies to illuminate the kind of process by which the label "mentally ill" is attached to some people in certain situations.

Concepts of mental illness have, until recently, been dominated by the "medical" model already described; here, because symptoms appear to be manifested (as in physical illness) by the individual, mental illness is thought to be a condition of the individual and to be "in" the individual. A "health–disease" continuum is applied to mental illness in much the same way as it is applied to cases of physical illness.

The sociological approach ignores, for the sake of analysis, individual manifestations of mental illness, and concentrates instead on the social situation in which mental "illness" becomes defined and the process by which role and status positions are created and proffered to those considered mentally ill.

In one of the most recent of these approaches, Scheff[13] has described what he terms the "social institution of insanity". Attitudes to and images of mental illness are built up in the individual during and after childhood; people learn from an early age to regard certain situations or people as "crazy". These stereotypes receive support in adult life through social interaction and through channels such as the mass media. Thus people use such phrases as "Are you crazy?" and "running like mad" in everyday conversation, so building up certain ideas of how "mad" people act. These ideas are supported by mass media reporting of events such as violence or murder in which it is suggested (often with little or no evidence) that the assailant has a "history of mental illness". All this serves to establish that mentally ill people are "different" from the general population and thus a dividing line is drawn between the two groups; thus "normal" and "ill" people are seen as occupying different social positions or statuses. Thus members of a particular society learn to respond in a definite way to what is termed "mental illness". One aspect of this response is "labelling"; this exaggerates and sometimes distorts the nature of the behaviour but enables people to respond to what is held to be bizarre or uncontrollable behaviour. This process is also recognized by the deviant himself and is seen as a way out of the situation. Thus when individuals are presented with a form of rule breaking which amounts to crisis, one way of "making sense" of the situation is to view it through ideas of insanity learned in childhood and reinforced in adulthood; action can be taken in such a way that rule breaking becomes labelled, and so controllable. The deviant also tends to react in similar ways, partly because he is persuaded by others to structure his experience in this way. The whole process is completed and stabilized when the deviant himself accepts this traditional way of looking at behaviour as the correct way to look at his own behaviour; he has adopted the proffered role of "deviant".

Thus mental illness can be viewed as a social role of a stigmatized kind which people accept and maintain. The processes which cause the deviant to accept and maintain this role include rewards for playing the role (from doctors and other patients) and the difficulty of re-entering non-deviant roles (e.g. of an occupational or marital kind) once the label of "deviant" has been applied. The suggestible nature of the situation in which the deviant finds himself at the point of entry to the role is another important factor; the deviant is sensitive to the opinions of those around him and shares their traditional and strongly held images of mental illness. The idea of mental illness becomes a way of organizing experience, particularly when this way of looking at things is encouraged by persons with prestige, such as doctors. Thus an individual can, in some circumstances, be launched on a "deviant career" which has features similar to those of a career in the occupational sense; the deviant moves, for example, from independent status to hospitalization, from institution to institution or hospital to hospital in much the same way as an employee moves from job to job within the occupational system. Scheff suggests that "labelling" is the single most important process in the launching of a deviant career; most rule breaking does not arouse a reaction in society. Once labelling has occurred this means a change in the status of the individual.

The idea of a deviant career has been elaborated in terms of the mental patient by Goffman.[14] His concern is with what he calls the "moral" aspect of the mental patient's career and the kinds of changes in a person's way of looking at himself and others entailed by this career. The first phase of the career is the period before entering hospital, the pre-patient phase. Here the individual gradually comes to see himself, or to appreciate that others see him, as a disturbed person. The process which leads from independence to hospitalization includes "contingencies" which move the individual on from one stage of his career to another; these include factors and circumstances which cause the individual to be labelled, including factors such as the availability of hospital beds and the tolerance level of the family or community. But other individuals in similar psychiatric conditions, or who are responsible for similar actions which cause others to be labelled, remain unlabelled and outside the hospital. As Goffman puts it:

> Society's official view is that inmates of mental hospitals are there primarily because they are suffering from mental illness. However in the degree that the "mentally ill" outside hospitals numerically approach or surpass those inside hospitals, one could say that mental patients distinctively suffer not from mental illness but from contingencies.[14]

Contingencies also occur because of the agents and agencies which participate in the individual's passage from society into the hospital. These include the complainant (the person who initially takes action against the pre-patient), the next of relation (the person whom the pre-patient sees as the most dependable in times of trouble), and the mediators, or the sequence of official agents (police, psychiatrists, social workers, etc.) by which the pre-patient is relayed to the hospital. Mediators, unlike other agents, bring a specialist and professional attitude to their role; they are also more psychiatrically oriented than laymen and may see the need for treatment where a layman may not. The pre-patient may see agents in the form of an "alienative coalition"; for example, the next of kin may also be the complainant, and may also be seen as conspiring with the mediator to effect the pre-patient's entry to hospital. The pre-patient becomes in various ways a spectator to what may appear a conspiracy in which he is abandoned by the person or persons closest to him; the fact that this has been witnessed by an outside agent makes a public or social fact out of the contingency in which he is involved which cannot be lightly put aside. The pre-patient appears to pass through a "betrayed funnel" in which at each stage he loses more rights as a free adult, despite the fact that this is often denied by each agent. The next of relation is in some cases the agent who most effectively leads the pre-patient to the point of hospitalization, although this may not be his specific purpose; he will also have to bear the guilt of this act. In order to rationalize the whole process of the pre-patient's hospitalization and his reaction to this, there may also be a restructuring of the patient's past to demonstrate that he was "ill" all along; even the patient may be led to believe in this psychiatric "work up" of his past which may allow him to enter hospital with greater equanimity.

One of the most important mediators in the case of mental illness is the psychiatrist, and Scheff has analysed the process by which decisions to hospitalize the pre-patient are made.[13]

In making decisions, doctors and other practitioners are guided by the norms of the professional culture to which they belong. In medicine one of these norms appears to be that to judge a sick person well is more to be avoided than to judge a well person sick; thus, when in doubt, an important guideline appears to be to diagnose illness rather than health—"better safe than sorry". This rests on two assumptions; disease is progressive and if it is undetected it may grow to such proportions that might endanger the life of the patient and others. Again, medical diagnosis and observation is neutral and innocuous and will in any case do the patient no ineradicable harm. Psychiatrists, being also physicians, are likely to accept these assumptions, but these assumptions may, when transferred to the field of psychiatric medicine, be questioned. Unlike medical treatment, psychiatric treatment can drastically change a person's status in the community; e.g. can remove rights that are difficult to regain. It is also by no means clear that mental illness, if untreated, leads to progressive deterioration in the individual; there is, for example, a large amount of undiagnosed and untreated mental illness in the general population.

If psychiatrists make such medical assumptions one danger is that a person, who may be highly suggestible at the time of treatment, may be led unnecessarily into the "sick role" in a situation where no serious outcome would result if his "illness" were left unattended. The patient may take the role of a sick person during the process of diagnosis and may infer from the physician's behaviour the nature of the diagnosis. In physical illness it is recognized that many patients will sometimes oblige with the appropriate symptoms if they feel there is a good reason for believing they are ill. The danger of this with mental illness is that this may lead the patient into a "career" of chronic illness from which he may have difficulty in escaping; this is particularly so when the role he has chosen in order to escape from a bewildering and frightening situation is validated by an authoritative figure such as a psychiatrist.

Again, to what extent is entry to a career of deviance unrelated to the actual condition of the patient? Scheff also studied the entry of patients to mental hospitals in a Midwestern state. Although the conditions under which patients are admitted in British hospitals differs considerably from the American setting, this study is nevertheless an important illustration of the process of entry to a deviant career which could with advantage be repeated in the British context. From a sample of newly admitted mental patients it was found that a substantial majority (63 per cent) did not clearly meet the statutory requirements for confinement but had nevertheless found their way into hospital on the recommendation of psychiatrists. The uncertainty surrounding these cases is attributed by Scheff[13] (and other writers) to the fact that in "doubtful" cases a presumption of illness is made by mental health officials during the process of examination before admission.

Factors predisposing psychiatrists to these kinds of decisions included financial, ideological, and political ones. The income of the examiners depends in part on the length of time spent with the patient—if this is prolonged the rate of pay is reduced. The ideology of psychiatric practice suggests, amongst other things, that mental illness gets worse if untreated and that the mental patient is potentially dangerous to himself and others. These assumptions strongly predispose towards a presumption of illness and the admission of the patient, but they are, in fact, extremely questionable. Political pressure from the community which acts directly on the officials is another important factor in the presumption of illness; here the risk of releasing the mental patient is seen as being greater than that of retaining him.

The motives of key decision-makers will thus substantially affect the way in which society reacts to deviance of this kind and will help to draw a status line between the deviant and non-deviant population. In the case of mental illness it would appear that, for a number of reasons related to the organization and ideology of mental health professions, once official reaction to mental illness is set into gear there is a strong likelihood that the deviant will be differentiated from the non-deviant and launched on a career of deviance, irrespective of the actual mental condition of the individual. This is an extreme contrast to the "denial" which is the response to other forms of rule breaking. Thus societal reaction of this kind is a vital factor in itself in explaining and helping to sustain what Szasz, one of the early writers on the subject, has called the "myth of mental illness".[3]

Finally, the pre-patient stage of the mental patient's career is followed by actual hospitalization, or what Goffman has called the "in-patient phase".[15] Here the fate of the patient is little different from other inmates of "total institutions", such as gaols, concentration camps, in which life is led entirely within the boundaries of the institution in the company of groups of persons of similar status. Here the changes in the outlook of the patient, which began in the pre-patient phase, are affirmed and continued by processes which are characteristic of total institutions. These include the "stripping" of the newcomer of his way of thinking about himself, and "mortification" through the restriction of freedom and the imposition of the authority of others; there is an assault on the "self" of the patient which is extraordinarily powerful because of the dependent role in which he is placed and because he has no control over the social setting in which this assault is mounted. One form of response to this, on the part of the patient, is to deny the circumstances which led to hospitalization and to assert his normality and health. The patient will hold that his presence in hospital is a mistake caused by the misdemeanours of others for which he is not responsible. But the mental hospital setting is not one which is favourable to such hard-luck stories; the staff have to justify their existence and their mode of treatment and do so by discrediting such stories and seeking to justify the patient's presence. The patient's case record is a powerful means to this end; this, as well as his present behaviour, can be "interpreted" to show that he is really "ill". Thus patients are encouraged to accept the hospital's version of the reason for their presence; this process has similarities with other forms of adult socialization, which proceed from alienation and mortification to the building of a new self through a new set of beliefs; the mental patient can take this path, e.g. can become devoted to the belief in the efficacy of mental treatment, but can also reject any new self that may be offered and remain in a state of total demoralization.

## CONCLUSION

In discussing the foregoing material it is useful to return to the idea that social work acts as a bridge between the deviant and society; by this means it is hoped that the deviant is reintegrated into society. This implies, amongst other things, that the deviant can be motivated to accept the norms and values which are commonly supported in the wider society. Much of the discussion so far, in particular the concept of anomie and its application, suggests that certain forms of deviant behaviour may be outside the scope of this approach. One way of looking at deviance is as the rejection of commonly accepted goals and means; here so-called "normal" behaviour has been entirely rejected. It is not as if accepted rules had been put temporarily aside and the deviant awaits a lead back into society through social work or some other form of counselling. As Pollak[16] has pointed out, anomie presents social work with its greatest challenge. For those who suffer from normlessness social work has

> no theory of helping, no tradition of success. Social work and psychiatry are without appropriate armamentarium because the helping professions have learned essentially only how to liberate people who have become beneficiaries of a norm directed life . . . here social workers will have to come to terms with a phenomenon of normlessness which makes liberating or improving efforts miss the mark.

Social workers can, for example, accept that cultural goals can vary from class to class and can use this knowledge on which to base an approach to treatment and diagnosis. But in situations where goals or norms have been totally abandoned, social work as a method of liberating the personality in order to achieve goals is rendered almost helpless

The situation which social workers face in such cases appears, however, to be much more complicated than this. In practice, as research on problem families who exhibit "retreatist" characteristics has shown, it is rare for commitment to established rules to be relinquished altogether. Instead, there is a gradation from families who, although below normal standards of efficiency, conform to certain generalized norms of standards to those families who have lost touch with social norms and have, in the main, rejected social goals. Thus a distinction can be made between "marginal" and "hard core" disorganization.[17] This distinction has practical implications for the social worker; in marginal cases "norm"-based casework has some chance of success, but in "hard-core" situations (where families have retreated from accepted norms and can justify their own deviant standards) casework with individual families is unlikely to work unless it is accompanied by attempts to get new norms accepted. If this end is in fact desired, casework may have to be supplemented by a process of re-education on community or neighbourhood basis. A similar point can be made about goals; the families in this study varied from those who had goals (however unclear) for the future to those who had retreated to the extent of abandoning all plans for the future. Again, casework based on clarification and strengthening of goals, which in the former case seems appropriate, will have little chance of success in cases of severe retreatism.

Thus severe withdrawal from goals or norms is difficult to meet at the level of the individual family by traditional casework.

A similar picture emerges from studies of the adolescent delinquent. The adolescent delinquent shares with the problem family the experience of being rejected by society although here the reaction to this experience takes a different form. While the problem family retreats into its inner world the adolescent delinquent, using Downes term, "dissociates" from the areas in which rejection and failure have been experienced, namely school and work. The ensuing emphasis on leisure often leads to delinquent behaviour. Because of the rigid way in which the lower working-class teenager is allocated roles of a subordinate nature, a situation in which the individual is highly prone to delinquency is built up. Here the important question is not why individuals adopt a delinquent solution, but why they conform in the face of this situation. Clearly no bridge exists here to the wider society because it has been effectively destroyed by that society. In a sense the only bridge that exists between society and many forms of deviance is found in the situation of the rebel;[18] at least the rebel seeks in one way or another a better society, a principle which would be widely accepted, and thus remains committed to some form of social order. The criminal and the retreatist are, on the other hand, withdrawing support from society, which in turn rejects them.

Again, it is difficult to envisage the success of the traditional methods of the personal social services in what appears essentially a problem of the social structure. Yet the solutions to such problems have continually been seen as extensions to social work and casework services with individuals and families. Sociological studies of delinquency and other forms of deviance, with their often explicit call for wider programmes of reform which transcend the individual case, appear to have fallen largely on deaf ears.[19] The work of Cohen, Cloward, and Ohlin in America, and Morris, Mays, and Downes in Britain all suggest in varying ways an attack on the problem at the level of the community or the society. Downes[12] suggests that the adolescent must be engaged in and rewarded by the society which at present rejects him; this can only come about through major changes in the comprehensive and further education system and in what is described as the "antiquated structure of manual work". The development of links between school and work, a change from subject- to pupil-centred teaching, and special schemes for areas with severe educational and social problems are examples of the kind of changes that are required.

The community and the social work profession have in a sense responded to this kind of analysis of the problem; a number of official reports on education and housing have stressed the necessity of a broader assault on social problems than in the past; the Plowden Committee's[20] proposal to designate educational priority areas is an example of such an approach. Social workers have been involved in this kind of thinking and have also begun to evolve their own approach; changes in the educational system can also be accompanied by measures designed to reduce the barriers to educational success outside the school, including a closer liaison between social workers and schools designed to solve some of the problems of family and neighbourhood which hinder attainment in schools. Again, social workers are evolving methods of working with communities; certain areas suffer from a marked lack of community identity, but, if this were fostered, individuals and families could look to each other for help as well as to the social services. The Seebohm Committee[21] recommended the institution of "social development areas" where needs are great but where resources of manpower and money could be concentrated.

Thus social work can help to grapple with such problems by intervention at levels which are intermediate between the individual and society—the school, the neighbourhood, and the community. But it is important to remember that there is some distinction between this kind of approach and a full appreciation of the nature of such social problems at the level of the total society and the social structure. Mills[22] distinguished a number of years ago between the social worker's considerable understanding of problems at the level of immediate social "situation" in which they are manifested and an appreciation of the same problems against the background of the total social structure; this distinction appears as valid today as in the 1940's. As Rea Price,[19] writing of the relationship between contemporary British social work and social reform, comments: "It is possible to be disappointed at the failure to trace sources of problems to the social fabric and to give sociological dimensions to the diagnosis." Although inroads have clearly been made into the traditional casework-oriented ideology, neither the official plans to involve social workers in reformist measures nor social workers' own awareness of the need for structual change appear to go far enough. One danger is that in the relationship between society and social work the latter will continue to be seen as the panacea for the evils of the former, but will lack the resources or equipment to achieve any sort of tolerable solutions to these evils. Some of the dilemmas posed for social work in its relationship with society, as well as the current debate about the changing role of the social worker, will be explored in Chapters 8 and 9.

Paradoxically, some of the changes suggested above could, as Downes suggests,[12] provide the basis for greater status consciousness and thus of status frustration characteristic of American society; efforts to reduce delinquency through changes in the school system might succeed in producing aspirations which could not be satisfied in the wider social system, whilst the main force for the control of such aspirations, working-class conservatism, is progressively reduced. These are important examples of the unintended consequences of social policies.

The idea that some rule breakers are, in certain situation, labelled as deviants and launched in this way on a career of deviance, has important implications for the professions which themselves play a part in this process. The label which society attaches to the deviant, whether it be that of delinquency or mental illness or rebellion, results from an essentially similar process. In the case of the young delinquent, labelling comes about through an emphasis on the purely legal and criminal aspects of delinquent behaviour. Thus laws relating to theft which are applied to a whole range of adult law breakers are also applied to very young children; criminal proceedings may, as Morris[23] has pointed out, provide "the first step in the process of stigmatization, the first stage of which Erving Goffman has called a 'moral career'. Application of the law of larceny to a twelve-year-old provides him with at least the preliminary qualifications for ultimately joining the ranks of Howard Becker's Outsiders." Thus in an entirely arbitrary fashion individuals can be launched at an early age on careers of delinquency in which formal court proceedings or admission to treatment can solidify the process of deviance through this important change in status. However, recognition is growing that distinctions between the deviant and non-deviant can rest on such slender threads as the social class of the offender or complainant, the area of the offence, current attitudes to the offence, and other arbitrary variables.

The 1968 Government White Paper *Children in Trouble*[24] appears in part a reaction to this situation. This shifts the emphasis away from the "criminal" definition and penal treatment of delinquent behaviour of young people between 10 and 17 towards the view that such behaviour is a product of the social situation of the offender and should be dealt with in relation to his social needs. For example, children under 14 would no longer be dealt with by the court except in exceptional circumstances; their cases would be considered by the police and local authority children's departments working together. Children taken to court would be dealt with by supervision orders (similar to probation orders) or by committal to care of local authority but not fined or discharged by the court.

Opposition to the scheme[25] comes from those who claim that it removes the onus for deciding on an individual's guilt or innocence from the law to other agencies, thus threatening the establishment of elementary justice for the child. The proposals also imply that social workers will play a much greater role in the treatment of rule breakers than before; doubts have been expressed about the capacities of social work agencies to deal with the increased volume of work which this will mean and the new problems which will be faced. There is also doubt about the extent to which many social workers actually share the assumptions behind the proposals. It seems important therefore that some of the theorization behind the proposals should be understood. It is also important to speculate about the extent to which the alternative forms of treatment proposed may launch rule breakers on different, but no less stigmatized, careers of deviance and to understand something of the possible character of such alternative "careers".

As Matza[26] has suggested, a number of problems arise from ideological support for the "negation of the offence", or the removal of the offence from a moral context. This "child welfare" ideology, which gains strength from psychiatric and other theorization, serves to shift "blame" for delinquent acts away from the young delinquent towards a variety of institutions and figures, including society, the family, the parents, and even the victims of the crime. Courts can become dominated by the ideology of child welfare and its appropriate treatment objectives and procedures; essential to this is the view that the family is part of a causal chain which led the child to crime and that parents are a particularly culpable part of this chain of circumstances.

However, in spite of such beliefs, it is still the delinquent rather than parents, kin, neighbours, or other citizens who receive, in a variety of ways, treatment or correction for the crime; there is thus a very considerable discrepancy between what is believed in theory and what is carried into practice. The juvenile courts, with their aim to rehabilitate rather than punish, rely for the success of this purpose on the trust of their clientele, precisely because these aims are so lofty; the capacity to accept this ideology on the part of young law breakers depends very much on the trust they can invest in the court and the degree of legitimacy with which they can credit its agents and officials. By attributing responsibility to social conditions outside the power of the offender yet continuing to hold the offender immediately responsible, the courts and their agents invite distrust and the charge of hypocrisy. Thus by persisting with the child welfare ideology, the court defeats its objectives—the offender withdraws belief in the legitimacy of the proceedings and thus the court's lofty aspirations cannot be achieved. A sense of frustration is engendered in the delinquent which facilitates what Matza has described as the continued "drift into delinquency". Although the proposals in the White Paper would, at face value, remove the punitive element from such proceedings and substitute for it a range of service and treatments based on what is described as the "child welfare ideology", it is difficult to see how the plan can escape entirely from the dilemma posed by Matza; it is still the child rather than the parent, the family or society which is "treated" and made the object of certain services. In the eyes of the recipient of such services, as well, perhaps, as some of the donors, the process may be much as before, only the name attached to it is different.

In the case of mental illness the "social system" or interaction approach has received possibly less attention and recognition from policy makers and practitioners. Mental illness is still seen by many in medical terms as a condition of the individual which requires diagnosis and treatment. This attitude appears in part a reflection of the current professional aspirations and status of social workers and associated occupations who function in many cases on the fringes of the medical world. The essence of professionalism is the possession of recognized skill which is not generally available; to use medical models and labels, which are in any case ready to hand, not only simplifies and rationalizes the work but also attaches to it a form of expertise and professionalism. It also simplifies the process of working with doctors, psychiatrists, and other medical personnel, and facilitates the exchange of information within this circle. This emphasis can be seen in the training of social workers, where the medical view of deviance is heavily emphasized. Teaching in some of the most important areas is frequently carried out by medical or psychiatric practitioners amongst others. Thus there are positive incentives to share certain medical norms, such as the "presumption" of illness, in the face of the difficult client. The implications of this are, again, to launch the individual on a career of deviance from which it is difficult to escape. Thus the cloak of mental illness can in particular circumstances come down over a wider variety of deviants or rule breakers, including the rebel and the innovator as well as the retreatist. Through this process it is possible to put aside the fact that many of the symptoms of the clients of social workers are in themselves criticisms of and comments on contemporary society and the kinds of demands this society makes on the individual or his family. It is by diagnosing such symptoms in medical terms, and such individuals as in the grip of a "condition", that society manages to disregard and set aside such criticism. The social worker, as a reviewer of Scheff's book points out,[27] is sometimes guilty of colluding in this deception of the individual; in this way the social worker exercises a conservative influence on the wider culture by emphasis on the protection and interests of the individual. However, "perhaps we [social workers] should not always collude in this deception. Perhaps we should reassert the tradition of looking to the needs of our culture as well as to the needs of the individuals. Mr. Facing-Both-Ways need not necessarily be a name to be ashamed of."[27] The practice of equating social deviance with social failure stems from the consensus view of society which social workers characteristically hold and which was referred to in the previous chapter.

The social worker is in a particularly good position to appreciate one aspect of the "social system" approach to mental illness, i.e. the process of the "extrusion" of an individual from a small social group such as the family. Here the tensions and conflicts within the family may be in part resolved by the selection of one member to play a scapegoat role for the group as a whole and for this individual to be "extruded" from the group; but the removal of a particular individual does not in itself solve the problems of the group. Social workers, with their special opportunities for the observation of whole families, may be in a position to introduce this kind of analysis into the whole diagnostic and treatment process.

Clearly the social worker's functions as a mediator in the complex chain of events leading from pre-patients to patient status is usefully illuminated by Goffman's account of the dynamics of the process. Here the reactions of the various actors in the process can be understood by putting aside the official account of the process and by taking into account the interests of the parties concerned; although the idea of an alienative collusion may seem, from the standpoint of the officials involved, to distort reality; from the standpoint of the patient this may, in fact, constitute reality only too clearly. Again, the social worker may be in a position to appreciate this position for he may be able to stand apart from the central positions (such as that of hospital psychiatrist) which constitutes the main basis of this collusion.

## NOTES AND REFERENCES

1. E. Younghusband, *Social Work and Social Change*, Allen & Unwin, London, 1964.
2. See H. Becker, *Outsiders—Studies in the Sociology of Deviance*, Free Press, New York, 1963; the two introductory chapters of this book constitute an exceptionally clear preliminary discussion of the sociology of deviance and largely form the basis of this introduction.

3. T. Szasz, *The Myth of Mental Illness*, Hoeber, New York, 1961; in Becker, *op. cit.*

4. It is also possible that some groups will see their rules as applying only to themselves and will not think it wrong for other groups to deviate from these, e.g. some religious or ethnic groups.

5. E. Durkheim, *The Division of Labour*, Free Press, Glencoe, 1947.

6. R. K. Merton, *Social Theory and Social Structure*, Free Press, Glencoe, 1957.

7. W. Baldamus and N. Timms, The problem family—a sociological approach, *Br. J. Sociol.* **6** (12) (1955); for an interpretation of the same material in terms of social work, see N. Timms, Social standards and the problem family, *Case Conference* **2** (9) (Jan. 1956). For a more recent but less sociological approach, see F. Philp, *Family Failure*, Faber, 1963. For a review of the literature on the problem family, see F. Philp and N. Timms, *The Problem of the Problem Family*, Family Service Units, 1957.

8. R. Cloward, Illegitimate means, anomie and deviant behaviour, *Am. Sociol Rev.* **4** (1959); see also R. Cloward and R. Ohlin, *Delinquency and Opportunity*, Free Press, Glencoe, 1960.

9. B. Green and E. Johns, *An Introduction to Sociology*, Pergamon, 1966.

10. A. Cohen, *Delinquent Boys*, Free Press, Glencoe, 1955.

11. See J. Mays, *Growing up in the City*, Liverpool University Press, 1956; T. Morris, *The Criminal Area*, Routledge & Kegan Paul, London, 1957. For a review of approaches, see J. Mays, Crime and the urban pattern, *Sociol. Rev.* **7** (1968).

12. D. Downes, *The Delinquent Solution—A Study in Subcultural Theory*, Routledge & Kegan Paul, London, 1966.

13. T. Scheff, *Being Mentally Ill*, Weidenfeld & Nicholson, London, 1966.

14. E. Goffman, *Asylums: Essays on the Social Situation of Mental Patients*, Penguin, 1961.

15. Goffman, *op. cit.* The concept of "total institution" is taken up again in Chapter 11.

16. O. Pollak, The social determinants of family behaviour, in Younghusband (ed.), *Social Work with Families*, Allen & Unwin, 1965.

17. N. Timms, Social standards and the problem family, *Case Conference* **2** (9) (Jan. 1956).

18. W. J. Sprott, *Science and Social Action*, Watts, London, 1954.

19. J. Rea Price, Social pathology—a dilemma for social workers, *Case Conference* **13** (12) (April 1969).

20. Report of the Committee on Primary Schools (*Children and their Primary Schools*) (Plowden Report), H.M.S.O., London, 1967.

21. Report of the Committee on Local Authority and Allied Personal Social Services (Seebohm Report), Cmnd 3703 H.M.S.O., London, 1968.

22. C. Wright Mills, The professional ideology of social pathologists, *Am. J. Sociol.* **49** (1943).

23. T. P. Morris, Children in trouble defended, *New Society*, 17 Oct. 1968.

24. *Children in Trouble*, Cmnd 3601, H.M.S.O., London, 1968; see also the Children and Young Persons Act, 1969.
25. See R. Sparks, Children in trouble attacked, *New Society*, 26 Sept. 1968.
26. D. Matza, *Delinquency and Drift*, Wiley, New York, 1964.
27. See *Case Conference*, **14** (8), Dec. 1967.

# PART III

# Introduction to Part III

In Part III attention is turned away from the study of aspects of the client's social situation towards a consideration of the position and role of the social worker. Clearly interaction between the client and the social worker hinges as much on the influences bearing on the social worker as on the client, and the following paragraphs are devoted to a preliminary analysis of some of these influences.

First, it is important to discuss the place of social work in society; one way of expressing this is to determine the kinds of functions that the institution of social work fulfils in modern industrial societies. Social work, like other institutions such as education, performs certain tasks on behalf of society and thus one of the pressures on social workers is to play their part in the fulfilment of such requirements.

At the same time social workers are themselves beginning to achieve a professional identity of their own and are taking on some of the characteristics of the established professions. Thus a further influence on the social worker derives from the social work profession, its structure, values, and goals; one of the principal ways in which any profession influences its members is through professional education and training, and it is therefore important to begin to explore something of the character of this process in social work.

Finally, the majority of social workers function within organizations, or agencies, such as local authority children's departments, hospitals, and a wide variety of other settings. Social work, like most other forms of professional or semi-professional work, is a highly organized activity and is therefore influenced by the organization and by its administrators, who may or may not be social workers. Again, the organizations in which social workers function are often devoted to ends (medical or legal) which may be marginal to the social worker's central concern. There are therefore a complex and powerful set of influences on the social worker in the organization which, to an extent, pull in the opposite direction to influences from the profession. Essentially the social worker has to reconcile his role as an individual citizen, as a member of a profession, and as part of an organization. It is important to determine the extent to which these roles are in conflict and to say something about the nature of the conflict.

In order to simplify the complex picture which is suggested here, it is useful to think of the social worker as occupying a position which is at the centre of a number of relationships, or roles, to which the term "role set" has been given by Merton.[1] Previously it has been suggested that each social position (or status) has a clearly defined role attached to it. But, as Merton points out, there are often many roles attached to any one position; the role set is the complex of role relationships in which individuals are involved by occupying a particular social position. For example, the status of school teacher has a distinctive role set composed of pupils, colleagues, parents, headmaster, school governors, the professional association, and so on. The social worker's role set includes (amongst others) the client and his family, colleagues, administrators, elected representative, members of other professions, lay experts (such as social scientists), and the professional association.

There are potentially differing and sometimes conflicting expectations of the behaviour appropriate to the occupant of the status among members of the role set. This reflects the fact that members of the role set are likely to hold differing positions, and thus have different interests, both from each other and from the status occupant. Thus parents may differ from school governors about the education of their children and thus have differing expectations of the teacher. Thus the status occupant is subjected to conflicting expectations which complicate the playing of the role. Merton[1] suggests that certain mechanisms operate to counteract such conflicts, and it will be useful to discuss the position of the social worker and the conflicting expectations deriving from the role set partly in terms of some of these mechanisms.

## REFERENCE

1. R. K. Merton, The role set; problems in sociological theory, *Br. J. Sociol.* **2** (1957).

# CHAPTER 8

## The Social Functions
## of Social Work—Social Control

### INTRODUCTION

In a previous chapter the family was discussed in part by asking the question: "What social functions does it perform?" One of the most important functions of the family was seen to be the preparation of individuals for their future lives in society. Thus the family functions as a socializing agent. This process was one of the main ways in which the family served the needs and requirements of the social system. A similar question can be asked about any social institution. Broadly this question asks us to consider the kind of consequences which social institutions or processes have for society as a whole. One way of looking at this question is to see social institutions as functioning to maintain or integrate society. Thus the family in its function of socializing the individual helps to maintain society by passing on certain values which will be important as guides to future behaviour. In the same way we can ask the question "What are the social functions of social work?" "What are its consequences for society and what part does it play in the integration of society and the maintenance of social equilibrium?" The question can be broken down into a number of parts; apart from the general relationship between social work and society, it is also necessary to understand the interrelationship between social work and other social institutions such as education. It is also important to understand the internal organization of the social work profession, which will form the subject of another chapter.

The question of the relationship between social work and society is an extremely complex but relatively unexplored one;[1] yet, because of many new functions that social work is being asked to perform on behalf of society, it is important to pursue the question.

One way of simplifying this task and of accounting for the role of the social worker is by stressing the organizational context of social work;[2] thus social work and its methods helps to achieve the ends of a variety of organizations, including the hospital, the court, and the local authority; thus the medical social worker will help the hospital to attain states of "health" for patients, the probation officer is part of the system for the treatment and prevention of delinquency. A modern society is characterized by a variety of such organizations which help to attain particular ends or values such as maintenance of law. Social work thus embodies certain of these values; and the social workers' purpose becomes identical to that of the agency. For example, social workers are concerned with the control of deviant or non-conforming behaviour in their role of officers of the court or in local authority children's departments. These clients may range from parents who fail to conform to social standards relating to the care of children or to other aspects of family life, to individuals or groups who threaten by violent acts the institutions of society. Such agencies, and the social workers within them, are thus part of the way certain values and norms are transmitted; social work agencies, like schools, function to transmit culture. Unlike schools their cultural transmission functions relate only to that minority of the population who have broken, or are unaware of, the rules of society or who require help or assistance with other problems of living or behaviour.

As well as exercising a controlling function in society through such organizations, social work and its associated agencies also have functions to perform in relation to social change. One way of viewing the emergence of social work is as a response to the needs of an industrializing society; because of the stresses of industrialization some of the functions of institutions such as the family could not be carried out and social workers, amongst others, were needed to "mop up" the problems resulting from rapid social changes of this kind. One implication of this view is that social work organizations are "residual" agencies which have developed temporary functions in an emergency and will disappear when the major social institutions regain their strength.[3] However, social work does not simply respond passively to changes in society for it can itself be the vehicle of those changes; for example, social work can help to promote the changes that society requires. In Britain it has been suggested that social workers play a more active role in attaining educational equality by mediating between the school and the community and attempting to reduce the social handicaps faced by some children. In the study of the New York casework agency[4] it was shown that social workers favoured in general the reduction of ties within the extended family and attempted to strengthen the nuclear or immediate family; this view may stem from the belief that changes in family structure are required if all families are to fulfil the functions demanded of them in a modern industrial society.

Again, social work through specialized knowledge and practice may itself be able to initiate or effect changes through influence on government by research and other means; as one writer has put it, "the profession is able, in short, to get its hands on the levers of social change".[5] Thus social work is one of the many means by which social change is promoted and directed. It is argued that social work, for these reasons, is an established part of society and not a residual institution that will wither away. This impetus will be related to the values of the social work profession as well as to the values of society; in many cases these values may coincide, and social work and society may agree about what is required. Professions are, in the last resort, accountable to society for their actions. In other situations there may be potential or actual conflict between social work and society; there may be conflict and disagreement about what changes are required. This has led some writers to describe social work as a minority culture which is alienated from the wider society, and social workers as a minority group in that society.[6] One explanation is that while social work is said to embody the "conscience" of society through its concern for the welfare of the individual and for social failure, this also makes it the target of society's ambivalence; social work stands as a painful reminder of society's failure to ensure the welfare of all its members. Again, with its concern for social change through planning, social work also mobilizes resistance and opposition to change from forces which seek to maintain existing social patterns. Thus the marginal position of social work relates not only to its existence in the shadow of other institutions, but reflects the fact that social work stands for values to which society may give only partial or contradictory expression.

Thus social work, as well as helping to maintain the social system and being shaped by social forces outside its control, also performs a role as a moulder of culture; for this reason, and because of the values embodied in social work which highlight the individual and the social pressures to which he is subjected, the position of social work in society is surrounded by dilemmas, conflicts, and ambiguities. One conflict arises out of social workers occupying positions in agencies and organizations; social workers may oppose the way in which society's values are expressed through such organizations or may oppose the values as such. Thus social workers differ markedly in the extent to which they accept the goals of the organization, and their positions as agency workers, members of a profession, and individuals in the wider society are often hard to reconcile.

This discussion is also important in relation to the emphasis in previous chapters on the differing cultural norms and values of social workers and the groups, and individuals, with which they are in contact. An emphasis has been placed on the potential and actual conflict between the "client system" and the "social-worker system". It has frequently been suggested that social workers should take into account and recognize such differences in their work. The idea of "cultural relativity" may suggest to social workers that actions must be taken based on the clients' rather than the workers' cultural preferences. One answer to this problem is to see social work (like education) as having certain functions to play in society which are dictated by society's needs, which are in themselves related to social work agencies and the social-work profession.

In what follows there will be a focus on the twin functions of social control and social change in social work, which will be prefaced by a brief sociological introduction to these areas.

## THE CONCEPT OF SOCIAL CONTROL

In attempting to understand the nature of social control it is necessary to return to the subject of deviance. Control can be seen in one sense as a response to deviance, and, in the same way as deviance, can be culturally defined and understood. That is, culture prescribes that "something is done" about deviance. Cohen usefully distinguishes between the latent and manifest structure of social control.[7] In the former there may be no social awareness that actions have anything to do with reducing deviance. However, changes in employment opportunities or the influence of the mass media may in fact perform such a function and may often be consciously incorporated into the manifest control structure. The manifest control structure includes the culturally accepted responses to deviant behaviour and the organization of such responses in which specialized occupational roles (such as magistrate, policeman, probation officer) are created for this purpose. In a simple society such roles are part of general role playing, and can be performed by such individuals as parents or kinsmen. Here control functions are allocated to roles which fulfil a variety of purposes at one and the same time. These roles can be described as "functionally diffuse". In a modern society control functions are increasingly allocated to functionally specific roles, i.e. where the sole purpose is to control deviance, although diffuse roles, such as that of parent, still play a part in control. These specific roles are often organized into special agencies to fulfil this purpose. These include the courts, prisons, hospitals, and some social-work agencies. Such a complex has its own organization, a network of agents or agencies similar to a series of stations in a communication network. In itself such a system has its own values or structure, and ways of operating which can themselves be subject to analysis. For example, questions are increasingly being asked about the effectiveness of this control structure and of different elements within it. Thus the effectiveness of social work and casework as a means of social control is increasingly being questioned.

An alternative way of thinking about social control is to see it as a more general property of social systems.[8] Here reference can again be made to the two major theoretical systems—consensus theory and coercion theory which have already been outlined in Chapter 2. In one sense social control is the basis of any social organization, for it denotes the ways in which the individual is limited in his behaviour by the group or community of which he is a member. But the way in which social control can be viewed depends on which theoretical system is adopted. Consensus theory suggests a set of values which are accepted by all and which the individual is asked to accept; such shared values underlie social equilibrium and make social interaction possible. Social control is the complex of forces which makes for equilibrium or restores society to equilibrium. For the individual it is his motivation to withstand deviant behaviour. In many circumstances self regulation may play a considerable part in the individual's behaviour. Here traditional or customary norms become part of the individual's behaviour at a very early age and are never questioned. However, in situations where such norms are weakened a more specific form of social control is required in order that the integration of society be maintained.

Alternatively it is possible to see all cases of social interaction as situations in which the individual's behaviour is limited by the actions of others or by groups and communities of which he may or may not be a member. This formulation allows for the fact that the control of the individual may not be in the interests of some assumed total value system or of the social system as a whole, but may be in the interests of a group of which the individual is not a member or whose interests may be different to those of the individual who is controlled. This view rests on the analysis of society as one of a series of conflict groups in which control is not seen as performing functions for society as a whole but for certain dominant groups who use their power to exploit others. Here types of control are seen as not only custom, convention, or ethical rules, but laws and specific institutional controls which may be applied in their own interests by one group to another.

## SOCIAL WORK AND SOCIAL CONTROL

The idea that social work is part of the apparatus of social control is not usually recognized or accepted in literature on the subject. Social work is instead seen as a form of treatment whose purposes include, amongst other things, strengthening of family life, the building of a wholesome community life, and the improvement of interpersonal relationships.[9] But social work and casework are not usually viewed by social workers as constituting the direct control of the individual, and are not seen primarily as a means of making the individual conform to society. On the contrary, one of the primary values of social work is an emphasis on the innate worth and freedom of the individual person. The social worker's potential power and authority is limited by two principles fundamental to the practise of social work and casework. Those are "acceptance" and "self-determination."[10] Acceptance implies an attitude of good will towards the client, a lack of hostility and condemnation irrespective of the feelings that the worker has about the client and his problem. It also implies an acceptance of the whole personality of the client and not just the aspects of personality which are being presented. Self-determination implies that where possible the client should be allowed to reach his own decisions about his problems and in general terms direct his own life. The potentially directive role of the caseworker should be reduced to the minimum and, although free to make suggestions, these should appear as ideas which the client is free to reject. These principles reflect the desire of social workers to escape from the authoritarian positions in which they found themselves in the past.

Another reason for increasing the area of freedom surrounding the casework relationship derives from the effect of psycho-analytic ideas on casework. If, as it is argued, unconscious motivations play a considerable part in human action, then the attempt to control and direct behaviour on the conscious level is bound to meet with failure.

Thus many social workers have seen and still see their role as a more or less independent one based on the freedom surrounding the client–professional relationship; here the client brings to the professional a problem for which he desires the solution. Although placing this problem in the hands of the professional, the client is free to withdraw from the relationship if he likes; an example of this kind of relationship, which many social workers appear to have in mind as an acceptable model, is that of the private psychiatrist–client relationship.

But, as many commentators have pointed out, this scarcely fits the facts of social work practice, and of client–worker relationships, at least in the British situation. The client must eventually, if not initially, be identified as having a problem which is not just his own but is the concern of the community and of society. Thus the "appropriateness" or "usefulness" of ways of functioning imply certain social standards or norms. There will be some idea or model of "social health" towards which clients, in one way or another, will be directed. Thus contemporary casework may not be basically very different from what has gone before. As Leonard[11] suggests, "the whole of social work is pervaded with concepts such as maladjusted, deviant, abnormal and neurotic, which are the modern judgemental equivalents of the older concept of good, bad, deserving and undeserving". Timms[12] points out that "self-determination often becomes 'best self-determination' ". Halmos[13] suggests that the caseworker's attempt to escape from a non-directive role may be a way of allaying anxiety about being "found in possession" of moral preferences. Greenwood,[14] in the American context, states that social work treatment is "concerned with action and change. It therefore belongs among the controlling agencies of society. Social workers by virtue of their technical knowledge and community sanction status possess a form of power which they exercise to reach certain ends."

Social workers have been the first to stress the limitations which beset such principles. They are seen more as ideals by which it is believed the goals of casework may be accomplished rather than principles which can be applied in all situations. Social workers, like any practitioner, must at times take decisions with and on behalf of their clients in relation to some assumed norm of behaviour. There will, therefore, be limits to the extent to which clients can in fact determine their own actions. Again, acceptance does not imply condonation of the client's actions. As Hollis[10] comments: "acceptance must not be confused with refraining from evaluating the appropriateness or usefulness of the client's ways of functioning. Self-determination does not mean the caseworker plays a passive role."

One way out of this apparent conflict between professional principles and the facts of the situation has been by the adoption of the idea of the social worker functioning within the agency or organization. "Agency function" implies the translation of such principles into practice and the identification of the goals of the social worker with the goals of the agency. Thus social workers could escape from the conflicts between the principles of casework and the realities of the casework relationship in agencies whose function was to control deviants' behaviour. There was a clear link established between the social worker, the agency, and the wider society; as Winnicott[15] expresses it, "in functioning within an agency a social worker, as well as being a trained professional person who uses her knowledge and skill to help people, also becomes something in relation to her clients on behalf of the whole community".

An important implication of this "agency-function" doctrine has been to narrow down the concern of the social worker to the individual and the immediate family situation and to ignore the wider social context in which social problems may have their origins. The social control aspect of the social worker's functions can perhaps best be understood by looking in more detail at the agency setting in which the social worker is employed. As Taylor[9] suggests, although the problems which are brought to the agency are ones of individual functioning, they are basically the concern of the whole community. The social worker's task can be seen as centring on the removal of the handicaps which prevent the individual from measuring up to the community standards. The agency is thus part of the way in which the community seeks conformity from its members and thus agency policy must reflect this. Social workers, because of their roles within the agency, must follow such policy and therefore become, in their treatment of clients, agents of the agency and therefore of society. Social workers thus become part of the way society secures conformity to expectations, and in this sense have social control functions. "The agency", Taylor states, "is by its very institutional structure and function, normative, evaluative and judgemental." One distinction that can be made, however, is between coercive and persuasive control. The former can be accompanied by the use of a threat of force, while the latter operates informally through the standards and wishes of groups which the individual is asked to accept.

In Britain many social workers function within statutory agencies, which are part of society's way of dealing with social problems. Here the local authority department administers statutes relating to areas such as child care and mental health, which represent society's attitude to such problems. These agencies are responsible in the last resort to a committee composed of lay representatives of the community.

Handler's[16] study of three children's departments in London clearly showed the crucial difference between the psychiatrist–patient and child care officer–client relationship. The main differences were that the casework agency dispensed rewards and benefits that families needed. These included the power to prevent family breakdown by casework and assistance in cash or kind. These powers were often used to get families to accept certain minimum community standards. The agency also constituted an important part of what has previously been described as the "manifest control structure", including judicial administration, the police, and the Ministry of Social Security. Children's departments have the power to bring children before the courts, to prevent the return of children to their parents; they are often seen as extensions of police authority through involvement with parents who are suspected of neglect or delinquency. In the minds of others, the social workers involved represent established authority and are seen to have extensive powers. Authority can either be exercised directly, by the threat of punitive sanctions, or indirectly by the granting or withholding of benefits in kind or cash; these latter sanctions can be used to change standards of behaviour in family or work situations. This coercive position relates not so much to the social worker involved but to the position in which the agency is placed in the control structure which gives it enormous power over clients.

The distinction made previously between persuasive and coercive control is in most casework situations one of degree only. Some casework situations are, as illustrated, highly authoritarian, but so, too, in a more subtle way are those in which authoritarian elements are not clearly present. Although in an earlier chapter it was noted that one characteristic of the therapeutic situation was that overt power and authority were suspended, it is possible that in casework a more subtle and bewildering kind of power has been put in its place. This can be seen where the caseworker encourages the client to talk about certain parts of his problem but not others. Responses from the caseworker such as grunting, smiles, sighs, or long pauses, appear likely to be interpreted by the client in one way or another to mean approval or disapproval of attitudes or actions. Thus the social worker, despite all attempts to the contrary, can hardly hope to play a non-directive role when face to face with the client, because this would mean suspending many of the conditions which surround any social relationship, whether or not it is a professional one. Clearly the degree of flexibility with which each client is handled will vary from social worker to social worker and agency to agency. However, the caseworker will always have a model of right functioning in her mind against which the responses and behaviour of the client are measured, and, moreover, the power (backed by community sanction) to enforce this in the last resort.

## CONTROL, CONSENSUS, AND CONFLICT

Much of the thinking about the functions of social work and the role of the social worker has rested on an acceptance of a particular model of society and of social organization which suggests a fundamental consensus about social values underlying the social system, and which allows for an interpretation of the social work task as one of helping to hand on accepted values to individuals and groups who have been insufficiently socialized into society and its value system;[12] thus social work clients are seen in terms of "failure" or "deviance" or "maladjustment", to which the answer is a resocialization of the individual in the direction of accepted values.

But relatively little consideration is given to the alternative model which stresses dissension and conflict and sees society as one of opposing group and opposing value systems. One form of this conflict is class conflict. Thus an alternative account of the control functions of social work is to see such control as exercised not on behalf of a unitary system of values for which there is general consensus and legitimacy, but on behalf of the values of a dominant or superordinate group in respect of some subordinate group or groups. Marx saw such domination as rooted in the capitalist system of production, in which the class with power of ownership in such a system was able to establish a dominant set of values and to seek legitimacy for them. Conflict became inevitable where the legitimacy of the situation was challenged and where the subordinate class attempted to gain positions of power by the use of force. This could only occur in a situation of class consciousness to which, as already shown, there are many obstacles. Again dominant groups would seek to reduce the likelihood of conflict and to protect their position. One way in which this could be achieved is by the creation of social or welfare services which, whilst not seeking to upset the distribution of power or wealth, would provide palliatives for social problems arising from social inequality between classes. Such social services are commonly seen, in the light of this approach, as stratagems by which the privileges of the dominant group are kept intact.[17] One of these services is social work, where one of the tasks is to deal with individual problems arising from the underprivileged stratum. Here individuals may come into conflict with the prevailing value system. One group of social workers have described themselves as "props to mask and perpetuate the under-lying injustices and inequalities of an acquisitive society".[18] In this analysis social work represents the interests and power of the dominant ruling class. Thus Taylor[9] comments that "the case-worker must help the client to know the real world, that is the dominant community values as they affect him". Leonard[11] suggests that social work can be seen as "a means by which society can ensure that underprivileged individuals are manipulated into adjusting to their position in society".

As already shown, the growth of institutions which manage or institutionalize class conflict as well as the increased affluence of the working class have challenged the Marxist thesis at a number of vital points. Although it is difficult to see the classes as confronting each other in the sense to which Marx referred, the clients of social workers represent more quasi group, a class in itself, and in Britain at least do not represent a group in fundamental opposition to the established order. However, both in the United States and in Britain there is evidence that such quasi groups are beginning to show greater signs of solidarity and opposition to the established order, and it thus becomes more difficult for social workers and others to seek the adjustment of individuals representing this stratum to the existing social system. In America social workers have had difficulty in formulating a response to this kind of challenge, e.g. from the civil rights movement. But this movement has been in little doubt about its attitude to social work and social workers, which have been dismissed as agents of a hostile *status quo*.[19]

In Britain also such groups appear to be growing in strength, although most are still in their infancy.[20] Although middle-class pressure groups such as the Child Poverty Action Group now have an established position, organized groups of underprivileged clients (e.g. Mothers in Action, an organization of unmarried mothers) are only just beginning to emerge. The extension of community work, the development of twilight zones in the cities, and the growth of an underprivileged immigrant population may all be factors in this awakening. The advantages such organizations could enjoy include the fact that they, rather than the middle class, are the recipients of inadequate welfare provisions. Their voice is thus all the more powerful. Again, because of the vast potential membership of these organizations, the possibility of disseminating information about the social services, including clarifying the rights of underprivileged citizens to appeal against official decisions, is very considerable. The implications of the growth of such client organizations for social work will be considered in the following chapter.

Alternatively, the conflict situation can be seen again in terms of the control of deviance and of the deviant act. If deviance is seen as behaviour at variance with dominant groups and their values, then the control behaviour which results will seek to legitimize the established order. One way this legitimation process can work is by defining a deviant or rebel as maladjusted, abnormal, or mentally ill. Laing[21] has suggested that where an individual is so defined, particularly in cases of schizophrenia, it is that society, or groups within it, have defined his values as wrong and threatening, and that the values that he rebels against are by definition right. Such a decision then takes on a political guise, and needs to be seen and understood in the context of the whole of civic society and of the political order, and of the control of behaviour within that wider context. So far deviance and its control has been seen in micro-sociological terms as, for example, the exclusion of the individual from the family or other small group. Here, on the other hand, is an approach which stresses the macro-sociological view of deviance and its control. Such a view has been developed again by Scheff,[22] who has enlarged upon the approach to mental illness already taken by writers such as Laing, Lemert, and Goffman. This approach sees mental illness as part of a social rather than an individual system. Scheff suggests that mental illness, and the definition of certain persons as mentally ill, has a part to play in maintaining certain ideas about society, and becomes integrated into the psychological make up of individuals. Stereotypes or bundles of psychological attitudes about mental illness, like racial stereotypes, are important points for social comparisons and self-evaluation. For example, discreditable references to Negroes fulfil, in the southern states of North America, functions for the white population because they brand a Negro as someone different, a group outside the normal society and by definition inferior. Similarly, references to mental illness also fulfil such functions by giving the individual a point of reference in comparison to evaluate his own position. Thus Scheff comments: "In the United States the average citizen resists changes in his concept of insanity or, if he is in the middle class, in his concept of mental disease because these concepts are functional for maintaining his customary moral and cognitive world."[22]

## CONFLICT REGULATION

In thinking of the complex relationship between the values of the social work profession and those of society it is important to consider the idea that social work constitutes a more neutral approach to such issues as conflict. One of the ways of interpreting the functions of social work and the welfare institutions is in terms of regulation of group or class conflict and the establishment and maintenance of a form of consensus. Here the assumption remains of groups in conflict over power, authority, or economic resources. But such conflict goes on within a broad framework of consensus. This consensus is maintained by certain regulators of conflict.[23] Conflict regulation is related not to the root causes of conflict, e.g. the abolition of social inequality, but to the expressions of such conflict and their regulation. Before regulation can operate the following factors are required: (1) recognition of the reality of conflict by both parties; (2) that the groups concerned are relatively well organized; (3) that both parties should agree to a set of formal rules that constitute a framework for regulation.

Conflict regulation takes various forms including quasi-parliamentary institutions and intervention from outside the conflicting groups in the form of third parties to the dispute, as for example in many cases of industrial conflict. Such forms of conflict regulation include conciliation, mediation, and arbitration which may be seen as operating as a succession of stages in each of which a degree of compulsion on one or other party to accept decisions grows. Entirely compulsory decisions run the risk of one party being dominated by an outside group or agency, e.g. the Government.

Although it is necessary to be cautious about extending the use of such a model, which has been developed for the analysis of industrial conflict, to institutions such as social work, some recent research by Rex and Moore[24] in a central area of Birmingham has suggested that social work may, in fact, play such a third-party function. In the Sparkbrook area of Birmingham, in which there were a majority of Irish, West Indian, and Pakistani immigrants within an indigenous English working class area, conflict centred mainly around the scarce resource of domestic property. In their study of interaction between the conflicting groups, the authors traced the growth of institutions of conflict regulation based on the growing recognition of conflict, the increased organization of groups, and an agreement to a formal set of rules to regulate such conflict. One major regulating institution was the Sparkbrook Community Association on which all groups were represented and which provided the main avenue for channelling grievances and complaints. To this association a trained social worker had been appointed, and many social workers in the area belonged to it. The tasks facing the social worker in this situation were "to understand the problems of a community in conflict, to have a shrewd political sense and to be able to act as a representative of the community".[24] In fact the social worker was able to play an important part in the fight back of the community against demoralization due to conflict. Here the function of the Sparkbrook Association, and of social work and community organization in general, was one of tension management. This function did not represent the "integrating" of various ethnic groups, a process which was in fact rejected by many of these groups, but ensured instead that the various groups represented were able to ventilate their grievances and to use the association and its services. In particular the staff of the association applied social work or bureaucratic categories to the problems of the area rather than racialist ones. In particular, they helped to restructure the interpretation of the situation by the indigenous English community along non-racist lines. Without the association many English residents of the area would have been members of an overtly racist organization. This function, and the community development approach which was adopted, therefore represented not the resolution of this kind of conflict, but the attempts to find a degree of consensus and of common interests as well as identifying and classifying diverse interests.

Finally, an alternative way of looking at the relationship between conflict groups and the emergence of welfare institutions is, as Rex[17] suggests, to see such institutions as belonging neither to the dominant bourgeoisie nor to the proletariat but to the social system of the truce itself. So far the emergence of conflict groups has been traced but little has been said about the nature of the conflict situation itself. Conflict can take several forms. There is, first, the ruling-class situation: here a dominant power group will attempt to get the legitimacy of its rule accepted by other groups. However, changes in the balance of power may occur which may result in either complete revolution and the replacement of the hitherto dominant group or some sort of compromise between them. This can be described as the revolutionary situation. However, this will imply a totally new social order. A third alternative arises where the old ruling class adjusts itself quickly to the new balance of power and gives up certain goals in exchange for a diminution of conflict and an avoidance of total revolution. Here the social values and accompanying institutions which emerge are of neither class, but are a product of the truce situation itself which opens up an area of limited co-operation between the classes. For example, the new institutions of welfare which may emerge belong to the truce situation rather than to either the ruling class or the proletariat. This interpretation offers an alternative to the purely Marxist view of welfare institutions as stated above. Out of the truce situation it is possible that a new unitary society will emerge as conflicts are forgotten, and such institutions will then come to be accepted by all. Alternatively, the old ruling class may take advantage of the weakening of morale to reassert its powers. Thus a balance of power is required if the truce is to remain, which poses conflicts for individuals and groups who will be under pressure to maintain such a balance. This situation may also have implications for the character of welfare institutions. For example, the ambivalence of social work as an institution might be explained by its existence as part of the truce situation in which participation with both sides in the conflict is necessary if the truce is to be maintained. Thus social work "faces both ways" in its advocacy of therapy or individual measures to ameliorate social problems and reform, or structural changes which would seek to eradicate these problems at their source. The uneasiness of the truce situation itself thus lends this kind of ambivalence to the institutions of the truce.

## NOTES AND REFERENCES

1. For one account see A. J. Kahn, The functions of social work in the modern world, in Kahn (ed.), *Issues in American Social Work*, Columbia Univ. Press, New York, 1959.
2. N. Timms, The role of the social worker, *New Society*, 3 Sept. 1964.
3. H. Wilensky and C. Lebeaux, *Industrial Society and Social Welfare*, Russell Sage Foundation, New York, 1958.
4. H. Leichter and W. Mitchell, *Kinship and Casework*, Russell Sage Foundation, New York, 1967.
5. P. Leonard, Social change and the social work profession, *Medical Social Work* **21** (3) (June 1968).
6. L. Rapoport, *Creativity in Social Work*, Smith College Studies in Social Work, June 1968.
7. A. Cohen, *Deviance and Control*, Prentice-Hall, N.J., 1966.
8. See J. Gould and W. Kolb, *A Dictionary of the Social Sciences*, Tavistock, London, 1964, and G. Duncan Mitchell, *A Dictionary of Sociology*, Routledge, London, 1968.
9. R. Taylor, The social control functions in casework, *Social Casework*, **39** (1) (Jan. 1958.)
10. F. Hollis, *Casework: A Psycho-social Therapy*, Random House, 1964.
11. P. Leonard, *Sociology in Social Work*, Routledge & Kegan Paul, London, 1966.
12. N. Timms, *Social Casework*, Routledge & Kegan Paul, London, 1964.
13. P. Halmos, *Faith of the Counsellors*, Constable, London, 1965.
14. E. Greenwood, Social Science and Social Work; a theory of their relationship, *Social Serv. Rev.* **29** (1955).

15. C. Winnicott, Casework and agency function, *Case Conference*, 1962.
16. J. Handler, The coercive children's officer, *New Society*, 3 Sept. 1968.
17. J. Rex, *Key Problems in Sociological Theory*, Routledge & Kegan Paul, London, 1963.
18. Socialist Medical Association, *A Socialist View of Social Work* (1965).
19. B. Davies, The jolt to U.S. social work, *New Society*, 25 May 1967.
20. R. Holman, Client Power, *New Society*, 31 Oct. 1968.
21. R. Laing, What is schizophrenia?, *New Left Review*, No. 28, 1964.
22. T. Scheff, *Being Mentally Ill*, Weidenfeld & Nicholson, 1966.
23. R. Dahrendor, *Class and Class Conflicts in an Industrial Society*, Routledge & Kegan Paul, London, 1959.
24. J. Rex and R. Moore, *Race, Community and Conflict*, O.U.P., London, 1967; see also R. Moore, Reluctant hosts, *New Society*, 9 Feb. 1967.

# CHAPTER 9

# The Social Functions of
# Social Work — Social Change

## INTRODUCTION

The subject of social change is not introduced here for the first time. Changes within the family and the class system have been discussed in some detail. These represent changes in sub-systems, but change can also be discussed at the level of the social system as a whole. The subject of change occupies a central part of the sociologist's concern and is one of the most difficult problems which he faces. One difficulty is that change is part of any social phenomenon and cannot, without difficulty, be discussed as a separate issue.

One way of simplifying the subject is to distinguish between the character, direction, and consequences of change and the various factors and mechanisms which produce change.

## THE DIRECTION OF CHANGE

The analysis of the development of society from simple to more complex forms has been central to the work of sociologists from the very early days of the subject to the present time. One influential writer was Tonnies (1855–1936),[1] who compared a form of social organization or collectivity described as "community" (*gemeinschaft*), in which members were bound to each other by social contacts in everyday activities, such as those in family units or small villages or towns, with "association" (*gesellschaft*), in which members were bound by rational interests and which is organized for specific purposes. In modern societies community relationships give way progressively to the rational and calculative relationships characteristic of large cities, in which, for example, links of kinship have been partly replaced by other relationships.

Another way of describing change is by the use of a rural–urban continuum in which an attempt is made to distinguish the characteristics of each type. An example of this approach, based on British community studies, is that of Frankenburg.[2] Here the concern is not so much with an historical comparison between a rural past and an urban present as with understanding important features of these systems which may exist together in the same society.

Replacement of community by association, and of rural by urban characteristics, has in the eyes of some commentators meant the destruction of vital social ties and has provided the basis for anomie and social disorganization, in particular in certain areas of large cities. Here there has been a breakdown in commonly held norms and in social control; in short a decline in community relationships, which has resulted in social deviance and in the dependence of some individuals and families on the social services and on social workers. In consequence, social policies have often been based on the idea of reconstituting community as a basis for social regeneration; this idea has formed the basis of town planning schemes and of policies for care of the old and of the mentally ill.

However, other writers have pointed out that the theories on which such policies are based often grossly oversimplify the situation. As Nisbet has recently suggested,[3] in a discussion of the "unit ideas" of sociology, there is always stress on elements (like "community") which relate to a stable, well-integrated society of the past by contrast to the disorganization of modern industrial societies. But this view may be based on a series of fallacies and misconceptions about the past (did community, in the sense referred to above, really exist?), and conjures up a jaundiced and inaccurate view of the present which provides an inadequate basis for social policy.

It is also important to assess the extent to which changes in one important aspect of society, e.g. technology, has repercussions throughout the system. Thus as technology grows education may be forced to reflect the needs of an advanced technological society, and this may also be true of other institutions such as social work. On the other hand, it is possible that such sub-systems may have a considerable degree of autonomy and may resist the demands of the economic system; thus the educational system may nurture values which are in opposition to economic needs and to technical advances and therefore may set up a resistance to these kinds of changes.

## SOURCES OF CHANGE

Sociologists have generally rejected the idea of any one factor as a determinant of change and emphasize a multi-factor approach, where the problem is to identify the strength and interrelationship of differing factors. For example, it is clear that technological factors have been of considerable importance in the process of industrialization; however, what are the conditions which have given rise to such innovations, and which have been favourable to the emergence of innovating personalities?

One view of change is as the adaptation of parts of a system to one another, or of a total system to its natural and social environment.

This kind of approach emphasizes the interrelationship between the parts of a society and suggests that change is a process of differentiation of functions by which new agencies emerge to perform specialized functions for society, as in the development of specialized agencies of social control outlined in the previous chapter. Each society is faced with the problem of survival and, it is argued, a differentiated system has greater powers to survive than a simple and undifferentiated one.

This approach has been opposed by those who argue that a theory which accounts for the integration of society cannot explain change. Change can only be explained by accepting the idea of conflict rather than integration. Thus change can occur as a result of group conflict, e.g. between social classes, which leads to the emergence of a new social order. Conflict will also depend on the extent to which "tension management" functions are performed.

Another way of understanding change is by stressing the fluidity of norms in a society rather than the rigid adherence to rules and regulations which is suggested by the idea of the internalization of norms and cultural values through socialization; thus norms may be so generally expressed that innovating behaviour is possible because individuals are able to interpret their role in a variety of ways. Again, strains or tensions can develop in a society which are dysfunctional for the system as a whole and thus can create pressure for change.

## SOCIAL WORK AND SOCIAL CHANGE

The relationship between social work and social change has already been outlined at the beginning of the previous chapter. Social work is one way of managing the social problems which are generated by rapid change, and can also help to promote changes desired by society. Social work can, through its own system of values, help to influence the course of change in a way which is independent of the requirements of society. It is important to see social work as one of the institutions which create, as well as conserve or promote, cultural elements.

One way in which the relationship between social work and social change can be illustrated is by reference to the values of social work, i.e. the generalized ends or purposes which are sought by social workers. These values will influence not only the part played by social work in the promotion of changes required by society, but also the kind of independent and creative role that social work can play as a moulder of culture.

Halmos[4] suggests that there are four main components to the welfare ideology on which social work rests; these can be traced historically but are in no sense distinctive or separate and interpenetrate in a number of ways. The first component is Christian charity, aimed at helping and inspiring the individual as a person of unique spiritual value through moral, religious, and material sanctions or aid; the second component is socialist egalitarianism; the third material progressivism and technological utopianism; and the fourth is psycho-analytical, psychiatric, and clinical humanism.

One approach has been to relate the value system of social work to the values of the capitalist economic system of production. It has been suggested, for example, that self-reliance, self-responsibility, self-determination, the need to achieve, and other economic traits are part of the value system of social work, but are also necessary characteristics if the capitalist system is to work.[5] Social workers, by encouraging these kinds of characteristics in their clients, are thereby functioning to support changes which will be favourable to the development of such a system. For example, social-work efforts in the anti-poverty drive in the United States are directed towards enabling the poor to overcome their own limitations, or those of their environment, and stand on their own feet. In the British children's departments studied by Handler[6] there was concern with the work records of clients; efforts were made to obtain better work records by the withholding of rewards such as the payment of bills; in the eyes of these agencies "failure to earn a living was a form of deviant behaviour". The encouragement of traits which will be favourable to this kind of economic system can be seen most clearly in social work with families. One of these characteristics, as already described, is a small, mobile, tightly knit, and independent nuclear family in which the motivation to achieve is maximized. A family organized in this way is thus "functional" to the development and maintenance of this kind of industrial system. There is evidence that social workers attempt to encourage these characteristics in their work with families. For example, in the study of family casework in a New York agency[7] it was found that a common factor in casework treatment was the goal of restricting contact with kin. In attempting to explain this, one possibility is that the caseworker may be acting as an agent for a particular set of values and is attempting to restructure the family norms of their clients in particular directions. Thus restriction of kin contact is likely to strengthen marital and parent–child relationships, thus promoting a more cohesive nuclear group. Kin ties which are wider than the nuclear family are, on the other hand, likely to result in a less cohesive nuclear family partly because of the greater number of affective social obligations which then exist. The needs of an industrial society will be met less well by this latter form of family organization. Another situation in which the social worker helps the family to adapt to new requirements is in the case of the large-scale redistribution of working-class families from cities to new towns and housing estates. Wilson[8] has shown how social work can help in the adaptation of behaviour to these new situations and describes the syndrome of problems which faces families in such situations of rapid transition.

Social work has, so far, been viewed as a sub-system which performs functions on behalf of the wider social system. But social work also has a degree of independence and stands for values and goals which may represent a critique of the dominant value system. This may in itself be an important source of change or influence on the direction of change. Thus in industrial societies where success and achievement are emphasized, an institution such as social work which, it is suggested, shows concern for social failure and which purports to accept the individual irrespective of his achievements, stands out as a sharp reminder of the dysfunctions of such a society.[9] This view contrasts distinctively with the previous conception of social work as a means of promoting welfare capitalism.

The social worker's concern for "failure" has been subjected to considerable comment and analysis. At its most abstract, this concern is expressed as the need to foster man's emotional or inner growth in the face of more rapid developments in material culture. Thus Younghusband[10] contrasts the tremendous development of material culture and technology with the less rapid growth in man's emotional life. By emotional growth is meant the capacity to pass through the stages of self-love to the further stage of love of others and of the world in general. This also includes, according to Younghusband, the constructive use of aggression, the achievement of self-identity, and a fusion of conscious and unconscious elements in the personality. Broadly, a love–achievement axis can be contrasted to a hate–hostility axis. The danger is, in the modern world where change has proceeded discontinuously and elements have got out of step with one another, that individually and collectively man will topple over on to the hate–hostility axis. Essentially, the broad task of social work is to make the process of change less discontinuous by fostering emotional or "inner" growth, in particular the capacity for disinterested "love", in the face of the materialism created by technology.

This concern for the growth of "love" and its triumph over "hate" has been analysed in some detail by Halmos in a study of all the counselling professions,[11] including psychiatrists, psychoanalysts, and clinical psychologists. He sees "love" as part of the "faith" of the counsellors, with often unacknowledged roots in religious feeling and psycho-analytical theory. In addition, this "faith" has far-reaching social influences on the moral and cultural climate of modern societies. Not only is the counsellor able to exert influence directly through the therapeutic worker–client relationship, but can extend moral influence in a deliberate fashion through the handling of colleagues and officials. The psychiatric social worker in the child guidance clinic will be in touch with local headmasters, and the medical social worker may perform therapeutic functions for the whole hospital. Again, although the counselling professions developed in an atmosphere of disillusion with political solutions, the counsellor will not miss the chance of influencing decisions about matters (such as mental health or the family) which are his everyday concern, even though such influences will not amount to a coherent political ideology. In these various ways, together with influences disseminated through the mass media, the counselling ideology will permeate to the rank and file of society. When such influences bear directly upon cultural or political leaders, they will be all the stronger.

The professional training of social workers constitutes a particularly powerful means by which the counselling ideology is passed on. The student in the school or department of social work will be heavily exposed to this ideology and may see his teachers as its major interpreters. The method of close tutorial supervision, which is often not confined to a purely educational context, is an

important mechanism for the transmission of such ideas. The influence of tutors on students, and through them on the wider
society, is therefore important. As Halmos puts it:

> A professional career of thirty or forty years in support of certain
> principles, preferences and practices may not be regarded as a decisive
> contribution to social change on a grand scale, but multiply this contribu-
> tion by the number of social workers trained by all the schools of social
> work and it may appear that the philosophical and social science principles
> informing the training of social workers are of sufficient moment for us
> to look upon training . . . as a political and ideological operation of some
> importance.[4]

Essentially, according to Halmos, the counselling ideology expresses belief in the need for self-knowledge as a means to the
acceptance and non-judgement of others, thus freeing counselling
from the charitable and self-seeking influences of the past. At the
same time, counselling stresses man's social needs, his needs for
others. Thus self-knowledge leads to concern for and acceptance of
others. The paradoxical nature of this ideology, the aims of both
objectivity and compassion, are evident. But their influence on
modern society, particularly towards a growth in fair mindedness
and a new form of idealistic intellectual frankness, can hardly be
doubted.

Critics of the counselling ideology often stress the undermining
of traditional morality, and charge that man is pampered, cor-
rupted, and made irresponsible by such aims. But the resemblance
between certain parts of the counselling ideology and some traditional, particularly Christian, beliefs, suggests rather that counselling
has reinforced such beliefs and has given traditional morals a kind of
clinical and psychological respectability. Such beliefs are not, of
course, referred to directly, but the aim of "helping people to help
themselves" awakens certain ecclesiastical echoes. In social work and
casework theory the influence of individuals such as Tillich and
Biestek is well known. The latter, a member of the Society of
Jesus, is the author of a standard casework text. The convergence
between counselling and Christianity is particularly close where
institutions such as the family are concerned. The belief in the value

of marriage, in the need to strengthen family relationships, and so on are much in evidence. The function of the Family Discussion Bureau (now the Institute of Marital Studies), for example, is "to prevent marriage breakdown".[11] This general concern with the stability of certain forms of marital and family life has a considerable, and possibly not accidental, resemblance to the moral influence of Christianity.

Although other forms of psychological theory are growing in influence, particularly those concerned with behaviourism and learning theory, Halmos points to the fact that counsellors have in the main rejected such mechanistic psychology in favour of vitalistic psychology of a mainly psycho-analytic kind which fits more adequately into the counsellors' world view of the triumph of love over hate.

In a more recent development of his theory, Halmos[12] suggests that the ideology of the personal service professions are beginning to influence professions concerned with impersonal service (professions such as engineers, architects, and lawyers) which are not concerned primarily with changing the personality of the client. As the professions grow in numbers and influence, so does the influence of the counselling ideology. Increasingly the interpretations of social reality made by members of the counselling professions are accepted by members of other professions; thus the former become the expert moral tutors whose authority in the field of human relations is accepted and whose dictas are passed on through professional education.

This suggests, again, that the counsellors, the purveyors of the personal service ideology, are not a residual and unimportant category but, instead, constitute a major influence on the occupational and social system.

Although Halmos' thesis is of exceptional interest and penetration, it is important to remember the speculative nature of much of what is being said. Essentially such propositions require further testing by research on counsellors "in action". A survey of the literature of any professional group or groups must inevitably discover the views of opinion leaders within those groups and may be inadequate to describe the activities of professionals in the field. Thus the extent to which the counselling ideology has permeated to all workers may be variable. Social work in particular, with its large number of untrained workers, may stand in sharp contrast to the other counselling groups. But with the rapid development of social-work training a distinctive counselling ideology may emerge in the future. Social work may also differ from the other counselling groups because of the extent to which it has been influenced by sociological as well as psycho-analytic theory. Again, the convergence between Christianity and counselling and the assimilation of religious elements into the counsellor's ideology cannot be entirely substantiated. The two ideologies may be in conflict at several points. As Martin points out,[13] social work may provide for the individual a frustrating alternative to the ministry because of its tendency to cloak the essentials of religious faith in professional and technical language and in its tendency to be excessively concerned with its own status and prestige in relation to other occupational groups.

## SOCIAL WORK AND SOCIETY

A two-way relationship between society and social work has been sketched out. Social work performs functions for society and, through its own system of values, gives a particular character and form to these tasks. In recent years in Britain the number and magnitude of such functions has increased until there are few aspects of the welfare services in which social workers are not involved. In recent years social workers have been asked to consider additional functions in relation to such diverse situations as the breakdown of marriage, children and their schools, and community problems. Society, it appears, has "discovered" social work, its ideology, and its methods, and is applying them to a range of situations and problems which before were the province of professions and institutions such as education and the law.

There is little doubt that social work, far from performing "residual" functions, is fast becoming itself one of the major welfare institutions of a modern society. This is the goal for which many social workers have also been striving; it is hoped by some that contacts with the social worker will in the future be accepted as part of the lives of individuals in the same way as visits to the dentist or the doctor.[14] The domestic adjustments which have been occurring in social work (such as the movement for a more unified professional organization) reflect not simply a desire for increased professional status, but results from the increasing importance of social work in society.

This change partly reflects, as Halmos[11] suggests, the discrediting of political or utopian solutions and the growing belief that measures which do not contain an element of personal counselling are of little avail.

But traffic between social work and society has for the most part been one way; social work has responded rather neutrally to society's requirements and has largely been unable to invest its functions with a distinctive character.[15] The kinds of tasks assigned to social work and the way in which these have been approached have been determined largely by forces external to social work. This may relate to the fragmented administrative contexts in which social work is carried on, to the lack of a fully trained corps of workers, and to other factors which make social workers a rather weak pressure group.

The relatively weak position of social work has raised a number of problems and dilemmas for social workers. Some of these derive from the general relationship between social work and the culture of capitalism.[16] Features of this culture have not only been responsible for the strains and social problems which social workers have to face, but have also influenced responses to such problems. Historically, the most obvious effect of individualism and of the market economy was to restrict social legislation which attempted to deal with such problems as poverty. Problems of this kind were associated with personal inadequacy, and in its initial stages social-work practice derived from this belief. The first social-work agencies in both Britain and America existed within a culture which emphasized self-reliance and self-responsibility.

Thus the response to social problems has always been an uneasy compromise between the values of humanitarianism and security, on the one hand, and self-reliance and competitiveness on the other. In spite of the development of modern welfare states, this uneasy compromise still exists. Social work appears part of this compromise in that it stresses security and humanitarianism and values the individual apart from his achievements, yet is forced to acknowledge and accept the values of a capitalist industrial society. Thus social work has been employed as one of the means of mitigating the worst effects of a capitalist market economy and of softening the blows delivered to those who have "failed" by a society dominated by profit and property owning. Yet at the same time social-work agencies have, according to one recent account,[17] philosophies little different from the past, and measure "success" by the extent to which clients have been helped to achieve the minimum standards necessary in a market-dominated economy. Thus while comforting the failures, social work acts also as a bridge back into a race which most of its clients cannot hope to win.

Again, there is the danger that society will see in social work a rationale for its problems and that social workers will be asked to collude with society that a panacea may have been found for them in the personal social services. As Rea Price[15] suggests: "The caseworker's approach is one which consoles, which detects the problem in the individual and not in his society. The community can retreat from the complexity of it all, delegate its responsibilities to its professionals . . . and forget."

Thus the social worker becomes involved, for example, in society's ambivalent attitudes to social deviance, and is forced into a position of tacking on services which aim to reform or rehabilitate to forms of treatment which are basically retributive. The attempt is made, through social work, to absorb or rehabilitate deviants, but nothing is done about the part society has played in producing deviant behaviour; again, the repressive use of institutions such as mental hospitals and prisons goes some way to confirming society's rejection of the deviant, whilst the social worker is attempting to form a bridge back into society.

A number of factors reinforce the narrow definition given to the social work task; as social work becomes more accepted by society, and has more resources and manpower invested in it, it is likely to become more wedded to the *status quo* and thus may be forced into a conservative or compliant stance.[18] Other factors which contribute to the narrow and non-structural definitions of problems include the restrictive nature of most social-work training courses which rely in the main on traditional agency training in casework and the adoption of the agency-function approach in which the aims of the social worker and of the agency (in many cases a statutory department of a local authority) are held to be identical.

Thus the new tasks social workers are being asked to perform on behalf of society may be defined in an equally narrow way, and there may be an extension of their role as purveyors of social palliatives. In the face of the conflicts and dilemmas surrounding their position, social workers may seek either to redefine their role or may attempt to incorporate new tasks into existing and traditional ways of working.

Just as society is in the process of redefining its relationship with social work, so social workers may seek to reinterpret their own roles. They do so against the background of a new climate of protest at traditional methods and traditional solutions, which is marked by a deep distrust of authority and bureaucracy; this will clearly have an effect on social workers and there are already signs that social workers are becoming more involved with political or pressure groups, such as the Child Poverty Action Group.

The Socialist Medical Association[19] called into question some of the tasks social workers were asked to perform, in particular the substitution of social work for inadequate social services, and stated that social workers should no longer be used as palliatives for problems which should be solved at a wider structural level. The report of the Seebohm Committee, in particular in its chapter on The Community,[20] contains an important reappraisal of the role and functions of the social worker in society. The proposals call for a wider conception of social service based on the community and the whole society rather than on its social casualties. In areas where there has been a breakdown in community relationships, social work with individuals alone is unlikely to be effective; what is required are efforts to co-ordinate services in relation to the needs of particular areas. One principle of such work is the involvement of individuals and groups in determining and meeting their own needs. Community development, such as that essayed by the Sparkbrook Association, has in the past been the province of voluntary organizations, but the report recommends that this work should be undertaken by local authorities. Implicit in this idea is "citizen participation"; the consumer should help in the process of identifying needs and defective services. Thus the distinction between the receivers and donors of services is reduced and it is possible for consumers to have some control over bureaucratic and professional power. One of the implications of this is that social workers may have to move away from a narrow definition of their functions; they may become involved with the community at several levels— one of these might be in helping to form and working with client groups.[21] Here social workers could be helpful in opening up channels of communication with the local authority and of indicating the most promising lines to follow by disseminating information about social services, in particular about appeals procedure and in preventing victimization of group members. Such forms of community work may bring conflict between the social worker and the agency, and the worker may be faced with conflicting loyalties; as the Council for Training in Social Work pointed out in their evidence to the Seebohm Committee, if local authorities are to undertake this work, they "will need to recognize the fact that some of its staff may be involved in situations which lead to criticism of their services or with pressure groups about new needs".[22]

Community work represents a considerable challenge to social work for these and other reasons. The boundaries of community work are so diffuse and the number and variety of those involved so great that this constitutes a challenge to the maxim that social workers, through specialist training, have exclusive claim to skill and knowledge in particular situations.

Pressure for a redefinition of role comes from another part of the social worker's role set, the lay expert; thus one sociologist[23] greeted the Seebohm report's plans for an extension and a restructuring of social work with a clarion call to social workers to change their conception of the task—"the provision of physical services and resources and the representation of the individual and the family in the struggle to obtain resources from other departments, and not the practice of individual casework, becomes paramount."

An alternative response to the new demands made upon social workers, and the conflicts and dilemmas which surround such demands, is for these to be interpreted in the light of what is seen as the basic values and purposes of the profession. This may also imply opposition to or modification of the demands of society. For example, the widening of the functions of social work in relation to child law breakers, as envisaged in the White Paper *Children in Trouble*, implies a considerable extension of the social worker's role to the protection of society. For some social workers this runs contrary to what is conceived as the basic professional task, the demonstration of concern for underprivileged individuals. The role of "agent of social control" which society seems increasingly to press upon social work, although paradoxically an expression of society's more humane and beneficient attitudes to rule breakers, still runs contrary to much of the ideological basis of social work.

Again, the view that social workers should necessarily involve themselves in the amelioration of the conditions which form the background to situations of individual distress also runs contrary to the beliefs of some; should social workers allow themselves to be forced into new roles as social reformers, so having to abandon their primary responsibilities to individuals? In the same way, should a doctor in the casualty department of a hospital be asked to concern himself directly with the state of the roads which produce so many of the casualties he treats?[24] Thus the priority stressed by recent government reports (including Newsom, Plowden, and Seebohm) for changes in the structure of opportunities in society and the community and for the participation of social workers in such policies, runs contrary to the supreme value attached by many social workers to the aid and succour of individuals. Social work has always faced in two directions—outwards towards society and inwards towards the individual. While emphasis is moving towards the former concern, there will still be some who will stand against the stream and reaffirm more traditional values. Thus new tasks will be interpreted in the light of such values and incorporated into existing principles of practice.

Social workers are not alone in experiencing conflict of different kinds between professional values and beliefs and public duties; the professions are frequently placed in this kind of dilemma by the demands of society. Thus some doctors find it equally repugnant that society demands that they now co-operate in ending the lives of unborn babies; teachers are faced with a conflict between the demands of society for a supply of skilled labour and a belief in the inherent value of certain educational experiences.

Professions have an "identity", i.e. a conception of what constitute its right and proper tasks, which can be threatened from outside and inside. Outsiders press upon the professions certain new tasks without considering fully whether these fit into the conception which the profession has of its own role; those inside the profession may be willing to take up new tasks and abandon traditionally defined ways, but may also be resisted by colleagues who refuse to accept such redefinitions. Such pressures can blur the nature of the focal task of professions, and can threaten the distinctive identity of the professional group.[25] Social work is experiencing just such an "identity crisis"; the increased importance of social work as an institution raises questions, although not necessarily new ones, about the purposes of such work. Such questions are no longer the preserve of a small group of professionals but are the concern of society; the interests of these two elements are not necessarily congruent. At the same time some social workers are seeking to define their tasks in new ways and are questioning established professional values.

It is important for any profession to find answers to such questions and to resolve in some way these conflicts. If this does not occur, social work is likely to be indicted for such failure by society; professions are to an extent under fire, and one reason for this is that they have begun to lose some of their mystique. Increasingly such groups are seen as working to achieve or maintain status for their members rather than squaring up to the problems that face society. Social work is clearly at a crucial point in its development. The answers to the conflicts it faces depend in part on the internal structure of the profession and the kind of professional organizations that emerge, in particular the character of the new professional association and the direction which training and education for social work takes in the future. It is to a consideration of some of these issues that discussion now turns.

## NOTES AND REFERENCES

1. F. Tonnies, *Community and Association*, Routledge & Kegan Paul, London, 1955.
3. R. Nisbet, *The Sociological Tradition*, Heinemann, London, 1966.
4. P. Halmos, Problems arising in the teaching of sociology to social workers, *Int. Soc. Serv. Review*, **8** (March, 1961).
5. P. Leonard, The application of sociological analysis to social work training, *Br. J. Sociol.* **19** (4) (Dec. 1968).
6. J. Handler, The coercive children's officer, *New Society*, 3 Oct. 1968.
7. H. Leichter and Mitchell, *Kinship and Casework*, Russell Sage Foundation, New York, 1967.
8. E. Wilson, Family casework in two new towns, M.A. Thesis, University of London, 1962.
9. B. Kent, The social worker's cultural pattern as it affects casework with immigrants, *Social Work*, **22** (4) (Oct. 1965).
10. E. Younghusband, *Social Work and Social Change*, Allen & Unwin, London, 1964.
11. Cited in P. Halmos, *Faith of the Counsellors*, Constable, London, 1965.
12. P. Halmos, The personal service society, *Br. J. Sociol.*, **18** (1) (March 1967).
13. D. Martin, *A Sociology of English Religion*, Heinemann, London, 1967.
14. Association of Social Workers, *New Thinking about Administration*, London, 1966.
15. J. Rea Price, Social pathology—a dilemma for social workers, *Case Conference*, **13** (12) (1967).
16. H. Wilensky and C. Lebeaux, *Industrial Society and Social Welfare*, Russell Sage Foundation, New York, 1958.

17. Handler, *op. cit.* See also comment by A. Miles, *American Social Work Theory*, Harper, 1954: "welfare programmes are, on the one hand, a Christian expression of compassion for our fellow men, and, on the other hand, insurance for the continued operation of the profit motive": cited in T. H. Marshall, *Social Policy*, Hutchinson, 1967.

18. P. Leonard, Social change and the social work profession, *Medical Social Work*, **21** (3) (June 1968).

19. Socialist Medical Association, *A Socialist View of Social Work* (1965).

20. *Report of the Committee on Local Authority and Allied Personal Social Services* (Seebohm Report), Cmnd 3703, Chapter XVI, H.M.S.O., London, 1968.

21. R. Holman, Client power, *New Society*, 31 Oct. 1968.

22. Seebohm Report, Chapter XVI, para. 494.

23. P. Townsend, Family welfare and Seebohm; *New Society*, 1 Aug. 1968.

24. L. Bell, Department of Social Science and Social Administration, London School of Economics; address to students, North Western Polytechnic, 1968.

25. For an interesting account of similar conflicts experienced by scientists see M. King, Science and the professional dilemma, in J. Gould (ed.) *Penguin Social Sciences Survey*, 1968.

# CHAPTER 10

# The Professionalization of Social Work

## INTRODUCTION

The movement of occupations towards professional status is one of the features of modern societies. This change carries with it far-reaching implications for the individuals directly involved and for society as a whole. Social work, like teaching, is one of the occupations involved, and at the time of writing the movement towards professional status appears, in Britain, to be gaining momentum. A drive to unify what has until now been a series of specialized professional associations is afoot. This may shortly result in the establishment of one national professional association of social workers. The recent report of the Seebohm Committee[1] has recommended a new administrative structure for social work in local authorities which may provide a basis for co-operation between workers in these services and thus make way for greater professional unity. Again, one of the most important features of the past decade has been the development of training courses in a variety of educational institutions.

Despite such developments, there is perennial uncertainty and continued controversy about the professional status of social work and the basis on which this status might be attained. Criticisms of social work's claim for a separate professional status and identity have been considerable.

The question "Is social work a profession?", posed by Abraham Flexner[2] more than 50 years ago, is still a very real one in Britain, although in the eyes of at least one observer[3] can (in the American context) be answered only in the affirmative. One problem relates to the skill and knowledge generally recognized as an important attribute of any profession. What precisely are the skills required by a social worker and what are the implications of the fact that large numbers of practising social workers lack any basic training?

Again, the title "social worker" is one to which many would lay claim. A roll call of all those claiming this title would produce a motley band ranging from the professional worker trained in a university or college department of social work to others for whom social work is a spare-time activity or an adjunct to some other form of work such as teaching.

The prospect of increasing professionalization in social work is not an unmixed blessing. While this may bring advantages in the sense of increasing the quality of service to the client, and of widening the responsibilities of the profession to society, there are also disadvantages. In the unification of social work services proposed by the Seebohm Report there is also the danger of *rigor professionis*[4] —of the greater unification and co-ordination of social work services leading to a loss of contact with the community outside the profession. Thus the advantages which increased professionalization will bring for social workers, including improvements in salary and status, may bring disadvantages for others.

Thus, apart from determining the extent to which social work can obtain professional status in the recognized way, another and possibly more important question relates to the process of professionalization in any occupation, to the particular character of this movement, and to the problems and conflicts which accompany it. The question of whether or not any particular occupation constitutes a profession is, as Hughes[5] has suggested, a false and unprofitable one. Thus the emphasis in the discussion which follows will be on the nature of the professionalization process in social work and on the problems this has raised for social workers and society.

It is also important to remember that professionalization is not a process that can be considered in isolation. It is related to other processes characteristic of modern societies, including the development of a system of social classes (already discussed in Chapter 5) and of complex organizations, particularly bureaucracies. The relationship between professionalization and bureaucratization is one of the most important issues in the movement of occupations towards professional status, and is particularly important in the case of social work. This topic is discussed in the following chapter, and the two chapters on the profession and on the organizational context of social work are highly related.

It is difficult to give clear and complete answers to all the questions posed above, and this is partly because the analysis of the social work profession in Britain has scarcely begun. There is, in particular, apart from a number of studies of social work in specific areas,[6] a lack of studies which suggest a general framework[7] within which these questions might be answered, and reliance must be placed on American studies, both of a general exploratory kind and those related specifically to social work.[8]

It may be useful to begin with a brief account of the nature of the professionalization process and to outline some of the recognized constituents of a profession before going on to a discussion of social work in the light of these approaches.

## THE STUDY OF THE PROFESSIONS

One approach to the understanding of the professions is by use of the ideal type or model concept outlined in Chapter 2.[3] An ideal type or model of occupational organization can be established. This is the situation which would result if any occupation became completely professionalized. It is possible that no occupation fully measures up to this model. From this it is possible to establish for any given occupation the extent to which it exhibits specifically professional characteristics. Professionalization denotes the process by which occupations change in the direction of the elements represented by this model.

Occupations can then be thought of as distributing themselves along a continuum at one end of which are the recognized professions all of which contain professional elements to the greatest degree, at the other the least skilled and prestigious occupations. As one moves away from the purely professional end of the continuum, occupations are met which contain such professional attributes to a lesser and lesser degree.

An example of the models sociologists have built up is that of Greenwood,[9] who has distinguished five distinctive attributes which make up the professional model. They are (1) a basis of systematic theory, (2) authority recognized by the clientele of the professional group, (3) community sanction and approval of this authority, (4) a code of ethics regulating relations of professional persons with clients and colleagues, and (5) a professional culture sustained by formal professional associations and other processes (such as socialization). It will be impossible to dwell in detail on all these, and for present purposes most importance is attached to (1) and (5) in the analysis of social work that follows.

Apart from the criteria by which success or failure in the struggles of an occupation to attain professional status are judged, is it possible to delineate a particular progression of events which have led to successful professionalization? Wilensky[10] has analysed the history of eighteen occupations in the United States and suggests that these show the following sequence: (1) the full-time performance of the occupation, (2) the establishment of a training system with an academic connection with the universities, (3) the founding of a professional association, first at local then at national level, (4) legal protection of the monopoly of skill, and (5) a formal code of ethics is evolved.

Deviations from this sequence occur because of power struggles within occupations and other reasons, and the more marginal professions often get out of sequence by, for example, proclaiming codes of ethics before the basis in knowledge and organization has been achieved, and by avoiding contact with the universities. The more established professions were more likely to follow the sequence set out above than the marginal professions or the professions which had not established themselves fully.

## SYSTEMATIC BODY OF THEORY

A major condition for the distinction between professional and non-professional occupations is the possession of knowledge and skill which is not generally available. The client must recognize that he wants what the professional offers and could not do the job himself. But skill alone is not sufficient, for many occupations involve considerable degrees of skill, in some cases greater than that of professions or aspiring professions. The real distinction rests on a fund of knowledge organized into a system, which can be termed a *body of theory*. Thus acquisition of skill depends on the mastery of a body of theory which underlies it, which in turn demands education and training of a high order. This is more than apprenticeship training "on the job", and implies the prolonged study of abstract principles and theories. Thus although there is medical or legal theory, there is no theory which relates to bricklaying. One aspect of professionalization is that apprenticeship learning gives way to formal education because theories cannot be learnt entirely in a practical way; they transcend particular situations.

Again, emphasis on theory implies an occupational milieu which encourages the critical development and discussion of theory, a situation which is not in general characteristic of occupations. Implicit here is a separation of the occupation from the more general occupational structure, which is again marked out by the development of special forms of knowledge in practice.[11]

The *technical* nature of such theory does not imply that it is necessarily scientific.[10] There is a variety of theory to which different professions lay claim. The contrast between medicine, with its roots in physical and natural science, and the Church, with its theory based mainly on propositions not subject to scientific validation, suggest that there can be a wide variety of "bases" for professionalism. In a society in which science has considerable prestige, professions based on this may seem to have greater acceptance; but the power of those who are identified with the sacred must not be overlooked.

There may also be a minimum technical basis to a profession.[10]

If this cannot be attained, a major barrier to professional status may exist. The twin dangers are to have a technical basis too broad and vague so that anyone can master it; alternatively, to narrow down this basis to a set of rules which, again, most people can learn. Professions in fact have an aura of mystery surrounding them, a set of tacit assumptions, which are more than skill or theory and which function to separate the profession from the more general occupational milieu but which are difficult for the layman to learn.

## SKILL AND THEORY IN SOCIAL WORK

The acquisition of specialized skills and theory and the separation of social work from other occupational groups has been one of the most difficult steps in the movement towards professional status in social work.

The attempt to develop an exclusive knowledge based on skill and theory in social work has centred mainly on the development of casework and casework theory. This is seen as the essential way in which social work is differentiated from the more general social service milieu and its many associated occupational groups (e.g. health visitor, Ministry of Social Security officials). Essentially the development of casework theory may be seen as the basis of the claim that social work is professional in the senses referred to above. Professional training (as distinct from other preparations for social work) involves casework training, and trained caseworkers—although a minority—stand out as the *élite* in social work; casework training is the basis for admission to some professional associations. So important has casework been to the professional development of social work that, according to Wilensky and Lebeaux,[12] "it is doubtful that there would be any such identifiable entity as professional social work without it". Although casework is only one of the approaches in social work, its principles and general philosophy strongly influence other forms of social work such as group and community work.

Casework evolved, in a sense, as a reaction to the problems of poverty and distress caused by industrialization and involves essentially the translation of a range of "problems" into individual "cases", to which certain kinds of skills and knowledge are applied.[12] Initially, casework was characterized by a kind of sociological bias. Individual problems were seen in the context of the social situation of the client; even at this time, however, this "situational" approach ignored the way in which social problems had their origins in the inequalities of the social structure.[13]

But casework has become increasingly centred on the personality of the individual, and has been influenced by theories of personality derived in particular from various types of psycho-analytic theory. This has been translated into casework terms and, together with theories drawn from other schools of psychology and material from the other social sciences, makes up substantially the knowledge basis of social work. Thus an important part of the training of caseworkers consists of the study of theories and explanations of individual behaviour through courses such as Human Growth and Development, the content of which appears to be based largely on psycho-analytic explorations of behaviour. The caseworker therefore carries a strong psycho-analytic orientation in many instances and "operates on the premise that any individual facing social stresses which he cannot deal with has strengths and inner resources which, if freed from the shackles of fear, inhibition and other types of psychological blockage, will enable him to become effectively self responsible".[12]

The process by which such theory is passed on from the practice and theory of psycho-analysis itself to the various counselling sub-groups and professions has been shown by Halmos;[14] he comments that:

> Most counsellors, no matter how different their clinical and social background, develop their ideas under the influence of published psycho-analytic reflection. It is easy to show how an insight or a new explanatory concept in therapy is passed down the line, usually starting with psycho-analytical re-appraisals and ending with the social casework theoreticians translating the thing into the idiom of the social caseworker . . . and so we can follow with ease the counselling ideology of psycho-analysts reappear in the professional journals of social work.

The fact that social work stands at the end of this line does not make the influence which psycho-analysis exerts through social work any the less; rather, as is argued in the previous chapter, the interaction between the social worker, other professional workers, and the community makes social work a powerful vehicle for such views.

Some idea of the importance of this approach in casework can be gained from the high status held by the psychiatric social worker.[15] By virtue of their training requirements and their occupation of many academic and higher administrative positions, this group appear to constitute an inner *élite* within the wider *élite* of trained caseworkers. The intellectual and ideological influence of this group on social work in general appears, through their output of books and articles, to be substantial.

## CRITICISMS OF CASEWORK

Criticism of casework as a basis for professional status in social work has focused in the main on the psychological and, more specifically, psycho-analytic basis of its theory and on the issues surrounding the casework relationship.

The most vigorous critic of casework in this connection has been Wootton.[16] Criticism is directed against the "casework relationship" as such and on the minutiae of the interviewing procedures as a basis for professional recognition. In the professions such as law or medicine the relationship between client and professional is not an end in itself but a means to solving some problem the client has; a service is performed which the client requires outside and irrespective of the interview situation itself. Thus the casework relationship in itself is not seen as forming the basis of a professional service. Again, the use by the social worker of the term "client" to denote the individual who is the subject of the professional relationship cannot be equated with the use of the term by other professions, where the client engages the professional to perform services which the client himself desires and which are performed through the use of professional skills. Here the client is free to enter the professional relationship and also specifies the ends he requires. For a sizeable proportion of the clientele of social workers these conditions do not apply; the social worker acts as an agent of society and seeks ends which are those of society rather than the client. Thus the client of the probation officer has little choice about entering the professional relationship. Finally, the nature of the case is not (as in other professions) specified. In the days before psycho-analytic casework, the cases in which social workers were involved would have been mainly of financial distress. Today, cases are likely to take the form of personality problems or adjustment between the individual and society. But cases are not seen primarily in terms of needing practical help or assistance with some problem of everyday living; this no longer forms the major basis of the casework relationship.

It is important to remember that these criticisms, although extreme in the way they were made, were not of social work as such but of the development of psychologically based casework and of claims to professional status made on this basis. Thus criticisms of this type would also appear to be a more general critique of psycho-analytic theory as such and claims to professional status made on the basis of such theory by the counselling professions in general. But, in Wootton's eyes, the social worker can still claim professional status by the practise of a more legitimate skill. By re-directing efforts towards more practical and material assistance, the social worker need not "fear that she must surrender her title to professional status. On the contrary an alternative and dignified conception of social work is entirely possible and a genuine professional status as well as a genuine parallel with other professions becomes actually easier to achieve."[17] With the unprecedented growth of the social services in the modern world and their accepted role in everyday life, the need for a middle man, who fills the vacuum between the services and the public, has increased. Although some 40 years before Wootton wrote, Flexner[2] argued that the middle-man function was the main barrier to the professionalization of social work, the growth in the importance of these services constitutes (to Wootton) a new basis for professional social work. To guide the individual through the labyrinth of services thus qualifies as a professional skill in its own right.

Although Wootton's severe criticisms have often been mis-construed as a total denial of social work as a professional calling, there is little doubt that the insistence that social workers are all minor psycho-analysts is exaggerated.

Caseworkers have utilized a wider range of theory, including that drawn from the social sciences, than Wootton suggests. More particularly, social workers have to an extent re-interpreted dynamic psychological theory in their own way and feel that they can lay claim to casework theory as such, which distinguishes their work from other counselling professions. Stevenson[18] suggests that the social worker (unlike the psycho-analyst) is not attempting to explore the unconscious but instead recognizes and works with the "little pieces of the iceberg" that show above the surface. Essentially casework is based on work with the "reality" situation, or the ego, which can be made the focus of the interview and of the casework relationship. Far from encouraging the superiority which Wootton claimed accompanied the casework relationship, dynamic psy-chology and the focus on the interview situation helps remove the "they–us" dichotomy and provides protection for the client by reminding the caseworker of her own part in the process.

But by transferring attention from the unconscious to the ego, the doubts surrounding the use of these concepts are not removed. Although the "many unproven assumptions" on which such theories rest are referred to by Stevenson, the overriding case for their use by social workers lies in the view that "this body of theory has offered much concrete help to social workers in carrying out their tasks". However, the criteria of helpfulness or usefulness are not the only bases for a professional skill. What has been described as "empathic understanding",[19] or the intuitive feeling of knowing another person from the inside, may have a vivid artistic quality and give feelings of satisfaction and relief that some sense has been made of puzzling behaviour; but there is no way of knowing whether such knowledge is accurate. There may be dis-agreement between individuals about the empathic understanding of another person; if so how is it possible for caseworkers to tell which opinion is right? Here the problem of defining a satisfactory theoretical basis for social work skills becomes related to the wider problem of the scientific status of dynamic psychology.

Such criticisms have been sharpened by the increasing interest of some social workers in theories of personality which involve a more scientific approach.[20] These stress the necessity of explaining behaviour by causal laws derived from hypotheses capable of being tested. Such theories attempt more limited explanations of aspects of behaviour but are nevertheless important for the social worker because of the greater certainty with which such knowledge can be used. Another function of this approach is to prevent the practitioner adopting theories uncritically and to develop a generally scientific attitude in which feelings and beliefs can be tested and new knowledge utilized. Such an approach may be important for the professionalization of social work, for it links the social worker to the more general scientific milieu which commands high status in society and provides substantially the basis for professional practices such as medicine.

However, irrespective of the state of development of such scientific trends, it has been strongly held by Halmos[14] that the skills of the social worker (and of counsellors in general) relate, in fact, not primarily to this kind of applied science but are rather a form of faith or love. This is in fact marked by a considerable rejection of a scientific way of thought and of empiricism. This, according to Halmos, can occur in two ways—a renunciation of the complete scientific basis for counselling and the attempt to obliterate the differences between objective and subjective observation. In the case of social work, rather than a disavowal of science as such, emphasis is given to the totality of objective and subjective experience. One view is that the reality situation cannot be understood without subjectively experiencing it; it is also argued that to attempt objectivity is to escape from personal and human contact with experience into impersonality. Essentially the skill of the counsellor here is in fact in the use of the personality in the helping process, the skill lying in the use of the self; thus a flight into impersonality, objectivity, and empiricism runs contrary to one of the central tenets of counselling.

This is, of course, not to suggest that the counselling professions do not use applied science, but, according to Halmos, it is constantly reiterated that this is of no avail without "faith". Such incompatibilities and dilemmas are not peculiar to counselling. In all professional fields (e.g. medicine) action is taken with insufficient knowledge. But in the helping professions the dilemma takes on a particular character because actions cannot simply be based on applied science (whatever the state of efforts made to apply it), but involve also moral and ethical decisions and judgements. But for all professional activities there appears, as Halmos points out, "no way of getting round the conflict between the cultural climates of a scientific and a professional way of thinking and acting".[14]

But in social work the conflict between differing bases for professional claims has been considerable and may be seen as one of the barriers to professionalization. Successful identification with one or other knowledge base functions, as Wilensky[10] shows, to stake out an area of exclusive jurisdiction. But social work has vacillated between the ministry (with a doctrinal or faith orientation) and medicine (science-oriented practice) as professional models on which to base its claims.

Another barrier relates to the basis of knowledge in social work, which appears too general and vague for the achievement of exclusive jurisdiction or competence—a dilemma which faces all human relations professions. This results not only from their newness and the undeveloped state of social science "but also from the fact that the types of problems dealt with are part of everyday living. The lay public cannot recognize the need for special competence in an area where everyone is 'expert'."[10] These professions suffer, in short, from "anomie" in this case the pursuit of vaguely conceptualized and ever-retreating goals.[21]

These points can be illustrated by a brief reference to what little is known of the alternative sources of help (other than social work) which exist in the community and to the extent of public knowledge of social work and the social worker.

## ALTERNATIVE TREATMENT RESOURCES

One way of illustrating the problem of the knowledge basis of social work and the question of "exclusive competence" is to look at the way services are actually used. One focus has been on clients who disengage or drop out of treatment before it is completed. A study[22] by the Family Service Association of America in 1960 found that nearly two-fifths of cases closed in the first year of treatment resulted from the client's unwillingness to accept a treatment plan or from premature withdrawal despite a plan. The importance of this, which parallels in some ways the problem of early leaving from secondary school, lies in the threat it represents to the practitioner's claim of competence, which is based on the understanding and treatment of clients' difficulties. Mayer and Rosenblatt[23] suggest that the problem should be viewed against a background of the individual's social environment. There may be other sources of help in the community to which the client can turn. Thus one hypothesis is that the number of alternative treatment resources available to the client effect his continuance in treatment. The absence of alternatives may induce the client to remain with whoever is helping him. Alternative resources include, at the professional level, people as diverse as psychiatrists and druggists; nonprofessional helpers range from lay consultants to friends, neighbours, and kin. Even though such resources exist, the client may not consult them; he may feel, for example, that they are inappropriate to his needs or that it is wrong to bring problems to certain people, such as close kin. Again, the client is in touch not only with the caseworker but with a variety of other individuals whose views may be relevant in shaping the client's views of and attitudes to treatment. The approval of these "relevant others" (e.g. the employer) may lead to a continuation of treatment, disapproval, or discontinuation of treatment.

Evidence relating to the first hypothesis, that the greater number of treatment alternatives perceived by the client the more likely he will be to disengage from treatment, was obtained by Mayer and Rosenblatt.[24] Size of city was taken to be an indicator of the number of treatment resources available; the larger the city the greater the number of treatment resources available. Thus city size is likely to be related to the rate at which clients break off treatment; the larger the city the higher the rate of disengagement. Basing their findings on a large sample of cases and cities, the authors show that this relationship holds and that client disengagement rates rose with size of city. It is clear from this kind of study that caseworkers are not regarded by clients as possessing exclusive jurisdiction in personal problems, and that where alternative resources exist considerable shopping around will take place. Although this may also hold for other professions, it is perhaps more difficult to visualize alternative resources for those seeking help with medical or engineering problems.

## PUBLIC KNOWLEDGE OF SOCIAL WORK

Public recognition of the exclusive competence of human relations professions such as social work is also influenced by the state of public knowledge of such services. If little is known about them then, irrespective of other factors, it is likely that they will neither be recognized nor used. A small pilot study by Timms[25] aimed to discover what a group of people of different sex, age, marital status, and occupation knew about social work and what kind of person they thought a social worker was likely to be. Respondents were shown a list of different social-work occupations and asked what each person did. The best known was the probation officer of whom only 2 per cent had not heard. In the case of others widespread ignorance was evident. A third of the sample could not say what the almoner's job was, and nearly half the respondents had not heard of a child care officer nor could they say what they did. Ignorance about psychiatric social work was at an even greater level—three-quarters of the sample had not heard of them and four-fifths could not say what they did. In answer to more general questions, a third of the sample did not know what social workers did; of the remainder the majority associated them with charitable organizations or voluntary work. Thus social workers are not in the main associated with the national or local social services. Most people thought that the social worker would require details of income if help was to be given, which indicates that the social worker is still thought of as performing charitable functions. No clear idea of how a social worker is seen emerged, but a sizeable minority had a stereotype of the social worker as probably female, middle class, unmarried, and over 40. Further research[26] carried out on a group of South African students broadly confirms these findings. Although this more middle-class group had a greater knowledge of social work than Timms's sample, there was still considerable vagueness and confusion about the social worker's role. The majority viewed the clientele of the social worker as mainly the poor or those suffering from social pathology or stigma. There was little understanding that the social worker helped with problems of personal adjustment. There was, again, little specific understanding of the duties of particular social workers.

The extent of the ignorance of social work and the social worker shown by such studies appears a serious obstacle to the professional advancement of the occupation although this is a problem shared by other occupations. One important feature of full professional development appears to be the recognition by outsiders (who also form the potential clientele) of the occupational group as forming a distinctive entity within the general occupational milieu, which offers specialized services based on recognized skills.

## PROFESSIONAL CULTURE

Although in any particular occupation skills applied to a well-defined and exclusive area of activity may exist, it is also necessary to organize, develop, and pass them on to new members of the group. Various forms of professional organization, both formal and informal, develop which fulfil such functions. These include organizations in which the actual service of the group is rendered (such as social-work agencies), organizations to provide for the recruitment, entry, and training of new members (such as schools or departments of social work in universities or colleges), and organizations which express group consciousness and provide means for discussion of professional matters and the development of the knowledge base (the professional associations). The way in which individuals interact in these organizations, the roles they play, constitute the professional culture. Although all occupations have such groupings and a form of organization, a culture is unique to the professions; according to Greenwood[9] this is "the attribute which most effectively differentiates the professions from other occupations".

Professional culture consists of certain values, norms, and symbols. Values in general (as distinct from the values of a particular profession) include belief in the essential worth of the service being rendered and the knowledge-based authority of the professional over laity. Norms represent guides to behaviour in professional situations, including correct ways of behaving to clients, peers, subordinates, and superiors. Symbols may include insignia, emblems, special dress, history, and folklore, stereotypes of the professional, the client, and the layman. Such culture also includes the career concept. This is an attitude which implies unswerving devotion, complete absorption, and total personal involvement in professional work. To embark on such a career is in some respects equivalent to entering a religious order. The process of entry to professions carries with it some of the characteristics of induction into a religious code in which novice and priest roles are enacted. Greenwood likens the process to that of the acculturation of the immigrant in a strange society. The career concept implies a stereotype of the completely adjusted professional, and, on the other extreme, the deviant who has only partially adjusted to these demands.

## SOCIAL-WORK CULTURE

In social work a professional culture has to an extent developed, based particularly on what Younghusband[27] has described as the "power house" of the profession, the professional associations, and training schools. These are staffed by individuals who seem likely to possess the cultural traits of the profession to a considerable degree and who have opportunities, away from the hurly-burly of practice, to develop the professional knowledge base. Such practices as student supervision and the training of supervisors also ensure that a wide range of practitioners are exposed to professional culture. Recent developments, such as greater unity of professional associations and the development of education and training for social work, are also conducive to the growth of this professional culture.

But these are very recent changes and may not in fact hold the key to the full development of professional culture. The fragmentation of social-work services into separate occupational categories, deriving from the way differing needs were met at different times, may not be overcome by formal changes in organization. More important are the different settings in which social work is practised, particularly the way in which these have become bureaucratized in such large-scale organizations as the hospital or local authority. These stand in the way of a distinctive *social-work* culture which overrides them all; in the words of Rodgers and Dixon,[28] "the professional qualifications and status [of the social worker] are those of almoner, probation officer, child care officer, not of the social worker".

## PROFESSIONAL EDUCATION AND SOCIALIZATION

Perhaps the most important influence in the creation of professional culture is the process of entry to the professions, in particular professional training. In most professions this means much more than the learning of technical skills and includes also the taking on of norms of professional behaviour and an acceptance of the values on which the profession is based. The process can be seen as part of the general process of socialization to which individuals are exposed during the life cycle and resembles in some respects the preparation of the child for its future life by the family. The process also seeks to establish a professional identity, a subjective feeling of belonging to a professional group and an acceptance of the more general professional milieu through the internalization of such cultural elements. Effectively, this is the process by which professionals are made; it is an important part of adult socialization as such and constitutes perhaps one of the most profound experiences of adult life.[29]

Although training for social work dates from the nineteenth century, the large-scale development of social-work training is of very recent origin, and this means that very large numbers of social workers have no training at all or have only pre-professional training of a degree or diploma type. For example, by the beginning of 1967 only 31 per cent of child care officers had professional training although this figure rose to 70 per cent for probation officers.[30]

Thus a varying, and in some cases very small, proportion of practising social workers have been through what is probably the key acculturation process—that of professional training. In the Rodgers and Dixon study only 9 out of 72 social workers had a full professional training; amongst those performing social-work functions there was little orientation to what might be described as a professional culture as described here. Thus only a minority of workers were "ready to talk about social work in theoretical terms and have a firm grasp of its principles and methods and consciously try to act in accordance with them".[28] In Jefferys'[31] recent study of social welfare services in Buckinghamshire only 13 per cent of social workers had education up to the level of a full-time university course, and 58 per cent had a recognized professional qualification.

This reflects a situation in which the development of professional education has not kept pace with the demand for social workers; employers are prepared to appoint the untrained or non-professionally trained rather than leave posts unfilled. This is a continuous process; whilst the number of fully trained child care officers rose from 422 to 612 between 1963 and 1965, the number without even a basic relevant qualification rose from 618 to 827.[32] This, as will be shown more fully later, has considerable relevance for bureaucratization of social work in large-scale organizations. Those social workers who have not been exposed to professional acculturation through training courses are most likely to take on bureaucratic characteristics, in particular to think about clients and their problems in bureaucratic rather than professional ways.[33]

Again, the organization of schools and departments of social-work training is a barrier to the passing on of an integrated set of attitudes to the profession. There are a very small number of fully established schools of social work in Britain (compared in 1966 with 63 in the United States).[34] and many departments are small and, particularly in technical colleges, exist within milieus with little tradition of social science teaching or professional training and education in the full sense of the term.

Although the generic principle in training, by which social workers irrespective of specialization are trained together, is widely accepted, these courses cater for a minority of social work students.

Thus the fragmentation of social work in practice is reflected by the fragmentation of training into numerous small courses (for medical social workers, child care officers, and probation officers) which cater for different occupational sub-groups. This situation reflects in part the divided administrative responsibility for training; in Britain three training councils (in child care, probation, and the council for training in social work) exist, which in the words of the Seebohm Report[35] are "each advertising for students, each directly or indirectly competing for teaching staff and field placements, each setting up or promoting a separate course, *sometimes in the same building*, adjacent but not integrated". This is "educationally and professionally unsound".

It is, then, difficult to accept that a full professional culture has as yet emerged in social work; education and training for the profession appears to resemble in some respects the stage of apprenticeship learning which most professions have experienced, where skills are divided and general theory is weak. Moreover, the fragmentation of training implies little sharing of major professional values among students, as well as disagreement about what is relevant professional knowledge and skill.

But as training schemes develop, the process of professional socialization is likely to take on greater significance in social work, and it is important to begin to understand some of its features.[36]

As in all processes of socialization, the kinds of questions that can be asked relate to the direction in which attitudes are modified and the mechanisms by which such changes are brought about.

The goals sought in professional training include the transmission of skills and cultural elements, which may involve a substantial reorientation of students' attitudes, and the filtering off (at the time of selection or during the course) of those "deviants" who are seen as failing to accept or as opposing professional values. The "cooling out" (or, in the case of social work, of counselling out) process and the ways in which it is legitimized, appears crucial to the process.

The main way in which social work courses meet these requirements is by emphasizing certain personality characteristics deemed essential in the light of what is construed as the primary professional task, that of casework. Here the primary instrument and skill is the use of the "self" of the caseworker, which must itself, therefore, be subject to exploration and study during the training process. Thus the capacity in the student for self-awareness and for psychological growth are emphasized at time of selection and throughout the course; these appear as guiding lines by which students' performance is measured. During the course the student meets a series of situations with clients, peers, supervisors, and tutors which are seen as testing out such capacities. By comparison the academic requirements of the course may, on occasion, appear of secondary importance to the exploration of self through exposure to practical situations, which appears the hallmark of such training. Work in the classroom and library makes up, in many cases, a small part of the students' curriculum, and is often so little emphasized by teachers as to appear an afterthought.[37] There appears in general an extremely uneasy relationship between the educational and the practical elements in training which has yet to be resolved by college and university departments. The interpersonal nature of the social-work training process marks it out from most other professional training and begins a process peculiar to social work as such, whereby professional relationships between social workers are carried on in a framework similar to that used in dealing with clients; thus begins a process of supervision and consultation which accompanies some social workers throughout their careers. In the training process psychological models in use with clients are imported into the training process. Thus, as in psychiatric training, the capacity to the student to play the client (or patient) role may be an important basis for successful socialization.

This process is continued in many social-work agencies in situations where supervisors control subordinates by indirect means rather than by the exercise of direct authority in relation to their work; again the emphasis will be on the personality of the worker and on inner conflicts which make it difficult to play the professional role in the prescribed way. Blau and Scott,[33] in a study of American social-work agencies, found that disagreements between supervisors and other workers were seen not in terms of differences of judgement or opinion but as resulting from the unconscious resistance of the worker; thus "workers found that they could not be right in any disagreement since their arguments were not accepted at face value but dismissed as being rationalizations to mask unconscious resistance".

It is important to remember that the way in which the professional task is defined in the process of education and training may vary considerably and will depend largely on the training and general orientation of the teaching staff; courses vary in the extent to which they lay stress on casework, with its associated emphasis on the self of the student as the central mode of working. In some courses emphasis is being placed on training the student to work as part of a team within the community or a complex organizational structure; where this occurs there may be changes in the character of the socialization process.

The process of socialization does not proceed without conflicts. These are part of role conflicts commonly found within social work and other professions and which are sharpened by professionalization.[12] Role conflicts in general derive from (1) social obligations in two groups which may produce contradictory behaviour (e.g. conflict in roles of married son and husband, in which roles are played in two families) and (2) conflicting expectations and therefore behaviour relating to the same role (probation officer as social worker and agent of court). There are a variety of responses to role conflict, including retreat or abandonment of one role or of part of one role. Role conflicts occur during the performance of professional roles, and in social work one of these derives from the clash between humanitarian values and professional norms.[12] It seems clear that the desire to help people is an exceptionally powerful motivation for entry to the profession. But, to their surprise, the newcomers find that the ideology of professional social work demands that direct help be abandoned in favour of the "exploration" of problems and the search for some underlying cause; expressed needs, the student is taught, are rarely the "real" ones. Again, the humanitarian desire to offer friendship to those who suffer runs contrary to the "distance" that must be maintained in a professional relationship. The conflicts and contradictions of learning the professional role in social work, made worse perhaps by the special demands of this particular culture, appear considerable, and some students are unable to reconcile such conflicts. Even those who manage to resolve such conflict in training often face them again in the field and, if the ambivalence shown by social workers towards social action is any evidence, are rarely successful in coming to terms with this strain. The blending of incompatible or potentially incompatible elements into a consistent pattern of professional behaviour appears, as Merton[29] suggests, a task in professional education which is shared by most professions.

A further conflict relates to the discrepancies between sex roles and professional roles in social work, which emerges particularly clearly in training. For women the role of social worker appears, although modified by professional and agency procedures, an extension of the female role in general. Part of the definitions of both roles are such traits as sympathy, understanding, and receptiveness. There is thus little discrepancy between the demands of these two roles. But for the male social worker there appear major discrepancies between the way in which the male role and the social worker role are defined; the qualities called for in the successful performance of the former (e.g. aggressiveness, self-assertiveness) may be denied by the requirements of the latter. Part of the problem is the presence of men in a profession traditionally dominated by women: most of the "folk figures" of the profession, whether living or dead, are female. Females often find themselves in super-ordinate positions as teachers or supervisors in relation to men. This situation again conflicts with the expectation that men will in their work (in general) occupy authority positions in relation to women. In the teaching situation the conflict between the female superordinate and the male subordinate is made worse by the process of self-evaluation which is characteristically demanded of social-work students; thus the mature male student may be placed in a position of revealing all to a succession of female tutors; it is little wonder that one male student described the social-work training process as, in part, an "assault on his masculinity".[38] The implications of this situation for male recruitment to social work and for the eventual definition of the professional role by male social workers are as yet unexplored.

Again, it is likely that the smooth internalization of professional values, which is the aim of the training process, is in fact attained only partially. Certainly as social work is a profession which is highly involved with social values, the internalization by students of social work values is an important part of the training process. One American inquiry[39] suggested that the difference between professional values held by students at the beginning and end of a social-work course was not as great as expected. A number of variables were associated with this; those students who might be considered "dependent" (i.e. young, with little previous exposure to social work, away from home, socially upwardly mobile) showed the greatest degree of change. These kinds of factors would make the student more dependent on the educational culture of the school and thus more open to its values and influence; by comparison, older students with experience of social work are more likely to be generally independent, and to resist the values purveyed by the school. Social class position was particularly important; students from upper-class positions made the least change, those from lower positions the greatest. Here the influence of reference groups might be important; these may act to provide an alternative set of values to that of the school or ones which might be in conflict with these, and thus neutralize the school's influence. Upper-class students probably had more reference groups available to them than lower-class students, particularly those who were in the process of moving from one group to another and who had left one set of reference groups behind. The class factor can also be explained by the fact that social work is in any case a profession with middle-class values and that middle-class students had been exposed to such values for most of their lives; it might be assumed that they would show little change in values during training for a professional life based mainly on these values.

An important factor in the socialization process is the presence of role models with whom the student can identify and who help to lead the student toward a professional identity of his own. In social work the tutor and the supervisor of practical work appear of the greatest importance in this respect and, with the student, this makes up a triangular set of relationships not unlike that of the nuclear family.[40] Tutors and supervisors present rather different models for the student. The supervisor's role centres around the delineation and facilitation of core professional tasks; there is also the task of utilizing and relating theoretical knowledge acquired in college. Identification of a very intense kind is thus possible for the student in this relationship; the supervisor and student are alike exposed to the everyday working milieu of the profession, to the rigours of the agency, and of practice. The supervisor also occupies a position to which most students may reasonably aspire. The tutor, on the other hand, may be seen as remote from the field. But she exercises a unique influence on the course and on the student from the time a student first applies for admission until the end of the course. In a sense she is the pivot around which other activities revolve. This role has its conflicts; in a practice-oriented profession such as social work, absence from the field may impose pressures; there may be a temptation to keep in practice by seeing students as "clients," which is heightened by the definition of the socialization process as mainly one of insight or psychological growth for the student. Something of the tension and strain of the tight family circle of tutor–supervisor–student may be worked out on the "extended family" of related but more distant figures on the course, including other departmental members. Again, there may be conflict between different groups of socializers (e.g. social workers and social scientists) about the purpose, content, and character of the training course. It would seem an important future research task to explore the dynamics of such courses in more detail.

## PROBLEMS IN THE PROFESSIONALIZATION OF SOCIAL WORK

The aim of this chapter has been to clarify certain aspects of the professionalization process in social work, in particular the basis of skill and knowledge and the development of professional culture.

Clearly social work in Britain is in the process of rapid professionalization; perhaps the most significant development at the moment appears to be the likely union of the various professional associations into a national body; this would parallel the establishment of the American National Association of Social Workers, generally regarded as a milestone in the history of professional social work in that country.[9]

In general in Britain social work appears to be moving along the path of professionalization outlined by Wilensky, although it is difficult to say whether all the stages in the process will actually be achieved. By comparison, it has been claimed that teaching in Britain has attained professional status. Thus Musgrave[41] points out that teaching became a full-time job well before 1800, a training scheme was established after 1839, a professional association for elementary teachers was founded in the 1870's and for secondary teachers at the turn of the century (and in some cases obtained legal recognition), and a code of ethics has been evolved. Although all these stages are not entirely complete in the case of teaching, it would appear that social work has a considerable distance to travel before gaining a comparable status.

Thus it is necessary to consider a series of dilemmas and problems which relate to social work in its drive for professionalism. One of these concerns the basis of knowledge and the area of exclusive jurisdiction claimed by social work. Social work, in relating so strongly to dynamic psychology, has laid claim to a knowledge base about which there is continuing controversy; it is no part of this work to evaluate the claims of rival schools of psychology, but it is clear that professions which utilize such knowledge then become involved in such controversy.

Again, it seems doubtful whether social workers will be able to claim anywhere near an exclusive role in the field of individual and social problems. Apart from competition with other members of the counselling professions, a very large number of other occupations, from priest to chemist, contain a "counselling" element. It also seems clear, from the state of public and professional knowledge of social work, that the specific function of the social worker within the wider range of helping professions is little understood. This suggests that a narrowing of the areas in which social workers claim special skills may be necessary before further progress can be made.

But, although the social worker's skills cannot be defined in a very precise way, it is also arguable that social work cannot be defined in terms of skills alone.[42] Social-work skills are linked with considerations of an ethical or political nature in ways in which the skill of other professions are not. The answers to the problems social workers and their clients face are rooted in ideas of what a good society should be like; social workers are asked by the society in which they function to lend their weight to certain kinds of "solutions" which have a strong moral content. Engineers or doctors rarely face in the same way the questions of what their skills are for—the need for bridges and physical health is virtually indisputable, even though ethical problems can arise in the exercise of such skills (to what ends are bridges or medical experiments, in wartime, to be put?), but a very great number of the problems faced by the social worker have a moral content. Yet the answers to such questions are difficult to give. It is easier to define an unsafe bridge or disease but, as Donnison[42] states, "there is no generally accepted state of social health which everyone strives to achieve—disagreements on such matters form the subject matter of politics the world over". This has implications for professionalization. Because social work appears so much the response to human needs and problems, it is difficult to define the skills required or to feel that these are the only basis for practice. This implies a degree of insecurity for social work and a status not as distinctive as in other professions. But social work can make a greater contribution to human happiness by "seeking to live with the insecurity of a profession devoted chiefly to recognizing and meeting human needs rather than seeking the more distinctive status and more vigorous *esprit de corps* of a profession defined by the skills employed in direct service to clients".[42]

Several critics have, in fact, highlighted the way in which social work, caught up in the general process of professionalization, has suffered from the negative aspects and dysfunctions of such a process. The movement away from the broader social basis is seen as the price that has been paid for a brand of professionalism, narrowly defined. Thus social workers "have gained a profession by forfeiting a mission".[43] Several factors outside social work have contributed to this development. Social science, especially in the United States, has in the past moved away from an interest in reform and in questions concerning aspects of the social structure as a whole, although there are some signs of a movement in the opposite direction now; at the same time the interests of psychologists have shifted in part towards psycho-analytic theory. Reforming zeal has also been reduced by the incorporation of social workers in large-scale organizations where there is more pressure to concentrate on technical details of the job than on broader social ends. In various ways, in particular during the process of professional education and socialization, the reformer in social work is cooled or counselled out or reorientated.

However, there appear various ways in which the kind of professionalization witnessed in social work may not in fact be incompatible with a reformist orientation and a concern with broader social questions. There appear, as Wilensky[10] points out, to be a growing number of individuals who, although retaining their basic professional allegiance, are drawn away from the technical considerations of practice into broader fields, such as welfare planning or creative and administrative work related to a particular professional activity; this is what Wilensky has termed the "programme professional". Here career paths which are created go typically beyond traditional social work roles and fan out into the community, planning administration and governmental advisory roles. Professional associations can also play such a role by performing a pressure-group function in relation to government welfare planning and programmes. The strength of this approach is that it comes from those at the grass roots of practical and administrative problems, yet is related to planning on a broad basis.

Thus what Wilensky has called a new form of "mixed professionalism" may be emerging in social work in which a number of career paths emerge which combine a variety of elements. The dilemma of the practising professional still, however, remains: to what extent is reform incompatible with roles in the organization and in the profession?

Perhaps the greatest danger of rapid professionalization is not that it destroys reforming zeal and creates trained incapacity to see how structural strains are related to individual problems, but that in the professional thrust, knowledge is used indiscriminately.[12] Here there is the danger of over-quick packaging for professional use of leads from the social sciences or other fields and the over-selling of such knowledge by others. This point will be taken up again in the concluding chapter.

## NOTES AND REFERENCES

1. Report of the Committee on Local Authority and Allied Personal Services (Seebohm Report), Cmnd. 3703, H.M.S.O., 1968.
2. A. Flexner, Is social work a profession?, *Proceedings of the National Conference of Charities and Corrections, 1915.*
3. H. Meyer, Professionalization and social work today, in Thomas (ed.), *Behavioural Science for Social Workers,* Free Press, New York, 1967.
4. A. Sinfield, *Which Way for Social Work?*, Fabian Tract 393, 1969.
5. E. Hughes, *Men and Their Work*, Collier McMillan, 1958.
6. See B. Rodgers and J. Dixon, *Portrait of Social Work*, O.U.P., London, 1960, and M. Jefferys, *Anatomy of Social Welfare Services*, Joseph, London, 1965.

7. Exceptions are R. Chambers, Professionalism in social work, appendix to B. Wootton, *Social Science and Social Pathology*, Allen & Unwin, London, 1959. P. Halmos, *Faith of the Counsellors*, Constable, London, 1965, is relevant but is neither a study of professionalization nor is exclusively related to social work; see also G. Millerson, *The Qualifying Associations*, Routledge & Kegan Paul, London, 1964.

8. H. Vollmer and D. Mills (eds.), *Professionalisation*, Prentice-Hall, N.J., 1966; E. Greenwood, The elements of professionalization, *Social Work (U.S.)*, **2** (3), 1957 (also in Vollmer and Mills; and H. Wilensky, The professionalisation of everyone, *Am. J. Sociol.* **70** (2) (Sept. 1966). Accounts specially devoted to social work include H. Wilensky and C. Lebeaux, *Industrial Society and Social Welfare*, Russell Sage Foundation, New York, 1958 ( ch. XI); A. Etzioni (ed.), *The Semi-professions*, Free Press, Glencoe, 1969; and H. Meyer, *op. cit.*

9. E. Greenwood, *op. cit.*

10. H. Wilensky, *op. cit.*

11. G. L. Millerson, *op. cit.*

12. H. Wilensky and C. Lebeaux, *op. cit.*

13. C. Wright Mills, The professional ideology of social pathologists, *Am. J Sociol.* **49** (1943).

14. P. Halmos, *op. cit.*

15. N. Timms, *Psychiatric Social Work in Britain*, Routledge & Kegan Paul, London, 1964. In the United States 83 per cent of P.S.W.s in clinics and 48 per cent in hospitals have at least 2 years in graduate social work. school, compared with 16 per cent of all social workers; Wilensky and Lebeaux, *op cit.*

16. B. Wootton, *op. cit.*, ch. IX. For further criticisms of more recent events in social work, including the Seebohm Report, see Sinfield, *op. cit.*

17. Wootton, *op. cit.*

18. O. Stevenson, The understanding caseworker, *New Society*, 1 Aug. 1963.

19. D. Jehu, Teaching growth and behaviour; a scientific approach, *Case Conference* **14** (2) (June 1967).

20. See, for example, D. Jehu, *Learning Theory and Social Work*, Routledge, & Kegan Paul, London, 1967.

21. P. Nokes, *The Professional Task in Welfare Practice*, Routledge & Kegan Paul, London, 1968.

22. D. Beck, Patterns in use of family agency service; cited in J. Mayer and A. Rosenblatt, The client's social context; its effect on continuance in treatment, *Social Casework*, **45,** Nov. 1964.

23. J. Mayer and A. Rosenblatt, *op. cit.*

24. J. Mayer and A. Rosenblatt, Client disengagement and alternative. treatment resources, *Social Casework*, **47,** Jan. 1966.

25. N. Timms, The public and the social worker, *Social Work (U.K.)* **19** (1) (1962).
26. S. Cohen, Community understanding of social work, B.A. Dissertation, Witwatersrand University, 1962.
27. E. Younghusband, *Social Work and Social Change*, Allen & Unwin, London, 1964.
28. B. Rodgers and J. Dixon, *op. cit.*
29. For an introductory account of the process see R. Merton *et al.*, *The Student Physician*, Harvard Univ. Press, Cambridge, 1957. See also O. Brim and S. Wheeler, *Socialization After Childhood*, Wiley, New York, 1966.
30. Seebohm Report, Appendix M, Part II.
31. M. Jefferys, *op. cit.*
32. J. Rea Price, Social pathology—a dilemma for social workers, *Case Conference* **13** (12) (April 1967).
33. P. Blau and R. Scott, *Formal Organizations*, Chandler, San Francisco, 1962.
34. Council on Social Work Education, *Contemporary Education for Social Work in the U.S.*, 1966.
35. Seebohm Report, *op. cit.*, para. 533 (italics not original). By 1970 the situation was showing some signs of changing, both in the organization of college courses and of the training councils.
36. What follows is an approach to professional socialization in social work arising out of research being carried out by the author; the approach derives in part from that taken by R. Bucher and A. Strauss, Professions in process, *Am. J. Sociol.* **66** (4) (Jan. 1961).
37. See R. Lubove, *The Professional Altruist*, Harvard University Press, 1965; this includes an account of the development and character of education for social work in the United States.
38. D. Keogh, Reflections on a two year child care course, *Child Care News*, Nov. 1968.
39. B. Varley, Socialization in social work education, *Social Work (U.S.)*, July 1963; see also D. Mcleod and H. Meyer, A study of the values of social workers, in Thomas (ed.), *op. cit.*
40. K. Woodcock, Tutor, supervisor and student, *Br. J. of Psychiat. Soc. Wk*, **8** (3) (1966).
41. P. Musgrave, *The Sociology of Education*, Methuen, London, 1965.
42. D. V. Donnison, The social work profession, *Case Conference* **3** (3) (Aug. 1956).
43. H. Bisno, How social will social work be?, *Social Work (U.S.)* **1** (1956).

# CHAPTER 11

# *The Organizational Context of Social Work*

## INTRODUCTION

Social work does not, unless it takes the form of private practice, go on outside an organizational context. Social workers are to be found in organizations ranging from social work agencies to such institutions as prisons and hospitals. Again, whilst social workers may operate in the context of one organization, e.g. the social work agency, their clients may at the same time be experiencing life in another kind of organizational setting, e.g. a children's home or old people's home.

Essentially such organizations can be seen as ways of co-ordinating and carrying out the many complex tasks of a modern society.

Thus a social-work agency performs some or all of the following tasks: services to clients, liaison with other agencies or organizations, recruitment, supervision, and training of staff. The relationship between the social worker and the agency is, as already shown, a particularly close one; one way of looking at the function of the social worker in society, the idea of "agency function", is as helping various organizations to fulfil their purposes. Here the social worker is closely identified with the goals of the organization.

Within the organization, the social worker comes into contact with further segments of the "role set", i.e. members of the administrative staff and, in a statutory organization, the lay-elected representatives of the community. Here the situation is complicated by the fact that social workers are themselves sometimes in high administrative positions; it is difficult therefore to draw a distinct line between social workers and other members of the organization, but it is important to understand the character of this interaction. Although the idea of agency function has been seen as rationalizing the relationship between social work and society, there is also a potential and actual conflict between social work and its organizational setting: this is part of a general conflict between a professional and an organizational or bureaucratic orientation. One of the tasks of this chapter will be to explore something of the nature and dimensions of this conflict.

Organizational analysis has an added importance at a time when British social work faces considerable changes in its administrative and organizational structure; there is the possibility that many social workers will find themselves in larger units with the likelihood of an increase in the amount of bureaucratic control and in the complexity of the tasks that face them. A further conflict is between the obligation social workers owe to the employing agency and to clients and the community; the changing conception of social work is likely to bring a new attention to this form of conflict.

There are many relevant issues that arise from the sociology of organizations, but here attention will be given to some of the issues arising out of the previous chapter on professionalization, in particular the problem of the use of knowledge by the organization, the position of the professional in the organization, and the relationship between the professional in the organization and in the community. Attention will also be given to certain reformulations of ideas about the organization of particular importance for social work.

## THE SOCIOLOGY OF ORGANIZATIONS

Sociologists have shown considerable interest in organizations both as illustrating certain general tendencies in modern industrial society and as objects of study in themselves, and have applied to organizations some of the approaches used in the study of other social systems and of whole societies. Sociology is only one of a number of social sciences concerned in various ways in the analysis of organizations, and makes up but one contributory discipline to the developing field of organizational theory. Here the concern will be to distinguish certain specifically sociological contributions to this field.

Organizations have been defined as seeking specific goals (e.g. education, welfare) by means of formally defined structures (such as committees). A division of tasks usually occurs if goals are to be realized in the most efficient way, which results in a hierarchy of officials. There is also the necessity to control and co-ordinate the efforts made to achieve goals, and this implies authority and the exercise of power: such authority relationships may be of a coercive or a persuasive type.[1]

One model (or ideal type) of the organization is that of bureaucracy. There are disadvantages in using this term for (like class) it carries negative and derogatory meanings. In modern sociology the study of bureaucracy has merged into the more general study of organizations, but it will be useful to pay some attention to this term as it is in constant use and represents one of the classic theories of organization, that of Weber.[2]

There are two main characteristics of bureaucracy—the division of labour and an hierarchical structure of control. Thus each official is allocated specific tasks for which he and no one else is responsible; he is controlled by the official above him in the hierarchy and controls those immediately below him. This ensures co-ordination and provides a formal channel of communication throughout the organization. The activities of each official are governed by the formal rules of the bureaucracy which prevent arbitrary action or actions based on personal considerations. The rules ensure that decisions are made in the most rational way and also ensure the continuity of the organization because any individual can take over any position if he knows the rules which govern decision making. Weber believed that this structure was the most rational and efficient way of organizing the performance of tasks in a modern industrial society.

More recent work[3] on organizations has criticized Weber's ideas and has suggested that there are a variety of types of organizations, and a variety of ways in which organizations can seek goals, which do not all correspond to Weber's model.

Another approach is to regard organizations as miniature social systems, or societies, in much the same way as social systems or parts of social systems external to organizations (such as the family) are studied. Here organizations can be approached by looking at the selection and socialization of members, the choice of goals, communication, rewards, and sanctions within the organization and relationship with the external social system.

Thus a second important concept of the organization is that of Goffman's[4] "total institution", already introduced in Chapter 7 on Deviance. This emphasizes in particular the influence of certain institutions, such as mental hospitals, boarding schools, prisons, and old people's homes, over the individual by virtue of their "impermeability", i.e. the barriers which exist between such institutions and the outside world. Such institutions can be described in terms of what Etzioni[5] has called their scope and pervasiveness. The scope of an organization refers to the number of activities carried out jointly by the participants, and pervasiveness refers to the extent to which the organization seeks to control the individual's life. In some organizations only some activities are carried out (leisure or work), but in total institutions maximum scope is attained. All aspects of life are conducted in the same place and under the same authority. Again, these activities are carried on in the company of large numbers of others, all of whom are treated alike. High scope can also give rise to a high degree of control of activity and, in particular, there is a breakdown in the barriers between sleep, work, and play. The processes to which individuals are subjected in the total institution have already been referred to,[6] but can be summarized as a severe process of socialization in which the individual's personality is subject to change in the direction of the norms of the institution by such methods as "degradation ceremonies", which are followed by a re-integration of the individual into the culture of the institution. Reactions include an obsessive acceptance of this new culture or an adoption of the perspectives and norms of the staff.

## USE OF KNOWLEDGE IN THE ORGANIZATION

One of the major problems facing any organization is the use of knowledge. Knowledge is used intensively by all organizations; Weber saw administrative authority as being based on technical knowledge and training. The higher the rank the more technical knowledge (based on examinations, etc.) the administrator is supposed to have and thus the more rational he is supposed to be. This forms the basis on which subordinates accept both a lower position in the hierarchy and the rules and regulations of the organization.

But, as Etzioni[5] points out, Weber overlooked the fact that some of the most well trained are to be found in the middle rather than the higher ranks of the organization, and that the principles of administrative authority and authority based on knowledge are quite incompatible. Effective administration depends upon the power invested in high rank; if the organization is to be controlled and directed, power must reside in positions of high rank or status irrespective of the knowledge of the incumbent. What is important are the rights and duties attached to these positions. But knowledge, and especially creativity, is an individual phenomenon and cannot simply be attached to a position and passed on from one incumbent to another. Even knowledge applied to a particular task is in the last analysis an individual act—the surgeon decides whether to operate or the social worker decides to terminate a case. Thus a degree of autonomy is necessary if professionals are to carry out their tasks. Thus the principles surrounding knowledge, which are basic to professional practice because professions rely on the possession of such knowledge, are in opposition to organizational principles of control by superiors. As Etzioni[5] states:

> The ultimate justification for a professional act is that it is, to the best of the professionals' knowledge, the right act. He might consult his colleagues before he acts, but the decision is his. If he errs, he still will be defended by his peers. The ultimate justification of an administrative act, however, is that it is in line with the organization's rules and regulations, and that it has been approved, directly or by implication, by a superior rank.

Although the professions have grown in power and importance, as noted in the previous chapter, in part this has been made possible through incorporation in organizations which have provided them with the necessary facilities and finance. Thus many doctors work in the context of hospitals and lawyers in large firms rather than in private practice. The problem of how professional knowledge is to be used is therefore a very real one. Organizations have also been faced with the problem of how to utilize such knowledge without destroying the basis of administration.

Etzioni[5] distinguishes three basic ways in which professional knowledge is used by organizations: in professional organizations knowledge is created or applied and used entirely for professional purposes; there are high proportions of professionals on the staff (and they have had at least 5 years' training) and professionals have authority over the major goals of the organization; examples include hospitals, universities, colleges, and research organizations. One sub-type are semi-professional organizations, in which the training of professionals is for less than 5 years; the concern is with the communication or application of knowledge and rarely with matters as important as life and death and in which the right of privileged communication is not guaranteed. The most typical semi-professional organizations are the primary school and the social-work agency. Secondly, there are service organizations in which professionals are provided with the facilities required for their work, but are not formally employed by the organizations (such as the service research organization which is part of a university). Thirdly, professionals may be employed in organizations whose goals are non-professional, such as industrial or military establishments.

## PROFESSIONAL AND ADMINISTRATIVE AUTHORITY
### IN PROFESSIONAL AND SEMI-PROFESSIONAL ORGANIZATIONS

Knowledge is the basis of professional authority, and therefore the relationship between professional and administrative authority will depend on the kind of knowledge the professional possesses. In fully professional organizations such as hospitals or universities, the dilemma of combining the two types of authority is resolved by giving control of major activities (in particular the goals of the organization) to professionals whilst the administrator is responsible for organizing the means to these ends. Although strains exist, the knowledge which is possessed by the doctor or professor is so important to the organization as a whole that it can scarcely be challenged on any administrative grounds.

In semi-professional organizations the relationship between professional and administrative authority is very different. In situations where professional training is short, where knowledge is communicated rather than created, and where life and death matters are not involved, there is, in the first place, less autonomy for the professional worker than in professional organizations; there is more control from those in higher authority and work is less subject to the discretion of the professional. In such organizations detailed supervision of work is commonplace. Nurses are directly observed by their superiors, and in cases where the performance of the task is invisible, as in teaching or social work, detailed inspection or reporting of the work is required. Social work is carried on within a complicated structure of supervision, although there are a number of limitations to supervision as a means of control. By comparison, the doctor or professor are not directly supervised by administrative superiors. Again, the qualities required for the communication of knowledge are often similar to those required for administration, and many semi-professional organizations are administered by those who previously held positions as professionals.

The social-work agency is a rather unusual example of a semi-professional agency as it is involved in the application rather than the communication of knowledge. But it shares other characteristics of the semi-professional organization in that it involves a fairly short training or in some cases no training at all. This serves to increase still further the amount of authority wielded by the administrator. In spite of the considerable increases made in the number of trained workers and in education for social work, organizations are still able, as was seen in the last chapter, to appoint as social workers individuals with no professional training; this makes it less likely that administrators will in all cases accept the professional advice and authority of social workers since it appears that the necessary skills can be easily acquired and that the welfare professions rest on little more than a sound common sense and good judgement.

Apart from differences in the nature of authority in professional and semi-professional organizations, there are other factors which serve to increase the power of the administrator or bureaucrat over the professional in this latter type of organization. Etzioni[5] suggests that one factor is the mainly female membership of the semi-professions (such as social work or teaching) compared to the more masculine professions (doctor, lawyer). Although the position of women has changed in the direction of greater emancipation, the way in which the female role is defined in general may still mean that women will be more submissive in an organizational context than men and therefore more likely to allow their work to be controlled by administrators. It is difficult to know whether organizations such as social-work agencies have taken this form because of the high percentage of female employees or whether they recruit females to fit into this kind of context. In social work the likelihood of an increasing recruitment of males may raise new problems for social-work organizations in the future.

Thus social workers in organizations are involved in a bureaucratic situation in which, for a variety of reasons, control of their work is in the hands of superiors (although these may themselves be professionals) and is carried through by a series of rules and regulations. The administrative and professional forms of authority and ways of proceeding may, of course, be entirely congruent, e.g. in situations where a social-work organization incorporates as part of the procedures a practice (such as supervision and consultation) which is approved by the profession. But there is not always a happy congruence between these two forms of authority in the same organization, and there is the likelihood of strain or actual conflict between them. In a sense, the growth of complex organizations and their ethos profoundly challenge the whole idea of autonomous and authoritative professional procedures. As social work becomes more professionalized and the knowledge on which social work practice is based becomes more distinctive, so the likelihood of this conflict grows. Leonard[7] cites the example of a family evicted by a London borough housing department who were to be rehoused by another authority. But the social workers involved in the case were instructed not to reveal this to the family, in consequence of which the family spent several weeks in acute distress believing they had no accommodation to go to; here the social worker was forced to behave against certain professional principles (e.g. respect for the individual), but to the organization the desired result, in bureaucratic terms, was achieved and the family were rehoused. Essentially the officials were behaving in a fashion graphically described by Merton[8] in his *Bureaucratic Structure and Personality*:

> The bureaucratic structure exerts a constant pressure upon the official to be "methodical, prudent, disciplined". If the bureaucracy is to operate successfully, it must attain a high degree of reliability, an unusual degree of conformity with prescribed patterns of action . . . but this very emphasis leads to a transference of the sentiments from the aims of the organization onto particular details of behaviour required by the rules. Adherence to the rules, originally conceived as a means, becomes transformed into an end itself.

As Leonard[7] suggests, this kind of conflict between administrator and professional is often seen by the social worker in psychological terms as the result of the personality characteristics of the administrator; but less often is this conflict understood as one which derives from different orientations and from positions in differing social structures. Essentially, as Wilensky and Lebeaux[9] suggest, there is conflict between the "colleague principle" and the "hierarchial principle"; professional colleagues have a similar technical training, common professional norms and formal equality with each other (hence professionals do not advertise for this assumes inequality in the service offered). Administrators are dissimilar in training and position, whose training has developed organizational norms and who are formally unequal within the organization. When the professional is employed in the organization these norms are inevitably in conflict, which results in a conflict between the roles of the social worker and the bureaucrat.

## THE ORGANIZATION AND THE COMMUNITY

It is also important to explore the relationship between the organization and its social context. The organization is not suspended in a social vacuum but consists of members whose activities are determined by external factors such as class position or peer group relationships. There may be different and sometimes conflicting orientations to the organization on the part of those inside and outside.[10]

Certain tendencies within social work may be bringing social-work agencies into closer contact with the community, particularly the possibility that more work will be undertaken with groups or communities. Because of an increasing involvement in work with the community, social workers may experience a conflict between loyalty to the organization and to the community.

Social-work agencies may, as a result of the changing social composition of their clientele, have to face increasing criticism and opposition from clients and the wider community. Other professions, such as doctors and lawyers, and the organizations with which they are associated, are also facing criticism from a client public who are less awed than before by professional expertise, are critical of the monopoly exercised by some professionals and, above all, are critical of the bureaucratic settings and organizational hierarchies with which they are confronted. Social-work organizations, with their relatively weak colleague relationships and their professional–administrative conflicts, may in fact be particularly good targets for client activism and attempts at client control.

Thus one important additional reason for understanding the way in which the organization constitutes for the social worker a hierarchy of power and authority is (as Ashton[11] points out) that this gives some idea of the kind of hierarchy of power and authority which confronts the client.

A further complication is that the social worker is not only controlled by administrators in the organization, but that the control of some organizations is in the hands of the lay elected representatives of the community, whose decisions may cut across both administrative and professional authority: little is known of the extent to which this form of authority is congruent with professional or administrative authority. In organizations in which decision making is of a highly technical nature and which are staffed by recognized professionals, there seems little scope for this form of control. But in social work agencies, which suffer from the anomie deriving from the welfare professions, the scope for lay decision making appears to be greater; there have been instances in social work agencies in which the authority of both professional and administrator has been overridden by lay authority. Thus decision making may be undertaken at three different levels by elected representatives, bureaucrat and professional, each of whom is essentially guarding a different interest to which differing weights will be given at different times.

Professional training also influences the degree of attachment that professional workers have to the organization as well as views on how work should be carried out. Blau and Scott[12] have shown in a study of an American casework agency how social workers who had professional training were more likely to select reference groups outside the agency than those who did not have such training (Table 5).

Again, the differences between social workers who were defined as "pure" professionals (with graduate training and outside reference groups) and "pure" bureaucratic social workers (no training and no outside reference groups) were considerable. Thus 86 per cent of professionals thought that supervisors should have a master's degree in social work against only 34 per cent of the bureaucrats, and 77 per cent of the former thought financial assistance to clients should be increased against 41 per cent of the latter. Loyalty to the organization, measured by whether the worker expected to leave or move to another agency, was also far less pronounced in the professional group than amongst the bureaucrats.

TABLE 5. PROFESSIONAL TRAINING AND LOCATION
OF REFERENCE GROUPS

| Graduate training in social work | Reference group | |
| --- | --- | --- |
| | Outside agency $N = 25$ | Inside agency $N = 61$ |
| Yes | 56% | 36% |
| No | 44% | 64% |
| | 100% | 100% |

Source: Ref. 1.   P. Blau and W. Scott, *Formal Organisations*.

Again, organizations which by their nature restrict professional advancement are less likely to retain the loyalty of professionals if they are in competition for manpower with others where this condition does not operate.

Thus for the professional in the organization, the "community within a community", as Goode[13] has described the professions, offers an alternative focus to that of the organization, and is a further illustration of the way in which organizations are permeated by influences from outside.

## NEW FORMS OF PROFESSIONALISM

An alternative way of looking at the relationship between professionalism and bureaucracy is not by emphasizing conflict but by considering the various ways in which the two cultures interpenetrate and some of the implications of the process. As Wilensky[14] suggests, "the culture of bureaucracy invades the professions; the culture of professionalism invades organizations". The result is something new, possibly a merging of the ways in which individuals see their roles in both spheres. Thus one of the types which is emerging is the professional service expert who is accommodated by the organization because his knowledge is useful, but whose professional training and allegiance to an outside colleague group enables him to resist the demands of the organization. Thus bureaucracy and professional commitment are not necessarily in conflict; professional training is a more powerful indoctrination than the influences of the workplace, while the organization may accommodate the professional because this is the best way of achieving its ends.

Thus the interpenetration of professional and non-professional forms of control leads to new kinds of organizational structures, and this characterizes, in particular, emergent professions such as teaching and social work in which professional careers may lead to managerial positions. Although professional social workers are achieving high administrative positions, and will increasingly do so as a result of changes in the organizational structure of social work, a great deal still depends on the existing power structure in organizations and, in particular, as Wilensky puts it, on "who got there first"—the layman, the manager, or the professional?

Again, although it is sometimes held that professional social workers should be appointed to high administrative posts as this will ensure the maximum co-operation between administration and professionals in social work agencies, it must also be remembered that the social worker, like anyone else in positions of administrative authority, is subject to bureaucratic pressures and may be forced to choose between an administrative and a professional role; for example, as Chrichton[15] points out, when a professional worker is appointed to a position of administrative responsibility within the organization this new managerial function is often seen by subordinates as being in conflict with professional needs:

> Once in the senior job they [the new administrators] appear to lose all sympathy and understanding for the problems of their subordinates . . . with promotion group loyalties change and there is some feeling on the part of subordinates that the earlier identification of the manager with their professional group has gone and the new identification with the management team gives insufficient weight to old loyalties.

## AN ALTERNATIVE VIEW OF ORGANIZATION

A final difficulty arises from the acceptance of classical definitions of the organizations: here organizations are defined in terms of a given goal or goals. Their structures are seen as means for the achievement of the organizational goal. But, as Albrow[16] points out in a critique of organization theory, organizational goals are not necessarily specific; it is very difficult to determine the exact nature of the goals of hospitals or prisons (or even social work agencies); they may vary from treatment to research, from punishment to reform. The structure of the organization may depend not on goals but on other factors, including the divergent goals of different individuals who recognize that they can only obtain their objectives by participation in the goals of others. Secondly, the formal rules by which organizations function are supplemented by an informal system; compliance with rules depends clearly on the way individuals interpret situations in which they may be applied—e.g. rules may not be seen as justified in particular situations. Therefore pure administration, the carrying out of completely rule-determined activity, cannot exist, and thus complaints against bureaucracy on this basis are misconceived. Again, organizational structure is as much determined by groups external to the organization as by organizational goals. Thus there may be different, and sometimes conflicting, orientations to the organization, and rules may develop which derive from differing power positions outside the organization. In general, the definitions of organizations commonly reflect a too simple and determinate view: some organizations do have single purposes, but such a common purpose is rarely to be found in complex organizations in a modern society.

These criticisms of conventional organization theory suggest that there may have been an over-emphasis on the potential and actual conflict between administrators and professionals (such as social workers) in organizations: if the organization is seen in terms of individuals or groups who attempt to gain acceptance for rather differing goals, and where rules relate to the resolution of potential conflict, then it is possible to be much more optimistic about the effects of the bureaucratization of social work, and of the chances that social workers may have in the future of influencing or changing the goals of their agencies or working in situations which appear to threaten professional goals. One of the few studies[17] of the process of innovation in a social-work agency (a local authority children's department incorporating new legislation) suggested that the organization was able to incorporate a variety of interpretations of these new tasks:

> The principal developments studied were accepted and welcomed by people who differed considerably in outlook and aims... different objectives derived from different frames of reference, even extreme diversity amounting to mutual incomprehension, need cause no serious conflict or administrative breakdown.

There is, therefore, the need to rethink constantly conceptions of the organization in order to have a realistic view of the potential or actual conflict between the organization and the professional. Albrow suggests an alternative model of organization to that in current use; while it is agreed that organizational goals do indeed exist, it is important not to assume unity or specificity as attributes of such goals: goals may derive from individual's roles outside as well as inside the organization. Secondly, goals are legitimized by all members of the organization, not just by management; hence there may be conflict over goals which relate to the power, class, or status situations of groups outside organizations. For example, if the agreed principle by which the activities of an organization is that of service to the community, attempts to substitute for this the principle of profitability will be considered illegitimate by many members.

Here there is the need for organizations to be studied in the same way as societies. But in the past one defect in organizational analysis has been the acceptance of the social-system approach, which attributes to the organization, as well as to society, a central value system. The organization has been substituted for society as an object of study, and organizational goals have been substituted for central values. This approach to organization runs into exactly the same problem as the social-system model of society, namely that societies cannot be thought of as integrated solely by means of basic values. Thus if organizations are characterized by a multiplicity and vagueness of goals and a conflict between members about goals, rather than by a set of simple goals and values to which all subscribe, then it is all the more likely that society must also be viewed in this way and cannot be fully understood through the social system approach.

It has already been suggested that this kind of sociological approach is of the greatest value to social workers in their understanding of the social worker–client situation. It appears an equally valuable, although as yet unexplored, approach to the understanding of the social worker in the organization.

Finally, concepts such as bureaucracy and total institution which have occupied a central place in the analysis of organizations, are also in the process of being reinterpreted, and this may highlight certain features of organizations in which social workers are involved which might otherwise be neglected. Smith[18] suggests that to the concepts of the bureaucracy and the total institution can be added those of the "front-line organization" and the "permeable organization."

In the front-line organization, by contrast to the hierarchical chain of command of the bureaucracy, tasks are initiated in the front line of the organization rather than being handed down through the chain of command from the top. An example would be in the children's department of a local authority where the initiative rests primarily with the child care officer in the field who often has a monopoly of information about how tasks are actually carried out. Although supervision is a means by which the organization can control the front-line worker, full control is difficult in situations of sudden emergency or where workers are very mobile between clients. A dilemma is created for those in the organization occupying positions where policy is made, for they have little opportunity, in many circumstances, to effectively exercise responsibility for such policy in the field.

Again, by comparison to the concept of the residential institution as an impermeable organization which is totally cut off from the outside world, another group of organizations (particularly some more recently developed residential care institutions) can be described as permeable. Here both the scope and pervasiveness of the organization, which is at its height in the impermeable total institution, are lowered. Thus participation in the activities of the organization is a matter of choice, a clear division between work, leisure, and domestic activities is maintained, and the organization does not hinder participation in activities and groups external to it. Thus children in residential institutions go to local schools and prisoners work outside the prison in local firms. Most important, the process by which the identity of the newcomer to the institution as well as his definition of the institution is changed (mortification) is replaced by a process of aggregation. Here the inmate is encouraged to retain his own identity and his definition of the organization and to participate in roles outside the institution by the retention of such symbols as his own clothes and name. There is no need to reorganize the culture of the newcomer to fit in with the culture of the institution, as this differs only slightly from the culture of the wider social system from which the inmate has come.

These two alternative conceptualizations of the organization may be increasingly helpful in explaining and understanding some of the new organizational situations in which social workers now find themselves.

## THE ROLE SET

In the Introduction to Part III it was suggested that the social worker could usefully be seen as occupying a central position within a role set, or a circle of associated positions such as client, colleague, administrator, lay representative, etc. One problem of the role set is that the central person has to deal with a series of expectations, some of which will be in conflict, emanating from the members of the role set. A number of these expectations have been illustrated as well as some of the conflicts between them.

Thus one problem raised by the idea of the role set is that of the resolution (from the point of view of the central person) of these conflicting expectations. Clearly if these conflicts are too severe, then the role set will cease to operate or will operate at less than full efficiency. Merton[19] suggests that several social mechanisms operate which counteract the potential instability of the role set and which lessen the conflict experienced by individuals within it.

Firstly, there are differences in the degrees of importance attached by members to their positions in the role set and in the power held by such members. This means that the central person (e.g. the teacher or social worker) is less vulnerable to expectations than if each member had similar interests in and also possessed similar power within the role set. Secondly, interaction with each member of the role set is not continuous and role behaviour is not observed by all members of the role set. This means that behaviour in one part of the role set is insulated from the sight of others and allows for behaviour which is at odds with the expectations of other members of the role set. Thus the work of both the teacher and the social worker is relatively invisible to certain important members of the role set; a teacher has certain freedom in the classroom and the relationship between social worker and client is often not observed by others and is protected to an extent by the professional principle of confidentiality.

Thus certain sectors of the role sets of teachers and social workers are effectively insulated from other important relationships (e.g. with administrators and lay representatives) whose expectations may not coincide with those of the central person. Insulation is not, of course, total, particularly in situations in which the minimum requirements of the role are not met by the occupant, in which case a spotlight is often turned on the behaviour of the central person from all sectors of the role set.

## NOTES AND REFERENCES

1. For an account of the various approaches to the study of organizations see P. Blau and W. Scott, *Formal Organizations*, Chandler, San Francisco, 1962; A. Etzioni, *Modern Organizations*, Prentice-Hall, 1964; and S. Cotgrove, *Science of Society*, ch. 8, Allen & Unwin, London, 1967.

2. H. Gerth and C. Mills, *From Max Weber*, Routledge & Kegan Paul, London, 1948.
3. For an account of these developments see Cotgrove, *op. cit.*
4. E. Goffman, *Asylums*, Penguin Books, 1968.
5. A. Etzioni, *op. cit.*
6. See Chapter 7, pp. 165–6.
7. P. Leonard, Social workers and bureaucracy, *New Society*, 2 June 1966.
8. R. Merton, Bureaucratic structure and personality, in Merton, *Social Theory and Social Structure*, Free Press, Glencoe, 1957.
9. H. Wilensky and C. Lebeaux, *Industrial Society and Social Welfare*, Russell Sage Foundation, New York, 1958.
10. For an analysis of the relationship between the organization and the community, see E. Litwak and H. Meyer, A balance theory of co-ordination between bureaucratic organizations and community primary groups, in E. Thomas (ed.), *Behavioural Science for Social Workers*, Free Press, New York, 1967.
11. E. Ashton, Organizational theory and social work, in Ashton, *Social Work and the Social Sciences*, Bala Press, Bala, 1966.
12. P. Blau and W. Scott, *op. cit.*
13. W. J. Goode, Community within a community; the professions, *Am. Sociol. Rev.* **22** (1957).
14. H. Wilensky, The professionalization of everyone?, *Am. J. Sociol.* **70** (2) (Sept. 1964).
15. A. Chrichton, Role conflicts in social work agencies, *Case Conference*, **12** (8) (Feb. 1966).
16. M. Albrow, The study of organizations—objectivity or bias?, in *Penguin Social Sciences Survey*, 1968 (J. Gould, ed.).
17. D. Donnison and V. Chapman, *Social Policy and Administration*, Allen & Unwin, London, 1965.
18. G. Smith, The organizational context of social work practice, *Case Conference*, **16** (4) (Aug. 1969); see also G. Smith, *Social Work and the Sociology of Organisations*, Routledge, 1970.
19. R. K. Merton, The role set; problems in sociological theory, *Br. J. Social*, **8** (1957).

# PART IV

# CHAPTER 12

# *Perspectives and Problems*

THE relationship between sociology and social work is, potentially at least, one of the closest that can exist between a social science and a professional practice. Both have their roots in a concern for the social problems and processes of industrialized (and industrializing) societies. The divergence which has taken place between them in more recent times, and which is showing distinct signs of a decline, should not be allowed to detract from this fact.

It has been one of the tasks of this book to demonstrate this relationship and to suggest a variety of sociological frameworks which the social worker may be able to utilize in a variety of situations, ranging from the confrontation between the social worker, the client, and the family, to the position of the social worker in the organization, the profession, and in society as such. At the same time, a clear distinction can be made between the role of the sociologist as social scientist and the role of the social worker as a practitioner in relation to social and individual problems.

This final chapter will be devoted mainly to a discussion of some of the factors which appear to stand in the way of a closer relationship between the two areas and to some assessment of future prospects.

The close relationship which exists in theory between sociology and social work is not matched by an equally close relationship in practice. For example, by comparison with their interests in other fields of professional practice, the interest of sociologists in social work appears to be very marginal. In the United States in 1959 while 126 sociologists affiliated with professional schools of medicine and 96 with schools of education, only 40 affiliated with schools of social work.[1] In Britain a survey (in 1966) of the membership of the British Sociological Association[2] revealed that 4 per cent (41) expressed a main or special interest in the sociology of the social services (including social policy and problems—there was, significantly, no special category for social work). This compared with 14 per cent (129) who expressed a main or special interest in education. These figures suggest that interest in welfare institutions, and in the institution of social work in particular, is still marginal for British sociologists, although in the British survey medicine and the law claim even smaller numbers of interested sociologists. The lack of interest in these fields shows up by comparison with education which, in Britain, claims the interests of the largest single group of sociologists in the association. A not insubstantial body of knowledge has grown up in this latter field, but one looks in vain for a similar development in the sociology of social work. This is all the more surprising considering that social work is one of the more important growth industries of the present day.

The currently underdeveloped state of the sociology of social work can be discussed by looking briefly at factors in the nature of both social work and sociology which have prevented a closer relationship from developing.

## PROBLEMS ARISING
### FROM THE NATURE OF SOCIAL WORK

The introduction of any scientific content into social work, whether it be of a psychological or sociological nature, poses a challenge to what is seen by many social workers as the essentially human and artistic quality of the work. This feature, which appears an important motivation for entry to social work, also appears to constitute an important part of the orientation of students and practitioners to their work. There seems little pressure on students to develop in any substantial way the scientific aspect of the diagnostic and treatment process and little belief that dealing with human problems can, in a major sense, incorporate this approach. This, as Halmos[3] has shown, is part of the unanalysable and holistic desire to help and as such resists the dissection and compartmentalization implied by a technology. Thus one barrier to the deeper interpenetration of sociology and social work is the general problem of the two cultures of scientific and artistic endeavour, made worse in the case of the social sciences by the widespread belief that the human condition is not susceptible to a scientific or rational appraisal, that the application of science to this field involves the manipulation or human engineering of groups or individuals and that love or faith (however this is encased in technical language) is the only answer, both practically and morally.

Although this view is receding in face of the prestige of science and the need to incorporate a more scientific approach as a basis for professional status, the residual view of social work as an activity springing directly from the personality of the counsellor remains a strong barrier to greater sociological sophistication.

Another way of expressing this point is to see the tasks of the social worker as requiring little more than experience and knowledge of society gained from living, in which a social scientific perspective plays little part. An American social worker, writing in response to a survey on social workers' views of sociology as preparation for their work,[4] gives details of her life experiences through working in the fields, washing dishes with coloured people, being a servant, being involved in trades union conflict, having a Polish social-work practice, etc.; she concludes "at the age of forty-seven I took a course in social psychology under Professor Mead at the University of Chicago. It was as interesting as a trip in an aeroplane would be to a person who had walked over the area and knew every road and path by heart."

Another substantial barrier related to social work is the way in which a psychological, and in particular a psycho-analytic, framework has been adopted as the vital model for professional practice. Through this, social workers have sought a recognized technique and status and have been able to identify with a practice which is derived clinically and which has direct therapeutic concerns. Sociology, with its concern for the analysis of social interaction on a wider scale, has been unable to offer these features and has not, in the eyes of many social workers, been able to provide a basis on which professional expertise could develop.

Thus, sociology suffers, in the eyes of many social workers, from the defect that it gives little idea of what to do in many of the situations in which social workers find themselves, which are more often than not face to face with the client and his problems. The message that sociology seems to bring is that both the cause of and solution to such problems lies somehow in society (or the social structure or social system), but this view is scarcely comforting.

The result is that many professional training courses are heavily weighted in the direction of teaching with a generally psychological and specifically psycho-analytic bias, whilst sociology appears to constitute a background to this approach. This is particularly noticeable in university professional social-work courses, where students are expected to obtain a grounding in the social sciences prior to the professional course. This then takes on a largely non-sociological character in which there is an emphasis on such subjects as social casework and human growth and behaviour. Sociology is seen as constituting in the main an empirical framework within which the more serious discussions of individual behaviour can go on. Such phrases as "the social framework" or "the social (and in some cases cultural) influences on behaviour" certainly imply this kind of thinking. But, as Timms[5] points out, this is a total misinterpretation of the nature of sociology, which (in his words) does

> not consist of a checklist of discrete characteristics (e.g. family, income, educational attainment and so on) nor exclusively of factors which can be described as external . . . such commonly used expressions as "the social influences on behaviour" seem to imply that neutral behaviour is from time to time pushed in one direction or another by external forces, whereas these "social influences" are a constituent feature of the behaviour.

Thus, although man is seen as being "in society", society is not really seen as being "in man". There is therefore some doubt whether sociology is actually "in" social work, as the author of a recent British text on the subject suggests by his title.[6]

A further problem is posed in the application and utilization of sociological knowledge in social work practice. Although little is known about the way in which practitioners use any of the knowledge gained in training, one problem is that knowledge may be put aside when practice situations arise and a reversion to a more personal basis for action may take place. As one probation officer,[7] in thinking about her reactions to difficult clients, confessed "my father's words, not those of my teacher's at the university, ring in my ears". Sociology may appear to the student, because of its diverse and wide-ranging character and the way it is seen by social work teachers, of least practical value, and may be the first to suffer in the hurly-burly of practice.

This is borne out by a recent survey of the reading habits of a variety of practising social workers[8] in which an attempt was made to assess the extent to which social workers continued to draw on disciplines such as sociology and psychology in their professional practice after the completion of professional training, and how the influence of these disciplines compared with other factors which influence social workers in daily practice. Literature on sociology (as well as social work research) was invariably placed at the lower end of the scale of usefulness by all the social work specialisms, by comparison to such factors as professional training, supervision, the personal experience and personality of the social worker.

One consideration here is that practical training in social work is almost exclusively concerned with casework and features of the practical work situation which may be useful in enhancing sociological understanding might not be exploited. Possibly very few supervisors, with their concern to teach the core skills of casework and perhaps with little sociological training of their own, are able to consolidate in a practical sense the sociological side of teaching, which is in any case a very difficult task. Thus in courses where sociology is taught, one side of the course becomes consolidated through field-work training, whilst the other side becomes merely a classroom subject divorced from reality. This is a serious defect when the student is taught to learn through practical experience, and results in a considerable weakening of the sociological contribution.

Related to this is the point that there has often been too little thinking out by social workers of the precise way in which they might draw on sociological knowledge. Obviously, in such a vast area as sociology, selection is inevitable, but there is often little thought given to the grounds on which some rather than other developments in sociology are heeded. Rather there is a general belief that certain concepts from this field are "relevant". This kind of "intellectual beachcombing", as Coyle[9] has described it, leads to the view that sociology may be of little value in practical situations and is difficult to operationalize. What is required, of course, is further research into the ways in which knowledge from a variety of fields is in fact utilized by the practitioner in the field.

This difficulty arises equally from the very amorphous nature of social work itself. The terms "social work" or "social worker" are attached to a variegated selection of processes and individuals, and it is very difficult for the social scientist to know precisely what he is applying his knowledge to. To be faced with the task of writing a book entitled "Sociology and Social Work" is a salutary reminder of this situation. One requirement is for social workers to clarify and sharpen the nature of the brief that is given to social scientists and to spell out the various key, or unit, processes of social work. Clearly, a detailed content analysis of social work in a variety of fields is required before contributions from sociology can be sharpened into distinctive professional tools.

The question of selection of material also poses problems for the sociologist. What may be uppermost in the mind of the sociologists in teaching in applied fields such as social work is the extent to which he should be prepared to compromise between the basic essentials of his subject and the professional needs of the student. What is the basic minimum of, say, sociological theory which any course in sociology, no matter to whom it is taught, should contain? To what extent should the subject stand and be understood in its own right? Possibly if this does not occur, to some degree at least, the whole flavour of a sociological approach is lost. These are some of the questions to which sociologists in applied fields must seek answers.

## PROBLEMS ARISING
## FROM THE NATURE OF SOCIOLOGY

One reason for the weakness of the link between sociology and professional fields such as social work relates to the nature of the occupational role of the sociologist. The way in which most sociologists define their role does not commonly include direct collaboration with the practising professions.[10] A normal career path appears that of teaching or research (in mainly academic institutions) with a particular commitment to theoretical ways of thinking. If practical fields (such as education) are entered, these may be seen mainly as vehicles for sociological theory building. Sociology, to a number of sociologists, still appears to have little or no practical relevance to areas such as social work. To enter such a field is to get drawn off into the irrelevancies of professional practice and away from the central concerns and essential business of sociology. Those who do enter such fields are often allocated low statuses in the social structure of the professions. These attitudes are associated with the dichotomy which took place between the interests of some early sociologists in the study of social problems and in social reform and the later concern for a more general and scientific study of society. This, as Leonard[11] suggests, may have been necessary for the development of sociology as an academic discipline and probably accounts for the continued hostility and opposition in the part of some sociologists to practices such as social work. In Britain, this led to the establishment of the new field of study known as "social administration", which has had an important influence on the training of social workers in the recent past.

If the sociologist does venture forth into professional fields there are various ways in which conflict is likely to develop between the sociologist and the practitioner. One of the ways the sociologist defines his role in such situations is to reflect on the nature of the institutions, whether educational, welfare, or medical, with which he is involved. Clearly if employed in a school of social work, the sociologist has the opportunity of learning a good deal about the beliefs and values, the ideology of social work. Reflection on the content of professional practice is likely to lead to the posing of certain awkward questions. Leonard[12] has described the sociologist as bringing a "Trojan horse" into social-work training, to the trepidation of social-work teachers. For example, social work is marked by a mainly therapeutic ideology which stresses that work must be done with the individual irrespective of the reform of the social structure in which the individual is placed. But sociological analysis illustrates the structural determinants of individual and family problems and stresses the part played in their problems by social inequality and by the differing life chances of social groups. There is also a focus on the wider functions of the social services as managers of conflict situations and in the role of social workers and others in adjusting individuals to such differences and in propping up the existing *status quo*. This analysis raises questions of a political or economic nature which social workers and other practitioners are sometimes unwilling or unable to answer and which highlight the ambiguities and dilemmas of their professional role.

On the one hand, as Leonard[12] shows, the sociologist may, through his technical contributions to social work, have an important influence on the ideology of social work; thus an emphasis on the environment in which client and social worker find themselves may cause the social worker to reflect anew on the kinds of tasks which he is asked to perform for society and the kind of organizational situations in which these tasks are performed.

On the other hand, the mutual hostility and suspicion which sometimes exists may cause the practitioner to withdraw into the inner world or community of the profession and into the relative safety of intra-professional controversy.

Thus to the practitioner sociology may be a double-edged weapon, a rose with a thorn. Although of vital importance to the practitioner in the search for a professional technique and for a recognized status, sociology also constitutes a considerable challenge to the ideological bases on which many professions rest. These situations are rendered all the more conflictful because the practitioner's expectations of the role of the sociologist do not appear to include that of social or professional critic. Instead, a rather simple service function is expected in which the sociologist should help the practitioner to achieve professional ends in the most effective manner.

The conflict between sociology and social work is well illustrated by the dilemma of the sociology graduate on the professional social-work course, in particular those who, sociologically speaking, have been exposed to the "conflict model" of society: one graduate in this position suggests[13] that

> Students holding such a model are placed in an extremely precarious position if they wish to become social workers. They may well find themselves suspended between two opposing ideologies with little support from either side. The social work idea has pretty low currency amongst many of the academics at the Universities . . . so that it is quite possible for [students] to arrive at their courses with a knowledge of, if not a full commitment to, the conflict approach. But the idea that social workers merely perpetuate the problems they are trying to solve is such a threatening one that it is rarely considered in the literature and by the teaching staff of social work courses.

With the considerable increase in the numbers of graduates coming from sociology courses, it is likely that increased numbers of sociology graduates will find their way into social-work training courses and into the profession, and will provide an important source of further recruitment. The need to understand something of the nature of this conflict therefore grows greater.

There are, in addition, other problems which stem from the application of sociology, or any social science, to professional practice. One relates to the rapid rate of growth of these areas of knowledge. Thus the teaching a student received 10 or even 5 years ago will soon be out of date. Growth derives not only from the development of existing areas of knowledge but from the creation of virtually new theory. Thus the social-work practitioner who was trained a decade ago will, for example, know little of Bernstein's socio-linguistic theories or of recent advances in the sociology of deviant behaviour.

Again, the possession of a knowledge base is, as previously suggested, an important step in the direction of achieving professional status. Although, in the case of social work, considerable reliance is placed on empathic understanding and on faith, it is also well recognized that one of the best bases for professional claims are skills firmly rooted in traditional scientific method. Social work has, as Kent[14] points out, grown up in an era of scientific ascendancy and eventually made the pretence of hopping aboard the scientific bandwagon. Thus, along with other emerging professions, social work has been anxious to incorporate knowledge from growing and increasingly influential areas such as sociology. But this has gone on without, in the main, the parallel development of a critical and evaluative perspective. The result has been that knowledge of various kinds has been accepted and utilized where it has seemed useful for practice. As Leonard[6] comments, the social worker frequently "endows knowledge borrowed from sociology with greater certainty and with greater simplicity than would the sociologist". Apart from the use of material of varying scientific respectability, the defect of this approach is that once a useful insight has been spotted and incorporated, this is taken as the last word on the subject, and the whole area tends to be shut off to further advances or discussion.

An example of the problems posed by new knowledge of a high degree of relevancy for professional practice is that of Bott's study of marriage and family life published over 10 years ago.[15] This work has been of considerable influence in social work and appears to many social workers one of the most useful contributions ever made to social-work practice by a social scientist. Yet one reviewer,[16] although welcoming the contribution this study made to the little known area of inner family relationships, made the following observations on the methods of the study and the way in which the material had been interpreted:

> The families actually studied were obtained through a variety of agencies (such as tenants' associations and schools) but not from the

general population: the result was a rather exceptional group of families which did not for example contain an unskilled manual labourer. Although each family was interviewed a number of times important information such as ages, family size and structure, frequencies of contact between relations, was not collected. This made it difficult to relate the theoretical terms used to the data which was collected: thus the "connectedness" of an individual's social network may take a variety of forms but it is not possible to work these out from the data. Thus the terms used (such as segregation) were not adequately explored. Certain leads, such as the role of relatives in the lives of the married couple, were mentioned but not followed up as important factors in immediate family relationships. Consequently the "facts" revealed by such a study need to be treated with caution if they are to be used as a basis for decision making by the social worker.

The need for the social worker to evaluate scientifically the mass of information which is in various ways available, provides some rationale for courses in the methods and problems of social inquiry during professional training.

Another problem faced by practitioners in their relationship with academic disciplines is that the knowledge which is borrowed remains essentially the property of such disciplines. The lack of specialized professional knowledge and theory, such as medical or legal theory, is another barrier to social work professionalization. Thus in social work there has been a movement to replace the knowledge borrowed from the social sciences by social-work theory as such. There is a tendency amongst some social workers to see social work as a distinctive and separate academic subject in its own right. This has meant in part an attempt to integrate the contributions of the various social sciences, in particular of psychology and sociology, and to apply this to social-work situations. The new psycho-social theory which results can provide one basis for social-work theory, thus eliminating the problem of borrowing from a sometimes bewildering variety of frames of reference. The approach also has the advantage that the practitioner seems unlikely to distinguish different frames of reference when actually using this knowledge in the field.

However, there are a number of reasons for believing that such an approach is premature and can lead to more confusion than gains. The desire for a synthesis of the social sciences to form an explanatory framework runs the risk of confusing the different types and levels of analysis and misunderstands the nature of scientific endeavour. Thus the sociologist, psychologist, and psychiatrist will have different explanations for, say, family behaviour, and will use different methods to obtain information. The sociological explanation is not more "right" than the psychological, but attempts to ask and answer different kinds of questions. Thus the social sciences cover an enormous range of interests, and to confuse these approaches may frustrate the attempt to understand, in different ways, certain problems. One particular difficulty which beset Bott's study of the family was that the attempt to relate the different approaches of the sociologist, psychologist, and psychoanalyst may have obscured rather than clarified the problem. By concentrating on a one-sided approach, all the advantages of a scientific division of labour may be obtained, as Weber[17] has suggested. But this does not mean that alternative explanations are rejected. Rather certain aspects of a problem are highlighted whilst others are left aside. Thus Scheff,[18] in his study of mental illness, left aside the psychological approach in order to concentrate exclusively on the relatively undeveloped relationship between mental illness and society; but this did not mean that he rejected the former. Another advantage of this approach is the idea that science develops through the crucial experiment, or the decisive comparison of two opposing theories, which may explain only part of the area under investigation. The intentional opposition of such distinctive models under circumstances in which one can be rejected is an important feature of scientific progress.[19]

In the present state of the social sciences it appears that a comfortable synthesis of the psycho-social variety may actually inhibit the growth of new knowledge and may be another way out of asking and attempting to answer difficult questions. The task of finding out how each of the different social sciences may be related to practical purposes is difficult enough without at the same time asking that these should all be related to one another.

It is perhaps more important for the practitioner to recognize the significance of the different frames of reference which are available and to judge which is most appropriate, or economical, for the task in hand.

Another disadvantage of interdisciplinary integration is that concepts which appear to perform the function of bridging the different disciplines are often, for this reason, inflated or reified to an unjustified degree. One concept of this kind is that of role, which, it is held, effectively bridges the disciplines of anthropology, sociology, and psychology. Consequently, role is perhaps the social science concept which is in greatest use amongst practitioners, and certainly this appears true of social workers. Thus the family, the organization, and the profession are analysed in terms of what is held to be a fundamental explanatory construct of human behaviour.

But, on examination, the actual development of the role concept, in particular its empirical testing in a variety of situations, has not proceeded very far. There has, for example, been little attempt to identify and critically examine the key assumptions which have been made about role behaviour, still less to develop this into any tool of systematic theory. Thus, after an exhaustive survey of the literature, one conclusion was that "role theory, as a set of unified propositions, does not presently exist".[20] This is not to suggest that the idea of role does not contain promising possibilities or cannot, in the future, provide a convenient and trustworthy bridge between several ways of thinking. The argument is rather that at the present it seems wrong to elevate to such heights such a concept for the sake of premature synthesis and professional convenience.

## THE FUTURE OF SOCIOLOGY AND SOCIAL WORK

There appears room for guarded optimism about the future of sociology and social work. The insecurity which has marked out their relationship in the immediate past appears to be on the decline as both areas become increasingly recognized as part of the institutional framework of industrial societies. In Britain, as the discipline of sociology becomes more established, the low status accorded to those who work in applied fields may disappear. Sociologists, like any group who exist within a wider community which offers them support, also have the obligation to justify their existence; sociologists will most likely be judged by the practical contributions they can make to professional fields of practice like social work. There are signs that the sociological study of social problems (as distinct from approaches in the field of social administration), and thus interest in associated fields such as social work, are becoming of greater importance to some sociologists.

This parallels a greater concern in the wider society for problems such as racial discrimination and poverty. Social workers are also becoming secure enough to move away from an emphasis on details of professional practice, and on psycho-analytic theory, to embrace a wider variety of approaches.

But serious conflict still exists between the two ideological positions; one way of reducing such conflict is by a greater understanding and acceptance of the nature of the distinctions between the role of the sociologist and the social worker. There is no reason, as Young[10] suggests, why sociologists should not accept the different ideologies and cultures of the professions in the same way as they accept differences in, say, the behaviour of social classes or ethnic groups. Similarly, the social worker could go a long way towards reducing this tension by recognizing and accepting the sociologist's role as not only providing an important part of the technical equipment of the social worker, but also as social critic of the professional and organizational environment. In this way, valuable contributions can be made to balanced professional self-criticism.

Perhaps the most promising developments lie in the convergence of sociology and social work in courses in education and training and in joint research. The development of new degree courses (such as those at the universities of Bath and Bradford) lays the foundation for a new type of education in social work in which professional training and academic education are combined in the same course over a period of 4 years. New degree courses in colleges outside the universities, under the auspices of the Council for National Academic Awards, also provide a means of closer integration between the social sciences and social work. One feature of these degrees is the stringent demands made by the Council in respect of academic standards and, implicitly, of standards of professional training. A further advantage here is the fact that both academic and professional interests are represented on the Council, thus providing in theory some balance between the two in the construction of these courses.

This point is made because the considerable developments in social-work training in Britain during the last decade, particularly in colleges outside the universities, has at times resulted in an imbalance in the delicate relationship between the social sciences and the demands of professional training. In some colleges, training courses have been developed in situations where there has been little or no tradition of academic social science teaching and in which the contributions of the social sciences have been restricted by narrow, professional demands. The risk here is that the contributions of, say, sociologists are limited to the imparting of certain techniques or skills, but where little scope for a wider role has been allowed. The danger is that such courses are dominated by purely professional interests, by professional associations, training bodies, and professional social-work teachers, so allowing for the growth of unbridled professionalism to the detriment of both the educational needs of students and of social-work practice.

The problem of the sociologist as a teacher in the course, department, or school of social work also raises a number of issues. One alternative is that the sociologist is based outside the department in which social work is taught, e.g. in an academic department of sociology, and performs a service function in his teaching of sociology to the social-work student. Alternatively, the sociologist may be employed directly and more or less exclusively by the department of social work.[21] There are advantages in both courses. If the sociologist is external to the social-work course this avoids competition between departments for scarce teaching resources and also enables the sociologist to take an entirely independent and critical stance on what may be very controversial issues. But if the sociologist is attached directly to the social-work course, this may allow for a clearer understanding of the problems facing social workers and a greater familiarity with practice. Hence the sociologist in this situation is likely to make a far greater impact than if he regards the teaching of social workers as a peripheral interest.

But this closer co-operation raises a number of problems. For example, the sociologist in a social-work department may not be able to achieve the same career advancement that would have been possible in an academic department of sociology. Jefferys[22] suggests that sociologists in the medical field have faced similar problems. Again, in a situation where professional interests on the courses are very dominant the sociologist may find himself in a very weak power position and may have difficulty in securing for his subject a sufficiently independent status. These are the problems which beset the applied sociologist in whatever field they are involved.

Jefferys suggests that one solution is to secure for sociologists in these positions status and prospects which would have been open to them had they remained in academic departments. This is an important point for practitioners to remember if a closer relationship between sociology and professional fields like medicine and social work is to be attained.

The sociologist's contributions to research which bears, in various ways, on the social work process is a further example of the importance of the relationship between the two fields. Examples have already been given of research with a sociological basis into the problem family and into working-class clients' perception of the casework process.

Another important area of research is the evaluation of the effectiveness of different kinds of social-work programme. Social work appears to have largely avoided any large-scale consideration of the success or failure of its techniques in attaining the goals that are set. But the development and increasing utilization of the various forms of social-work practice as part of more general welfare programmes should presumably be accompanied by apparatus by which the effectiveness of this instrument can be measured, as in the study carried out in the United States by Henry Meyer, *Girls at Vocational High*.[23]

It is also important to consider the kind of contributions that social workers themselves can make to social scientific research, particularly to research in the field of social policy. Social workers, by virtue of their intimate contact with and experience of everyday social situations, are in a strong position to contribute to the research process and to such tasks as the suggestion of hypotheses and the adaptation of research methods.[24] More specifically, the social worker may be able to participate actively in policy making through social science research; there is a considerable need for research related to both the intended and unintended consequences of social policy, to the goals and aspirations of groups and individuals, and so on; there is a considerable need in the initial stages of such research for intuition and speculation. Instead of using only the sociologist at this stage, who may be a distant figure, the social worker may have an important role to play, and could function "as an intelligence agent of the sociologist and of the policy maker, and a trusty pilot of the sociological researcher".[24]

In the aftermath of the Plowden, Seebohm, and Gulbenkian reports, one area in which joint research of this kind might be mounted is in the assessment of the problems, needs, and resources of communities with special problems in which it is necessary to involve the people themselves in working for an improved community life.

The importance of a specifically sociological orientation to these problems and to social-work training needs to be specially stressed. Social-work training has, in the recent past, been heavily influenced by the teaching of social administration which stresses the detailed analysis of the social services, but rarely penetrates beneath this to an analysis of social relationships, and is as yet generally weak in its theoretical approach. For example, the authors of the study of race relations in Birmingham[25] note that the success of the appointment of an all-purpose social worker to the Sparkbrook Association rested not so much on a general grasp of the way in which the social services work or of orthodox training in practical work, but rather on an ability on the part of the worker to understand the problems of a community in conflict, on the possession of a shrewd political sense, and on the ability to act as a representative of the community and to do casework in this context. A sociological training appears an essential basis for the development of these kinds of skills.

However, a major problem arises out of the current practice in many courses of professional training in social work (particularly at the universities) of virtually excluding sociology as a formal teaching subject. This derives from the fact that most of the students on such courses have previously taken social science courses, including sociology, at pre-professional level and it is not considered necessary for the subject to be pursued much further. However, pre-professional courses in sociology, e.g. at undergraduate level, are not designed to contribute to courses of professional training, may not cover areas relevant to such practice and are often not seen by students as having any particular practical relevance. They are also frequently taken by students at formative stages in their own development when career plans are not at all certain. By now areas of sociology which have particular relevance for social-work practice and research have been mapped out[26] and it is of the greatest importance, if social work is to draw more heavily on sociology, that students should be exposed to this in their professional as well as undergraduate courses.

Clearly, these developments in teaching and research will require a larger group who have been trained in both sociology and social work. Thus the recruitment of graduates in sociology to social-work practice is of great importance in long-term developments of this kind.

In the meantime, there is the need for social workers, particularly in teaching and supervisory roles, to accept to a greater extent sociology as part of the total educational and training process and to play a greater part in the teaching of sociology themselves. In social-work courses it should be somebody's job, as Halmos[24] has put it, "to sociologize over individual cases"; this cannot be left entirely to the professional sociologist. In this direction the fellow-ship course at the National Institute of Social Work Training is providing a useful experiment in the provision of this kind of equipment for the teacher of social work.

Possibly the most significant development of all lies in the reaction of social work to the almost exclusively therapeutic bias of the recent past and the growth of concern with the political and economic questions surrounding the institutions of welfare. It has taken many years in social work for the pendulum to begin to swing back in the direction of the original reformist orientation, but this is unquestionably what is occurring now. In Britain the concern of social workers for the wider issues of the social structure is evident in organizations such as the Child Poverty Action Group and in the recent Seebohm and Gulbenkian reports on the future of social work in Britain. The situation of the client, normally viewed in casework terms, is now increasingly seen against a background of social inequality and injustice; students in particular, close as they are to the new political climate, have a new awareness of such issues. The widening social origins of recruits to social work may be playing an important part in this process. In the United States widespread political conflict seems to have had similar repercussions on some elements of the social-work profession; in some quarters casework is a discredited term. Such developments draw the social worker and the sociologist closer together; it is also important to recognize the part played in such developments by the ideological influence of sociology itself, an influence which looks like increasing in the future. Thus the dilemma of the politically committed sociology graduate in social work, whilst real enough at the moment, may be resolved by long-term changes in professional attitudes, which he may himself powerfully influence, and which are only beginning to show themselves. It will be important to document in the im-mediate future the ideological impact of sociology on social work and on the rapidly growing institutions of welfare and, through them, on the wider society itself.

## NOTES AND REFERENCES

1. M. Riley, Membership of the American Sociological Association 1950–9, *Am. Sociol. Rev.*, Dec. 1960; quoted in J. Mayer, Sociology and social work, *Case Conference*, **14** (5) (Sept. 1967).

2. M. Carter Report of a survey of sociological research in Britain, *Social. Rev.* **16** (1), (March 1968).

3. P. Halmos, *Faith of the Counsellors*, Constable, London, 1965.

4. T. Eliot, Sociology as a prevocational subject; the verdict of sixty social workers, *Am. J. Sociol.* **29,** 726–46 (1924).

5. N. Timms, *A Sociological Approach to Social Problems*, Routledge & Kegan Paul, London, 1967.

6. P. Leonard, *Sociology in Social Work*, Routledge & Kegan Paul, London, 1966.

7. M. McCullough, Social work in no-man's land, *New Society*, 4 April 1968.

8. M. Brown and J. McCulloch, Some characteristics and continuity of learning in child care practice, *Child Care News*, Oct. 1968.

9. G. Coyle, *Social Science in the Professional Education of Social Workers*, Council on Social Work Education, 1958; cited in Mayer, *op. cit.*

10. D. Young, Sociology and the practising professions, *Am. Sociol. Rev.* **20** (1955).

11. P. Leonard, The application of sociological analysis to social work training, *Br. J. Sociol.* **19** (4) (Dec. 1968).

12. P. Leonard, *The Contribution of Sociology to Social Work; Some Ideological Implications* (unpublished), 1967.

13. Sociology and social work—a student's dilemma, *Child Care News*, Aug. 1968.

14. B. Kent, Friend or foe?, *Social Work* **23** (1) (Jan. 1966).

15. E. Bott, *Family and Social Network*, Tavistock, London, 1957.

16. P. Townsend, Sociology and the relationship between man and wife, *Case Conference* **4** (10) (April 1958).

17. M. Weber, *The Methodology of the Social Sciences*, Collier McMillan,1950.

18. T. Scheff, *Being Mentally Ill*, Weidenfeld & Nicholson, London, 1967.

19. T. Kuhn, *The Structure of Scientific Revolutions*, Phoenix Books, 1962; cited in Scheff, *op. cit.*

20. B. Biddle and E. Thomas, *Role Theory: Concepts and Research*, Wiley, New York, 1966; for a critical comment see also M. Banton, Roles, *New Society*, 7 May 1964.

21. A further complication is where a social work course is located within a department of sociology.

22. M. Jefferys, Sociology and medicine—separation or symbiosis?, *The Lancet*, 7 June 1969; this article also contains an important analysis of

some of the other problems in the application of sociology to professional fields.

23. H. Meyer *et al.*, *Girls at Vocational High*, Russell Sage Foundation, 1965; see also D. Plowman, What are the outcomes of casework?, *Social Work* (U.K.) **26** (1) (Jan. 1969).

24. P. Halmos, Problems arising in the teaching of sociology to social workers, *Int. Soc. Serv. Review* (8) (March 1961).

25. J. Rex and R. Moore, *Race, Community and Conflict*, O.U.P., London, 1967.

26. For an account of developments in the United States see H. Meyer *et al.*, Social work and social welfare, in Lazarsfeld *et al.*, *The Uses of Sociology*, Weidenfeld & Nicholson, London, 1968; for an account of British developments see Leonard (1968), *op. cit.*

# Author Index

# Subject Index